"A reference the digital signage industry was missing. Now the digital signage networks operators, creative agencies and advertisers have a method to Unleash the power of Digital Signage."
—Christian Vaglio-Giors, ceo, Neo Media Group

"... a great primer for the ad agencies, and a great reference for the pioneers in the digital signage industry. It's an excellent resource for anyone planning to use this medium effectively."
—Jake Lambert, vp, content director, Draftfcb

"... everyone, from digital signage novice to expert, will learn something to achieve better results with digital signage, regardless of goal. Kelsen covers it all, from the basic mechanics of digital signage, to the breadth of content types, delivery mechanisms, execution methods and performance measurement."
—Leslie Hand, research director, IDC Retail Insights

"Keith truly illustrates, that with proper planning and a solid content strategy, digital signage will return on its objectives and provide uniquely targeted, relevant messaging."
—Michael Chase, vice president, marketing, sales & creative, St. Joseph Content

"Finally a must read comprehensive book that addresses the issues of content. ...Keith Kelsen has brought forth the ingredients to create great content for any of the diverse types of digital signage networks."
—David Drain, executive director, Digital Signage Association

"Good content is a large reason why digital signage networks are successful, but up until this point there has not been one comprehensive reference point on the subject. *Unleashing the Power of Digital Signage* fills a much-needed gap in this industry."
—Bill Yackey, editor, DigitalSignageToday.com

Unleashing the Power of Digital Signage
Content Strategies for the 5th Screen

Keith Kelsen

Focal Press
Taylor & Francis Group

NEW YORK AND LONDON

First published 2010
This edition published 2013 by Focal Press
70 Blanchard Road, Suite 402, Burlington, MA 01803

Simultaneously published in the UK
by Focal Press
2 Park Square, Milton Park, Abingdon, Oxon OX14 4RN

Focal Press is an imprint of the Taylor & Francis Group, an informa business

Library of Congress Cataloging-in-Publication Data
Kelsen, Keith.
    Unleashing the power of digital signage : content strategies for the 5th screen / Keith Kelsen.
       p. cm.
    Includes index.
    ISBN 978-0-240-81302-8
    1. Digital signage. 2. Advertising–Audio-visual equipment. 3. Signs and signboards. I. Title.
    HF5841.K44 2010
    658.13'6–dc22
                                   2009042442

ISBN: 978-0-240-81302-8 (pbk)
ISBN: 978-0-240-81303-5 (ebk)

Contents

Dedication

To all the media creators that have come before us and to the ones that shall follow...

Acknowledgement

It takes many hands to write and coordinate a book. One hand that is always in my life is God's hand. To the rest of the many hands that helped, I would like to thank foremost my family, my three beautiful daughters and my handsome son, for their support.

Additionally, thanks to my executive assistant, who was relentless in tracking down graphics and setting up interviews. And of course the rest of my family, Mom and Dad and my four brothers, for just being there throughout my life.

I would also like to acknowledge my board of directors and my colleagues at MediaTile for all the support they offered during my months of a closed office door while writing.

And last, but certainly not least, to all who participated in the interviews, conversations, and reviews about a sensational medium that is coming into its own. I must say this has been a fantastic and remarkable experience that I anticipate will uplift our industry in the understanding and use of this medium.

Foreword

Keith Kelsen does a masterful job in *Unleashing the Power of Digital Signage* of introducing this new technology to the business world. All marketers need to pay close attention to what is going on here, for as Kelsen points out, what we are witnessing is the birth of *the 5th screen* – beyond movies, TV, computers, and mobile phones – which provides companies with a new tool in the arsenal of how to interact with people. Whether you are already deeply involved in using digital signage in your enterprise, are just starting to investigate it, or are reading about it for the very first time, this is the ideal book to learn what it's about, what it means, and what you should do about it.

But understand that digital signage is not just about interacting, nor just about marketing, nor even about technology per se. What Brenda Laurel said in *Computers as Theater* about the third screen – "Think of the computer not as a tool, but as a medium" – applies to the fifth screen (and, come to think of it, each of the other ones as well!). So think of digital signage as the birth of a new *medium*. Not a communications medium, however; think of it as an *experience* medium, a place that engages people in the experience.

So make your use of digital signage an experience! Certainly make it entertaining and whenever possible an element of the design esthetic of your places. (We love the example of the video wall in MGM Grand's Shiboya restaurant that furnishes a level of ambience perhaps unachievable without this technology.) But across each of the three types of networks that Kelsen has identified – point of sale, point of wait, and point of transit – don't just make it a passive endeavor to entertain people momentarily, but an *active* experience that engages them over a duration of time. That's not always easy, of course, but read about Oblong in the last chapter and see what it is doing to take interaction far beyond today's simple touch interfaces into analyzing and responding to people's gestures. Then envision how you could use a digital signage network to engage, educate, and offer people an escape from the humdrum commonality all too often found in each of the three networks: the drudgery of waiting, waiting, waiting.

Interestingly, John Underkoffler, the chief scientist and a cofounder of Oblong, was the chief science advisor to Steven Spielberg's *Minority Report*. The movie provides a great caution to consider as business employs this new medium: be wary of the director's vision of marketing. Recall how wherever Tom Cruise's character John Anderton walked in public, he was bombarded by advertising messages aimed directly at him, by name. We do not know anyone who would want to live in that world, where we so obviously become unremitting targets for the slings and arrows of outrageous fortune-seeking missives. We're not arguing against the customized messages – indeed, anything you can digitize you can customize, so it ought to part and parcel of any digital signage network – but the technique. Don't cosmetically customize your marketing messages, but rather *transparently* customize them – with no specific, personal entreaty until the person himself actually assents to interact with you. Don't be so overt (and so crass) as to constantly use people's names and other obviously distinguishing characteristics; rather, let them discover the value you have for them, as if by serendipity (something we call *diaphanous marketing*).

Moreover, don't just customize the message, but the offering as well. If you know so much about a person that you can target them individually, why then offer them the same standard stuff you offer everybody else? This need not be expensive if you embrace the principles of Mass Customization to efficiently serve customers uniquely. If you're unwilling to treat your customers as the unique individuals they are, why are you addressing them by name in the first place? We are not entries in a database; we are human beings.

And as human beings, what consumers seek in today's Experience Economy, where life increasingly becomes a paid-for experience, is *authenticity*. We no longer want the fake from some phony; we want the real from the genuine. So don't make the mistake of so many marketers and their complicit ad agencies by letting your marketing, and your advertising in particular, become a phoniness-generating machine. Whenever an advertisement exaggerates the features, benefits, or sensations of any offering, the disconnect between what the ad says it is and what people actually encounter in that offering gets it, and the company, branded as inauthentic.

What demand generation needs to become in today's day and age is *placemaking* – creating physical or virtual places where people can experience your offerings directly. Then there can be no disconnect between what you say about yourself and what people encounter, for it becomes one and the same thing! Think of manufacturer American Girl (a unit of Mattel) with its amazing American Girl Places as well as its Boutiques and Bistros; ING Direct with its Cafes that have generated over a billion dollars in new accounts for the bank; the United States Army with its online game at AmericasArmy.com and its real-world recruiting vehicle the Army Experience Center; or LEGO with its entire portfolio of placemaking experiences, from its LEGOLAND theme parks through its Discovery and Education Centers to its online experiences such as LEGO DesignByMe and its virtual world LEGO Universe.

Digital signage, therefore, shouldn't just be part of a traditional communications and marketing strategy, but an element in creating your own portfolio of placemaking experiences. Go to an ING Direct Cafe, for example, and note how it uses digital signage facing outside the place to attract passersby, and inside the place to engage, inform, and even sign-up coffee-loving consumers. The bank's usage effectively integrates the 5th screen into an appealing real-world experience that renders it authentic, while it uses the third and fourth screens through an alluring web site that, when the Cafes first opened, encouraged people to "come to one of our cafes to experience who we are".

As these examples attest, digital signage can be the entrée to a brave new world out at the edges of the digital frontier, one that merges the real and the virtual. But if it is not used to make a *human connection* with your current and prospective customers, what is the point? Don't use this new technology, nor the principles Kelsen outlines in this insightful book, merely to sell more stuff. Use it to connect with people on an authentic human level, and then the stuff will sell itself.

B. Joseph Pine II and James H. Gilmore are co-founders of Strategic Horizons LLP, an Aurora, Ohio-based thinking studio dedicated to helping companies conceive and design new ways of adding value to their economic offerings. They are co-authors of The Experience Economy and Authenticity: What Consumers Really Want. *They can be reached at Pine&Gilmore@StrategicHorizons.com or +1 330 995–4680.*

B. Joseph Pine II and **James H. Gilmore**
Co-authors,
The Experience Economy and Authenticity:
What Consumers Really Want

.

Introduction

The sophisticated nature of communication sets humans apart from other creatures. Since prehistoric times, as evidenced in cave paintings, people have used images, placed where others would encounter them, to communicate important information.

For the past 120 years or so, rapid advances in technology have transformed human communication faster and to a greater degree than in all the time before. Since the development of the motion picture in about 1890 with the advent of Dickson and Edison's Kinetoscope, the screen, with moving images and text, became a dominant form of communication (Figure I.1). At first a source of novelty, then entertainment, it also became a source of news, information, propaganda, and advertising within its first decades.

From this 1st Screen, it was another half century before the first electronic screen, television, entered daily life. Although movies had been a very public form of communication, experienced en masse, this 2nd Screen was one that spoke to people in a much more intimate setting: their living rooms (Figure I.2). Because of that, it was able to deliver different kinds of messages that were perceived differently by viewers.

Another 40 years passed before the 3rd (and first digital) Screen, the personal computer, came to market, and it wasn't until the early 1990s, with the advent of the Internet, that its potential as a communications medium became clear (Figure I.3). For the first time, individuals had a personalized, on-demand screen for viewing the information they wanted at any time and in (almost) any place that suited them.

When PDAs met cellular technology, the mobile phone came into its own and took its place as the 4th Screen—the most intensely private and controlled screen yet (Figure I.4). This revolutionary handheld screen accompanied people into the real world and let them access information wherever they were at any moment.

All of these screens enable people to communicate with one another, whether providing information or stimulating purchases. Each screen has unique characteristics, and each of them reach people in different places, offering different degrees of viewer control. Yet, as a whole, they do not fill the gaps in the communications grid; there are myriad places people go every day where none of these screens can deliver messages from a marketer, employer, or other entity to inform a recipient and guide decision making.

Enter digital signage.

Figure I.1 The 1st Screen, the silver screen.
©2007 Baldur Tryggvason.

Figure I.2 The 2nd
Screen, television.
©2009 Pixelery.com.

Figure I.3 The 3rd Screen, the personal computer.
©2003 Ayaaz Rattansi.

Figure I.4 The 4th Screen, mobile phones and PDAs.
©2008 Steven Smith.

Figure I.5 The 5th Screen, digital signage in Times Square. ©2009 Jeremy Edwards.

Today a combination of technical advances—low-cost flat panel screens in a range of sizes, digital cellular and Wi-Fi networks, web-based control software—make it possible to create a 5th Screen that can be encountered in all places where the presence of the other four screens is diminished (Figure I.5). From miniature screens on a retail shelf that inform consumers about products and shape their decisions to buy, to bright, ever-changing highway billboards that convey the right messages at the right time, digital signage offers a powerful new medium for communications in education, marketing, retail, and employee communications environments. This 5th Screen creates a crucial visual connection with messages delivered on the other screens we encounter daily, intercepting our inquisitive nature at our points of decision.

For the first time in history, there is a screen that matches what consumers want to see and interact with. The business of digital signage is in alignment with the consumers' experience, purpose, and mind-set. This truly is a winning combination for advertisers and consumers alike.

Of course, digital out of home (DOOH) is much more than a digital billboard. With a combination of dynamic content that is highly adaptable to its audience and environment, high-definition video imagery, and often interactive features, digital signage can help us, motivate us, provoke us, and unite us. Whether you watch them, touch them, step on them, interact with them, or pass them by at 70 miles per hour on the freeway, these new screens will have a powerful influence on our decision making and our experience.

As with every screen that came before, the most important element of the 5th Screen is not the technology behind it but the content it delivers. Without the right content, delivered with a clear understanding of the power of digital signage, the technology can't deliver value, can't motivate consumers, and can't bolster brands. Those who understand how to create content that works for digital signage will be the ones who will reap the benefits.

Throughout this book there are more than 160 illustrations and images as examples. The video and Flash productions from which some stills are taken are available in full color and full motion along with color illustrations on www.5thScreen.info, the companion web site for this book. In addition, the companion web site will carry updates on the latest industry content trends, video interviews, and book updates.

1 The New Medium: Digital Signage and the Power of Content

One finds oneself faced with a plethora of choices for media placement and creativity in the vast digital landscape of information and advertising. Whether an agency, creative production facility, brand, or media conglomerate, one now must consider the latest installment, digital signage or Digital Out Of Home (DOOH). This latest screen, the 5th Screen, has its own characteristics, its own content methodology, and its own strategy to ensure success.

Every screen has been used in one way or another by advertisers to deliver messages. Just as the Internet, in the beginning, became part of our daily lives, content was approached from a printed brochure mind-set as opposed to creating media true to the medium itself. Advertisers have to consider the special nature of each screen to maximize the opportunities. Making the most of digital signage is no different. Because people have learned the visual language of movies and television and standards of interaction with the Internet and mobile devices, those habits will transfer to DOOH. But there are also characteristics of where and how viewers encounter each screen that make communicating through them different. It is the viewers' relationship to the screen and the mind-set they bring to the encounter that changes from screen to screen.

To understand how digital signage provides unique value to viewers, we should consider their expectations when they encounter it.

With television, for example, the viewer generally wants to be entertained; this mind-set dictates how the consumer absorbs the message. On the other hand, the producers of television programming have a different interest: they are intent on providing entertainment value that will capture enough attention so that consumers will also watch the advertising messages that pay for the entertainment. This creates a fundamental conflict: the viewer simply wants entertainment and resents the interruption when commercials interfere with that goal.

The entertainment mind-set goes back to the original screen—the silver screen—but consumers paid for that entertainment directly in the form of tickets. Television turned to the entertainment–commercial break–entertainment model instead and set in motion a long-running emotional battle. Television viewers accepted this model until they found a way around it, first by videotaping shows and fast-forwarding past commercials, and more recently with digital video recorders such as TiVo. Television producers are trying to deal with this disconnect by taking another cue from the movies: using product placement within the entertainment itself—from a soft drink can to a pop song—to present products and charge a fee.

Now consider using the Internet on a computer. Here the viewer is engaged differently because the technology is interactive and the content is more personal. Again, as advertisers try to reach consumers through this screen, they encounter the same problem as with television: their goals are at odds. In this encounter, the viewers' reaction is even more aggressive. Pop-up ads, designed to interrupt users like the ads that interrupt viewers in the TV model, were quickly slapped down by irritated viewers with the use of pop-up blockers. (Proof of the demand for pop-up blockers is that they are now a built-in feature in most web browsers.) Banner ads are the most popular method for getting the attention of viewers, showcasing products related to the web site being visited or search words the viewer used to get there. Unfortunately, viewers usually ignore these ads unless they are seeking related products or services. Now banner ads employ animation and video in attempts to catch the users' eyes with movement—a different form of interruption to garner attention (and a potential click through).

The issue with advertising and the Internet is that viewers may or may not be engaged in an activity where they are receptive to advertising. When searching for products or services, a viewer is more inclined to click on a banner ad or a paid search advertisement. If, in contrast, the user is searching for more general information or viewing entertainment, ads are an interruption. Yet advertisers and marketers want to reach as many viewers as possible, so they are developing ever more sophisticated methods to generate a positive response and additional interaction by consumers. Sometimes these can be very unnatural, but in other cases, such as social networks, they can even be fun.

The mobile screen presents a challenge that makes it even more difficult for advertisers to engage the viewer. Mobile handheld screens fit into the pocket, purse, and palm of the viewer, making it very intimate. Initial tests for reaching viewers using this screen failed miserably. Direct delivery of messages was viewed as spam—spam that most consumers paid for by the kilobyte. People regarded it as they would junk phone calls and faxes: something unwanted that arrived on a device they considered to be personal and inviolable. Because of this, the mobile screen is the only one so far in which the consumer opt-in model is widely used.

The mobile viewer sees the phone as a personal tool. Add a media component, and it becomes a personal toy. The viewer's mind-set is about him- or herself and nobody else. The key for the marketer is to get the individual to choose to participate and to engage the viewer in alternate ways. Involving user generated content and DOOH is one way marketers have recently engaged mobile more effectively.

Clearly, marketers have a tough time getting their brands and messages to the viewer in a relevant way on most screens. It takes thoughtful, engaging tactics and downright trickery on all of these screens except one: The 5th Screen. For the first time in the history of media this medium matches the expectations of the viewer with the medium.

This is where, by providing the missing link connecting the other screens, the 5th Screen shines more brightly than any other. Its business model, content, and placement make it ideal for advertising. It is designed to bring relevance to viewers in many ways. When done well, it has delivered results that rival the fresh and personal nature of the first commercial televisions spots.

1.1 Types of Digital Signage Networks

Employing digital signage to best advantage requires understanding the different networks in which it can operate.

There are three basic types of digital signage networks that determine both the placement and approach to creating messages for these installations:

- A point of sale (POS) network is what you might expect: digital signage that consumers encounter close to a product or service for sale. These screens are usually composed of in-store or retail digital signs. Sometimes they include screens placed on the end of an aisle, or end cap, near the deli in a grocery store. These viewers are shoppers (Figure 1.1). The power of this type of network is that the call to action is immediate; the screens are placed where consumers make their buying decisions. The content is attention grabbing and relevant to the product and brand while the consumer is focused on buying.

Figure 1.1 Point of sale networks are typically found where there are shoppers. ©2009 Neo Advertising.

Figure 1.2 Point of
transit networks are
placed where people are
on the go.
©2009 Lamar
Advertising.

- Digital billboards, along with screens associated with transit hubs and store windows,
  comprise the second type of installation, point of transit (POT) networks. These are
  arguably the live poster of the industry. They work by grabbing the attention of passing
  consumers for a brief period of time. The consumers are on-the-go viewers (Figure 1.2).
  These screens are mostly focused on establishing brand identity or value and parcel out
  visually attractive or active content in short bursts. Many consumers are already familiar with these types of POT networks. Even an exterior screen on a taxi that functions
  as a moving billboard is considered to be a POT screen.
- The third type is known as the point of wait (POW) network—one targeted to consumers waiting for a product or service. Usually we encounter these in retail lines
  and healthcare and hospitality locations, as well as internal corporate communications. The consumers watching these screens are dwell time viewers (Figure 1.3).
  One typical POW network is found in retail banking, where consumers are entertained in a queue while also being exposed to advertising and general feel-good content. Good content, usually lengthier, results in a happy customer for the teller. It is
  all about perceived wait time. Digital screens installed inside elevators present a
  quick news bite, an ad, and perhaps a weather forecast during the short trip from
  one floor to the next and enable advertisers to reach viewers during this dwell time.
  Another area where screens are putting everyone on the same page is internal communications. Simply put, one cannot avoid digital signage in the work place. Some
  of these networks are interactive, such as screens facing passengers riding inside
  taxis. In those cases, the viewer has more dwell time and can take in a longer message or series of messages. The common thread is that consumers viewing a POW
  network screen are both receptive and have sufficient time exposure to allow for
  longer messages and several repetitions.

Today most agencies think of the 5th screen as Digital Out Of Home
(DOOH) as many within the industry do, but mostly when it refers to ad-based
networks. The advertising agencies are driving this. Simply put, it fits their
Out-Of-Home (OOH) advertising nomenclature which has been in place since
television came into force and brought advertising inside the home. There is a
distinct difference between ad based networks (DOOH) and non-ad based

Figure 1.3 Point of wait networks take advantage of dwell time.
©2009 The Wall Street Journal Office Media Network.

networks (digital signage). And within one of the three network categories POW, DOOH and digital signage are used interchangeably, whereas POT networks are mostly referred to as DOOH. And POS networks are primarily called digital signage networks.

1.2 Keeping it Relevant

Each of these networks uses the technology of digital signage in remarkably different places and ways. In turn, they require marketers to develop specialized content for screens that hold relevance for the viewer when they are engaged in the primary activities of being on the move, waiting in line, or shopping. When the content touches viewers where they are and relates to their mindset and lifestyles, then it is relevant and powerful.

Relevant content can be displayed to the consumer through the manual process of creating playlists. Or it can occur in a more personalized way by using sophisticated search engines that couple available content with the type of network and exact placement of a given screen. Matching content with networks and venues provides useful information to the viewer and creates a more thoughtful, engaging experience.

All digital signage networks can change dynamically to keep up with the events of the day to deliver messaging that is relevant and targeted to a viewer's needs. Adding interactive capabilities to any of these networks naturally increases relevance and engages viewers in a sticky manner, meaning that the message sticks with the viewer because the experience is prolonged and the viewer is physically engaged. The tactile experience adds to the viewer's feeling of connection. The interaction ranges from the use of mobile phones and touch screens to gesture interaction. Gesture interaction is a very interesting facility where the movement of the participant in front of a screen or projection causes the content to change.

Data about viewer selections that are collected from these interactions can be very valuable for marketers who are fine-tuning messages and products to be more appealing to consumers.

1.3   Where is the ROI?

Return on investment (ROI) is measured in many forms depending on the type of digital signage network. For a POS network, sales ultimately drive the success of the network. For POT networks, return is driven by the number of eyeballs or people reached. For POW networks, there is a combination of call to action, eyeballs reached, and behavioral change in attitude of the viewer based on the experience.

Although each of the types of networks are measured by different metrics, these networks are almost always more cost-effective in delivering the same messages when compared with traditional media—including paper. After installing a network, resources used to keep it fresh are all digital all of the time. Delivery of content is electronic, modern screens are energy efficient, and the creation of content is digital. More resources can be invested in the creative side of the equation—the side that actually connects the message to the consumer—and much, much fewer resources are needed for production and distribution. The savings over time for printing and delivering paper and cardboard can be significant. So can the savings on the materials involved: paper, ink, and the energy to produce and transport them.

In some cases, as with digital billboards, this technology lets owners capture additional revenue by changing messages every 15 seconds or so. This reuse of the same electronic real estate allows for more brands to share the screen—something that is impossible with most paper signs. This has the added advantage of allowing fresh content to be displayed relative to the time of day, increasing consumer response. However, the most valuable part of ROI is in the effectiveness of the message delivery. Because DOOH connects so closely with the consumer, it can be made more relevant than other screens and reach consumers in places that other screens cannot (and in places when consumers are receptive); it simply can deliver better and more consistent message transfer.

That transfer, in turn, generates returns in the obvious form of greater product sales or the less obvious benefit: boosted brand value.

Because of this, marketers are able to reallocate less efficient market expenditures to digital signage to further increase ROI. Pulling budget from traditional media is a common occurrence. This is happening across many sectors and many types of networks. It is being done because of the proven results of deployments that are being tallied by network after network. The ROI in most cases can easily be proven in pilot phases of a network.

1.4   A Green Solution

The question that is asked daily in businesses across the globe is, How do we help our business become green? Digital signage is no different, and the same question is being asked of panel manufacturers, retailers, corporations, and the print world. According to the U.S. Environmental Protection Agency, 246 million tons of trash were created in 2008, but only about 50 percent (42 million tons) of all paper products were recycled. When it comes to printing posters, one must consider all aspects, including the inks, chemicals, adhesives, solvents, packaging, transportation, delivery, and then the disposal and recycling of the old posters. Common sense suggests that using fewer resources on a daily basis to deliver messages with energy-efficient displays is a more green solution than traditional paper-and-cardboard methods.

Does the energy required to operate displays outweigh the energy resources required to design, print, deliver, and install new signage on a monthly or quarterly basis? An extensive study of digital signage carbon emissions compared with traditional signage shows that the carbon consumption of a projected display is 7.5 percent lower than a traditional poster package. The independent study was commissioned by MediaZest, cosponsored by Cisco and Panasonic, and carried out by leading consumer research company ROI-Team and Brunel University. It took into account the emissions from warehouse to warehouse and compared all aspects of types of installation, performance, maintenance, and decommission, and it assessed consumption of electricity, diesel, paper, and ink. The digital display that was analyzed was a Panasonic PT-D4000 projector, 3M Vikuiti Rear Projection Film applied to the window, and a Cisco media player. All changes of content were sent via a broadband line, thus eliminating repeated printing of materials and road distribution. The lifetime of the display was set at 3 years.

Panel manufacturers are also making strides in creating panels that are energy efficient. New LED technology used as edge lighting instead of florescent backlight is an example of how the technology itself is changing to a more compelling green solution (Figure 1.4). The energy saving over florescent backlighting is, on average, 30 percent.

Figure 1.4 Edge lighting using LEDs are reducing power consumption.

Although all the data is not yet fully available, we do know that a single screen can effectively replace alternatives that require thousands of pieces of paper, hundreds of gallons of fuel, and the energy consumed by hundreds of hours of personnel resources over a short period of a year. From this, we can infer that a digital signage network is indeed likely to be a very green solution relative to existing approaches.

1.5   How DOOH will Change Marketing and Communications

Today's marketers already make use of most of the first four screens in an attempt to reach consumers. From product placement in feature films to TV ads, web banners, and even delivery of coupons via SMS text messages to mobile devices, each screen has a function in the marketing toolbox.

Marketers also know that the effectiveness of each of these screens is, in many cases, diminishing. Digital video recorders have created the TiVo effect, where consumers fast-forward through television commercials. On the Internet, most users reject paid search engine results in favor of organic selections while using blockers to counter pop-up ads, a common tool that marketers use (with limited success) to compete with the attention-grabbing motion and video on web sites. The mobile phone screen is, by design, personal and a highly controlled environment, making it a difficult place to direct marketing content.

Effective marketing means working with the strengths, and taking into account the weaknesses, of each of these media. The power of digital signage lies in its ability to connect the dots effectively among other screens and to help ensure that an appropriate message is communicated to consumers with each step of their daily movements. Because consumers may encounter several types of digital signage in POT, POW, and POS environments during a given day, a coordinated use of digital signage can help a brand marketer ensure that engagement with consumers continues in a variety of ways from first contact until the point of decision.

Digital signage can work with other types of screens to deliver a marketing message more effectively to consumers. A product shown on a TV ad, with its brand reinforced by a digital billboard and again by a digital sign at a retail outlet, followed by an interactive digital sign on the store shelf, backed by an offer sent to the consumer's mobile screen all can be orchestrated and intensified as the day progresses.

The best way to understand this is to imagine a typical day for a consumer and how he or she might be reached. How are the consumer's decisions affected by digital signage? In the morning, our consumer arises and switches on the television, where he first encounters an advertisement for a brand of frozen pizza while watching the news. Going online to check his web-based email, he encounters a banner ad for the same product because the marketer is targeting the consumer's city as part of a promotion.

Driving to work, our consumer encounters his first piece of digital signage, a large billboard along the highway. Because roadway sensors are able to signal that traffic is slow in that section of the freeway on this morning, the sign intermixes images of people eating the freshly baked frozen pizza, the brand's logo, and timely traffic information. Between the parking lot and the office is an ideal time to stop and buy a latte—and encounter a smaller digital sign inside the retail location while waiting in line. The pizza maker is one of several brands whose wares are shown in 15-second video clips on part of the screen, which it shares with headlines and sports scores. The clip mentions the local 50-cent discount promotion.

On the drive home, the digital billboard on the freeway has changed. Now the time is approaching the dinner hour, and now an ad is presented with a specific call to action to purchase a frozen pizza for dinner on the way home.

At the local supermarket, our consumer encounters a small, shelf-mounted digital sign next to the frozen food case, near the pizzas. The themes of the other pizza company messages of the day are repeated in a 15-second clip, including the 50-cent off promotion. The end of the spot includes a call to action for the consumer to send a text message to the pizza maker and in return receive a 50-cent off coupon directly to his cell phone. At checkout, the cashier will scan the coupon's bar code, and our consumer is on his way home with dinner.

Of course, it is likely that anyone would encounter additional digital signage during the day while waiting for lunch or waiting in line at the bank to deposit a check. Not every encounter will reinforce one particular brand or message. But the concept is clear: a single message or set of related messages can follow the consumer's physical path during the day, providing consistent reminders and eventually a call to action at the point of sale or decision.

Working in concert with print ads, TV ads, billboards, and the like, digital signage enables advertisers to reach consumers in places where, today, marketers typically are unable to deliver messages. Because the signs are dynamic and can adjust to real-time variables, such as time of day, they are more effective than static delivery systems.

1.6   Digital Signage as an Internal Communication Tool

Digital signage is not only useful to companies in outward, customer-facing applications. It can be an incredibly effective tool in communicating with employees about everything from company news and policies to the latest products and offers.

Placed in areas where employees congregate—cafeterias, break rooms, locker rooms, and stock rooms—digital signs can readily become a focal point of those areas and command attention. Because they provide high-resolution moving images, these screens are much more effective in capturing attention than email (and are much harder to dispose of without reading). The messages on these screens, because they are pushed to employees where they naturally assemble, are much more likely to be seen than similar content placed on intranet sites, which employees must actively choose to visit (Figure 1.5).

The video capability of screens makes them very effective for demonstrating a new product or procedure.

Content also takes on a peculiar psychological tone when presented on a large screen to a number of employees at once. It can take advantage of group dynamics by generating discourse or provoking group action about matters that are important to the company. These signs are especially useful for companies that have many workers without regular access to company computers and who would otherwise need to be reached with bulletin boards or printed newsletters. The latter media are more limited in their abilities to command attention, particularly when a workforce is mobile.

Once again, content is crucial; mixing softer material with more serious company information is most likely to keep employees' attention.

Figure 1.5 Rolls-Royce internal communications lobby screen.
©2009 Rolls-Royce Corporation.

1.7 Why Content Matters Most

Although all the evidence makes it easy to conclude that digital signage has an important place in the communication grid, that doesn't guarantee that an individual marketer, network, or screen will succeed with its deployment. Where the technology itself is a proven delivery mechanism, it is the content that often fails because marketers don't adapt their thinking to produce new content that matters.

This is not a startling revelation; each of the previous screens has either succeeded or failed in a particular case because of the content and how it was presented. The beauty of the 5th Screen is that its heritage comes from the previous four screens. DOOH, like the latest iterations of the TV screen, utilizes high-definition video, and like computers and the Internet, it uses Flash-generated content. As with mobile phones, it is personal and can be directed to an audience of one. Content for digital signage must stand alone during its creative production, but it must have continuity with the other four screens to echo its message across the digital landscape of screens.

In this communication grid, digital signage requires special attention to a number of unique details that are all distinctive within each and every network type, whether it is point of sale, point of transit, or point of wait. The messages change as we arrive closer to our point of decision to make a purchase. The message on the billboard may be brand driven, where at the shelf it will be product driven, all the while maintaining consistent creative elements across all the screens and throughout the campaign.

The elements from high-definition video produced for TV or the Flash and digital artwork from computers and the Internet can be reworked and effectively repurposed for digital signage; the content is different from any of the other media and is unique to the 5th Screen. We can build upon the visual cues that have been developed since the beginnings of film, where color can drive an emotional cue and graphic forms can offer perspective. These cues are a familiar visual language delivered in a new setting: digital signage.

Refreshing content for DOOH is no small task, but when utilizing creative assets with slightly modified content, those assets will keep the messaging fresh in the mind of the consumer. Other considerations we will discuss in later chapters, such as dwell time and frequency of visit, directly affect how often the message is refreshed. In addition, by introducing time of day into the mix, messages can be altered to target an audience, at that precise time, in that precise place. Fine-tuning content to match the audience by age, income, and behavioral attitudes will also add to the creative workload.

When objectives for creating content include interactive features, the first inclination is to draw from web-based content that has already been created. Fortunately, design and graphic elements do translate, but interactivity for digital signage requires larger buttons and single-purposed actions on the screen at one time. This type of content also includes interaction with the 4th Screen, mobile devices, where digital signage is designed to promote and cause a call to action. Content downloaded or browsed on the mobile screen will share some of the same assets, but the context and messages will be different.

1.8 Summary

Digital signage is as diverse as the content that is displayed. It is technology that meets viewers in their environment with potentially the right message at the right time. I challenge the industry to drive toward a 25 percent penetration by 2015 based on the success of today's networks. And in a world where there is less than 2 percent penetration in retail, this means millions of points where digital signage will become present, and with that, billions of pieces of content will be created.

Creating content for digital signage is no different from creating content for any other screen. It takes thought, process, and strategy to create compelling, effective content. With digital signage, content (*with relevance*) is king.

The power of digital signage is delivering creative, compelling content that is relevant to viewers, and it will have an impact on the out-of-home experience in more ways than any other medium ever invented.

2 Content Strategy: Methodology and Process

Before a marketer can create any content for a digital signage program, it's important to understand a number of things about the network—to make a kind of preliminary survey of the landscape. If it is a new network then a strategic blueprint will have to be created before screen one is deployed. What you learn in this initial phase will inform a host of later decisions that are vital to the network's success in communicating your messages to the intended audience. It can take some time to create a strategic plan and will require those new to digital signage to learn some new concepts and terminology. This often runs into a countervailing force—the pressure to get a network developed and operational quickly, with a minimum up-front investment. Because of this pressure, there can be a temptation, even by experienced marketers, to skip this step, particularly when a marketer has a wealth of existing content to tap—television commercials, print ad campaigns, and the like. But as we learned in the Introduction and Chapter 1, DOOH has its own unique characteristics that most often prevent that content from being used as is.

The focus of discussion for this book is content strategies and how they relate to digital signage. It is, however, important to understand that there are strategic steps that need to be followed when building a new network from the ground up.

The top 10 basic steps for network success include the following:

Strategic planning; establish type of network
Content relevance and audience research
Content creation; network guidelines
Programming the network
Choosing the right technology
Pilot rollout
Measurement of the pilot
Roll out the network
Measure the entire network
Continuous refinement and measurement

Starting from the beginning will also help marketers identify responsible decision makers who will help guide or provide the content. They can be internal to your organization—from executives to different brand owners—or external (partners, for example). Understanding who else is involved is important to planning and implementation and the ability to put into action a digital signage campaign in a timely fashion.

Pat Hellberg, a partner in The Preset Group who also formerly ran the Nike network for 7 years, agrees that planning is critical. "Clear vision and the road map really provides the network a reason to *be* and in turn, the audience a reason to *watch*. Those two are huge issues that require planning."

Finally, by considering how the particular digital signage network will interact with other types of communication between an organization and its target audience, a marketer can help ensure that the work of digital signage reinforces business goals, sales campaigns, or other objectives.

2.1   Establishing the Type of Network

In Chapter 1 we outlined the three basic types of digital signage networks. Although it's possible—even probable—that marketers will use a mix of these networks with a single brand or for one organization, the content considerations for each are significantly different. When one understands the type of network and its relevancy, then one can create the right content for the viewer.

Within each of these main network types, one can identify a series of subcategories (Figure 2.1) that will further identify the characteristics of viewers and their experiences and refine the type of content that is most appropriate.

Point of Wait

Service Lines
Healthcare
Fitness Centers
Elevators
Office Buildings
Corporate Communications
In Taxi, Subway, Train
Bars and Restaurants

Point of Sale

Brand Shelf Network
Brand Owned Store
Convenience
Mall
General Retail

Point of Transit

Airport
Bill Board
Bus Station
Store Front Window
Subway Station
Train Station

Figure 2.1   Three types of networks and subnetwork categories.

2.1.1 Point of Transit

A point of transit (POT) network is one in which the viewer is in transit past the sign and is not expected to linger. These networks are tailored for "on the go" viewers. These can be signs along the side of a highway, where they are visible to large numbers of diverse viewers passing at fairly high speed, or they can be in airports, train or bus stations, or other locations where people are passing more slowly. Content on a POT network is most like a traditional billboard in that it needs to quickly create a thought-provoking impression and is usually more focused on a brand rather than a particular offer. Its value over traditional paper is twofold. One is motion; with the exception of a handful of mechanical billboard arrangements, a digital sign is the only way to produce movement that will attract an otherwise inattentive eye. The other is that a digital sign's message can be changed at frequent intervals or to match the time of day or other external conditions. A digital sign along a highway might highlight a coffee brand during the morning commute, and the evening commute message might relate to a chicken dinner.

POT networks break down into a several subcategories:

- Digital billboards
- Signage inside transit hubs
- Exterior-facing retail signage

Digital Billboards

True digital billboards alongside highways or next to pedestrian walkways in urban settings are probably the easiest subcategory to understand. These tend to be larger signs made to be viewed at a distance and with an extremely short time window to deliver a message. In fact, the speed at which consumers are likely to pass a given sign of this type is probably the most important factor in determining the type and mix of content that will be effective. Tommy Teepell, chief marketing officer of Lamar Advertising, explains why digital billboards are so attractive to advertisers. "Because it's digital, I can, for the first time in the history of billboard advertising, change my ad anytime I want anytime of the day." Given only a few seconds, these signs are best for brand awareness, pithy messages of few words and provocative images, and frequent repetition. "One of our clients was basically selling lemonade at a fast food restaurant. So they put a lemonade stand up on the billboard," explains Teepell. "The first thing they put up was a dog and a lemonade stand. And a lot of background creative. So we put that up and we measured the responses and then we said, 'Let's just eliminate all that and just have the lemonade stand and the dog in a black background. With the message on selling the lemonade and see what happens.' All of a sudden the concept of lemonade for sale popped out [Figure 2.2] as opposed to people driving by going, 'Oh isn't that funny. It's a lemonade stand and there's a dog running in it.'"

Some restrictions do apply to the speed at which these ads can be refreshed. Most local ordinances will state that the ads can change only every 10 seconds, for example. In addition, the ads can have no animation. This is all done for safety

Figure 2.2 Simplifying messages for digital billboards is critical for the fast paced, on-the-go viewer.
©2009 Lamar Advertising.

of the drivers. Teepell has done extensive studies on length and loop times. "Typically what we have, and of course it's based upon what the local governmental restrictions are but typically what we're going to have are six advertisers and their message is up from 8 to 10 seconds depending upon the regulations."

Transit Hub Signage

Depending upon their point in the travel process, viewers tend to have more time to devote to signage inside transit hubs, such as airports, train depots, bus stations, and subway platforms, than they do to digital billboards, offering some flexibility with the length of contact segments. For marketers, that offers an outlet for advertising seeking to establish brand awareness (Figure 2.3). What will cause people to watch these ads? The key is to be thought provoking and unique—traditionally the way these ads have drawn attention in printed form. But digital signage offers two powerful extensions to the print ad.

The first is that other relevant content can be mixed with advertising to keep the viewer engaged. Viewers in these locations are looking for transit-related information—schedules, weather reports, anything related to their trip. For example, a passenger who has just landed at LAX may be interested in knowing not only the weather but perhaps what major events are happening in the area that day, or perhaps the latest movie releases and where they are being screened. DOOH creates another layer of relevance that was not possible before.

Kelly McGillivray, president of Peoplecount, has experience measuring what works and what does not. "In anything that's in transit, I would say it has to be

Figure 2.3 Transit hub DOOH can also have relevant information along with full-screen advertising.
©2009 Neo Advertising.

5 to 10 seconds, bites, and it has to have the product or logo on the screen virtually all the time and no sound. It would be better off to run something 5 to 8 seconds long several times through the loop. I have never tested any multiple split screens that have worked. People remember the weather, the sports, the other content but they don't remember the advertisers. I would say that you need to rotate content and advertising but have it on the full screen or most of the screen for a few seconds. And then change it to something else. Have something dominate, whatever it is, dominate the screen because people really aren't multitasking that they're looking at four things at once. If it is not just purely advertising, if it is content, then it needs to switch back and forth somehow so that people know if they just wait a second, they're going to get something for them. So it's always what's relevant to them."

One significant refinement that's possible in these networks is to actively match the departure point and the arrival city. Signs at a given airport gate can change to display content that is relevant to the city to which the viewer is traveling and be matched with similar marketing messages upon arrival if the network has access to flight data and gate information. Screens along subway platforms can be programmed on the fly to match the destination of the next train.

The second advantage is the ability to add the time of day into the determination of the marketing content for greatest impact. Passengers on a morning flight are likely to be more open to advertisements that are relevant to what consumers do in a typical morning—Gillette for the overnight flier or Jimmy Dean sausages for those who might want breakfast.

In all of these cases, careful attention needs to be paid to the type of hub and the time of day. Subway commuters, for example, will spend less time in proximity to the sign than the average airport passenger.

There is also a significant potential in these subnetworks to add an interactive component. Given the controlled environment, some of these signs can be placed in such a way that consumers could touch the screen or interact with one's cell phone and obtain information or even make a purchase as they might in a point of sale network.

Exterior-Facing Retail Signage

Retail signage that faces a sidewalk and is seen by passing viewers through a window is a kind of merger between the digital billboard and the in-mall network. There's not as great a chance that potential viewers are predisposed to buying as when they are at a mall—people have many reasons to walk past a particular retail establishment. But there is a greater chance to create an interaction with a passing viewer than with a roadside digital billboard. Here content is most likely to be effective if it is both directly relevant to the retailer (brands, products, and special offers) and unusual—something that has the potential to catch the eye. Vincent John Vincent, cofounder and president of GestureTek, echoes this sentiment: "Retail window installations really capture people's attention as they are going by on the street, and then engage them in an interactive and fun way. Some of the installations are by retailers themselves and some are using vacant spaces as an advertising venue to promote a movie release. [Digital signage for the film] *Coraline* is a great example of this [Figure 2.4].

Figure 2.4 The movie *Coraline* is promoted in a storefront window using interactive gesture technology to engage the viewer.
©2009 GestureTek and Laika Films.

It was simulation of some of the movie scenes and people could interact within the scene, so they became part of the experience and the movie."

Content segments for these subcategories can be longer than on a digital billboard but not overly long, unless, as in the *Coraline* example, it is an interactive experience. In that case, then one can build segments that have shorter introductions to attract attention but much longer interactive material that allows for the person experiencing the interaction to determine how much time he or she will spend on the content. The content can also vary according to time of day—when a shop is open the messages would be largely aimed at drawing the viewer inside at that moment; when it is closed, the messages would be more focused on branding and encouraging a return. This is a popular approach in the real estate business, where offices can promote properties for sale through the use of interactive screens that allow people to browse or even tour homes on the screen (Figure 2.5) when the real estate office is closed, and if they choose they can leave their contact information so an agent can follow-up with them.

Figure 2.5 Projected window screen in front of a real estate office in Malmo, Sweden.

2.1.2 Point of Sale

A point of sale (POS) network exists in retail environments and can be at the shelf, or elsewhere within a store, and even in the public areas of a shopping mall. These networks of course are tailored toward the "shopper" as a viewer. When they are in a store, consumers are predisposed to shopping and are in the ideal mind-set for making a purchase; they are often actively searching for information about products and services or weighing one brand against another. Thus, content on a POS network can help drive these consumers to make a particular purchase through presentation of a value proposition along with a call to action (Figure 2.6). Unlike a POT network, here you have the opportunity to present a longer message (the viewer is already at the shelf and engaged) or even an interactive one (because of the proximity of the viewer to the screen).

When digital signage is properly incorporated into retail environments, our experience is that the quality of the content leads directly to higher levels of sales uplift and enhances the shopping experience. As with the other types of digital signage networks, content on a POS network can be targeted toward the time of day and any additional demographic knowledge a retailer might have about the customers who come to the store at a given time. In addition, in-store signage can be tailored to precise product offerings and, if connected to an inventory system, can change or stop offers based on the availability of an item.

Figure 2.6 Retail screen built into the environment, Lindri Clothing, Sweden.

Within the POS network category, there are at least three relevant subcategories to consider:

- Brand-owned network
- Retailer-controlled network
- Signage in the public areas of shopping malls

One of the most obvious places where digital signage provides direct value to marketers and consumers is at this point of decision. In most cases, this will be at the shelf where a retail product is displayed or in a service environment at the place where orders are taken. The reason for this is simple: consumers are most receptive to a call to action or purchase when they are at the shelf or immediately prior to receiving service delivery.

This is, of course, the same strategy behind the use of static shelf signs—whether to simply reinforce other marketing messages or offer a coupon on the spot. However, digital signage can take the strategy an important additional step further. Because the content displayed on the sign is dynamic, marketers can vary messages, from reinforcing product attributes, to making an offer, to providing additional information about the product or service. The offer can vary by time of day or even based on the rate at which a product is selling.

The most significant differences among these subnetworks are less about where the screens are located and more about who controls them. What they all have in common are the goals of creating sales uplift, increasing brand equity, and creating a better shopper experience, putting together two otherwise separate marketing functions into a single device. Digital signage is about "bridging the gap between branding and merchandising," says Lyle Bunn, CEO of BUNN Co. "Where we would have typically had branding budgets and promotional budgets, I see this as combining the two." Branding content "helps develop recall and aspirations" while the merchandising part of it "activates the sale."

One step beyond that is the creation of interactive environments for point-of-sale screens. If placed in an environment where consumers can interact with a screen by touch, content can be displayed that answers consumers' product questions, provides personalized offers, or allows for further message delivery based on consumer feedback and even can connect a live person via video conference. This is something no static sign can do, and, because the other four screens (silver screen, TV, computer, mobile) are not typically located right next to saleable products, they cannot compete on the same level.

Digital signage, therefore, can play an important role in driving sales and influencing buying decisions in most retail environments. But these are only some of the ways in which digital signage helps guide consumers' behavior in the retail environment. At its most effective, digital signage appears in a number of zones throughout a store, beginning with large screens in various departments, leading to smaller interactive signs at the shelf, and finally to signs while customers are waiting in line to pay for their purchases.

All these signs share the common goal of presenting products, ideas, and concepts to consumers while they are positioned by relevant goods or services. Their differences, as we will see later, have to do with distinct ways in which one uses content to reinforce the brand and the buying decision.

Brand-Owned Network

A brand-owned network is one that is deployed by a specific brand at the shelf or on the end cap and is independent of the retailer (Figure 2.7). It seeks to promote products from that particular brand and relies on the brand value along with special offers to steer consumers away from nearby competitors. Using screens in these locations can make a huge difference to the brand because consumers today make nearly 74 percent of their purchase decisions at the shelf.

These screens are more commonly found in smaller retailers or in certain sections of larger retailers' stores. Marketers will want to have a detailed understanding of each store where their screens are displayed and manipulate the content according to demographics, time of day, competitive realities in that geographic area, and their own current sales objectives. This will require building a

Figure 2.7 Brand-owned retail screen at the shelf. ©2009 Hunters Specialty.

significant library of content templates with targeted themes that can be swapped in and out to match the customer demographic traffic and maximize sales.

One brand that has used this kind of digital signage network to stand out from larger competitors is Buffalo Technology, which makes wireless networking equipment aimed at consumers. The company competes against larger brands with household names, such as Cisco, and this competition is particularly intense in the 45 stores of the Fry's Electronics chain. Working with Fry's to install digital signage into their end caps, Buffalo was able to direct educational and promotional video content directly to consumers, standing out from competitive paper-based displays and pop-ups (Figure 2.8). The company also inserted training content for store sales personnel and ensured the content was tied to stock levels. Buffalo reported an 18 percent uplift in gross sales

Figure 2.8 Brand-owned Buffalo digital signage display at the shelf reported an 18 percent uplift in sales.

from the installation and an 11 percent cost savings over delivering traditional paper promotional products to the store.

Retailer-Controlled Network

A retailer-controlled network exists where the retailer—typically a major chain—wants complete control of its space and the digital signage network. These networks will likely combine shelf-side screens, whose content is largely specific offers, with larger screens in each of the in-store zones into which large retail stores are segmented. The content on these larger screens is more specific to the types of goods offered in that segment—appliances versus cameras in a consumer electronics store, for example.

What's most important to determining content for these networks depends on the retailer's overall objectives. Is it to increase sales of cameras? Get customers to add service contracts to their purchases? Promote a brand that is new to the retailer? Clear out older merchandise? Whatever the answer, a long-term content plan can be created to accomplish those goals.

One successful deployment of this kind of in-store zoned network has been at Incredible Connection, a technology retailer in South Africa. When designing a major new store in KwaZulu-Natal, the retailer incorporated digital signage at four separate levels throughout the 20,000-square-foot location. At the top level, Incredible Connection installed a large video wall (Figure 2.9) visible to entering customers that combined customer welcome messages, store

Figure 2.9   A large video wall greets shoppers at Incredible Connection in South Africa. Image courtesy of Tactile.

branding, and current promotions. At the next level, strategically placed kiosks incorporating interactive technology combined self-service assistance with virtual product browsers. Next, kiosks along product shelves provided content specific to the products and services within customer reach. Finally, digital signage clustered near checkout lines provided a combination of entertainment content (to reduce perceived wait time) and additional promotions (a final opportunity for sales uplift).

The digital signage strategy at Target provides a prime example of how to use specific content closer to the product in the in-store zones. Mark Bennett has been involved with Target's digital signage team from its early stages, working with the supplier brands to create content that is specific to the product, yet also has continuity across the network, in an effort to drive overall sales. "There was the TV wall because Target sells TVs. So all of those TVs got wired and then there is a music and movies area where there are DVD and CD sales, and then the kids' entertainment area and a video games area. So those all seemed like very low hanging fruit at the time. And so that's how we initially launched the network. So as a part of our relevancy guidelines, our guests were only going to see content relevant to the area on the screens in that area. So in the video game area, for example, you were only going to see video game trailers. The kids' entertainment was all going to be about Curious George and whatever Disney programs there were and so on and so on."

For apparel stores, the content can be totally different. Whereas Target is creating specific vendor content that is related to in-store zones, Brian Hirsh of Retail Entertainment Design is creating engaging entertainment content that drives sales in a different manner.

"If you look at a point of sale category, you have lots of different ways to have a media play in that space," he explains. "From a content perspective, obviously if it's in the front of the store, it's [a] short, smaller loop. It could be some ambient footage, meaning quick edits of us being on-site during a photo shoot where it's live product shots and merchandising shots, but it would be real fast. You have about a second to attract the consumer. And then again the goal is to get them to walk inside the store."

When the potential customer is in the store, Hirsh's strategy changes. He expands on concepts and ideas and creates longer and more engaging segments (Figure 2.10).

One temptation in a retailer-controlled network is to craft a kind of hybrid network that couples outside advertising with the retailer's own branding and offers. Often this is done to provide an additional revenue stream for the retailer, but to do so as the sole or main reason for creating a hybrid network is not smart use of the technology and does not create value and relevancy to the viewer.

Let's consider a retailer that operates a chain of women's shoe stores and installs a retailer-owned network. The messaging that network would seek to create in the stores would have to do with the company's vision of its brand, its current product offers, and perhaps some educational content.

Figure 2.10 Apparel stores are using digital signage to enhance the experience.
©2009 Retail Entertainment Design.

Supplementing that with other advertising requires choosing carefully to ensure the relevance of the network to customers isn't compromised. Advertising for jewelry might be effective and relevant, even giving the shoe store a share of the halo effect of the jewelry brand and helping to reinforce its position in terms of market segment. By the same token, subjecting customers to soft drink advertising would likely be ineffective and create a negative association for the retailer.

The issue here, as with almost every decision concerning digital signage, is relevance. How relevant is the message to the viewer with respect to the venue? The in-store network is poised to succeed in driving sales and strengthening brand value when the retailer's first concern is the objectives and the content that will run on its network. The best choice when it comes to reselling screen space and time is to cater to the same brands that are in the store. And rather than compromising coop money, look at digital signage as an opportunity to secure new money for in-store media.

At long last retailers that have been struggling with digital signage are now beginning to embrace the retail network as a useful tool that helps the shopper make a purchase decision right then and there. One such agency that is taking this task seriously is Studio Square. "When I look out in the world of most digital signage companies, they think that people in the store are eyeballs and they sell them like eyeballs," says Bruce Fougere, creative director. "They sell them like impressions. They sell the network to whoever wants to buy it. In retail shoppers are looking to buy something right now. Our philosophy is simply help our customer shop today. There is no do this later. There is no go somewhere else. There is no check out the web. There is simply an understanding of what you need to do today."

Public Areas of Shopping Malls

Signage in the public areas of shopping malls may at first seem to be POT networks, but they are fundamentally different. Even though these signs are not next to a product, they do provide a direct sales opportunity within the mall. They do offer the chance to direct messages at viewers who are already in a frame of mind to make purchases—after all, that's why they have come to a mall. But there's also a sense of escape about it; to many people, women and teens in particular, a mall is an escape. For women, it's an escape from their kids and their husbands and their everyday life; for teenagers, it's an escape from their parents and their teachers.

At the same time, this is an environment where there is a great deal of competition for the consumer's attention—printed signs, store displays, lighting, and activity around them. So a successful digital sign needs to display ad content that is unique and thought provoking but is also mindful of the clutter of messages surrounding it. Again, here's a place where digital signage has an advantage. Because it can mix other relevant content with specific marketing messages, a digital sign has a greater chance of attracting the attention of consumers.

This suggests a content mix that combines general branding along with specific mall information—for example, matching available brands or products with the merchants offering them. Mixed with these messages, consumers might be attracted to information about the other services in the mall, such as food or entertainment, as well as future events to create an incentive for a return visit. Adspace Networks CEO Dominick Porco approaches content on this type of network very specifically, based on the category of shopper (Figure 2.11). Some, who are in the so-called mission shopper group, do not pay attention to the screens; they simply accomplish their mission of buying a specific item and leaving. But shoppers who spend a few hours on a Saturday afternoon (the average shopper) and take time to browse "can be very engaged with these screens."

As with most other digital signage networks, time of day combined with demographic knowledge can be a powerful tool for making content decisions—moms with kids on weekdays at lunchtime or teens after school or on Saturday night.

Fine-tuning any of these networks—point of transit, point of wait, or point of sale—requires creative thinking, research, and great technology. But relevant content in context is what will make or break them every time.

Figure 2.11 Essentials is engaging
content that attracts shoppers in
malls.
©2009 Adspace Networks.

2.1.3 Point of Wait

A point of wait (POW) network generally has a different purpose than the previous two networks. These networks are tailored toward "dwell time" viewers.
There are two basic types of subcategory networks: one is waiting and the
other is dwell time during an activity. Often there are three primary goals.
The first is to provide key messaging geared toward brands and products
related to the service provider. The second, equally important, is to increase
customers' satisfaction by altering their perception of how long they are actually waiting. The third is to provide interesting, relevant content in various
venues. These networks might be found in a hospital or doctor's office, health
and fitness centers, a corporate lobby, break rooms, or a bank—anywhere that
individuals gather and wait for services or have dwell time. Because of their
dual nature, these networks perform best with a mixture of messages that combine brand, product, or service information along with segments that offer

entertainment and educational value. Depending on the nature of the service provider's environment, the expected real waiting time, and the needs of the brand, the entertainment and educational content may be as simple as a weather forecast, or it could extend to brand-building community messages, longer news segments, or games. The disadvantage to the viewer of having dwell time *is* the advantage of these networks; at times the content can be lengthier, more complex, and more nuanced than is possible in a 5-second drive-by of a POT network.

POW networks have at least five subcategories:

- Health care and fitness
- Bars and restaurants
- Service lines
- Elevators and office networks
- Internal communications

Health Care Waiting Rooms

Health networks include screens placed in the waiting rooms and common areas of hospitals, doctors' offices, veterinarian clinics, and dental offices. In these situations, people are accustomed to fairly lengthy wait times—a half hour would not be uncommon. People here are also very closely focused on the reason for their visit.

These networks offer a prime opportunity to provide a mixture of informational content that can be educational (how to exercise and diet to lower cholesterol); might market additional services (tooth whitening) or products (special pet food); or help remind viewers of things they might need to do at this visit (time for a flu shot). These segments can be several minutes in length because it is likely that most viewers will be motivated to watch the screen for much of the time they are in the waiting area. Captivating segments will reduce the perception of waiting time while creating a positive experience for the consumer, which transfers as an increased positive perception of the health service provider. Integrated informational content and advertising garners the highest approval level from viewers. Conversely, rapid rotation of content along with frequent repetition of segments will be very noticeable to viewers and likely cause them to lose interest through boredom and actually increase the perception of the time spent waiting.

Fitness Centers

Fitness centers offer network operators and advertisers a unique opportunity reach high-dwell-time viewers. Viewers are engaged in exercise activities, which are usually on machines that can face monitors. Zoom Media has the largest fitness network in North America. They categorize their network into three uniquely different types of networks for special purposes. The obvious screen that Zoom Media programs is the one that is seen while a viewer is on a particular exercise machine. "The first screen that we have is on the cardio machines," clarifies Francois Beaubien, CEO. "If you get on the cardio machine, our server powers that screen [Figure 2.12A]. You have an opportunity to see an advertisement that opens up and you then can see whatever you want to but we're in the process now we're putting in our own channels. So that you can not only see CNN, ESPN, or whatever you want from the cable feed that goes into that gym, but you'll have to have long programming. I'll give an example of something we did with HBO. *Entourage* is a big show on HBO. When they were launching season 3, they wanted us to play season 2 and they paid us for that. So we played season 2 in New York Sports Club."

The second screen that Zoom Media programs in fitness centers is the general ambient screens that are scattered throughout the gym. "There are certain venues you walk in and you feel like you're in a television shop it's so amazing. You can imagine how many screens we have in those," says Beaubien. "And that's the screens [Figure 2.12B] that tie back into our music video content. Remember that we are the entertainment system for the gym industry. So when you walk into a gym and they're playing music and that's part of the entertainment for their members, we provide that and they pay us a monthly subscription fee to provide content."

The third type of screen is really closer to the digital signage model. Zoom Media provides three types of content on these screens: club messaging to their patrons, editorial content, and advertising [Figure 2.12C]. "We have the digital screen without sound and we tailor that to the venue," explains Beaubien. "You can have the time, the weather, the class schedule, and specials, like a Bally special on the trainers today. It's whatever the venue wants. We also have editorial content that's playing on that screen. Again no sound, but think fitness content. Think of health and wellness. Think about hydration, think about tea, and think about a whole bunch of tidbits of information which are educational and health related. And of course the other part of it is advertising."

Bars and Restaurants

Bars and restaurants are under the category of POW and are similar to fitness centers because the audience is dwell time viewers. Ron Greenberg, Touch-Tunes CMO, says that the company has digital jukeboxes that consumers interact with to select and purchase music. "I think our application is a bit different from other types of digital signage [Figure 2.13] because people are actually seeking this out, paying for it, and spending a lot of time in front of the screen and learning about new songs available and new artists. In addition there are advertising messages that are presented. So you get a highly vested, highly engaged audience that you know is pulled in by the content. We can track the responses by touches to the advertising and how they respond to that as well."

Ripple TV has networks in coffee and bagel shops. When a customer sits down to drink coffee or eat a bagel, the Ripple TV network keeps the viewer

Figure 2.12 Fitness centers often have several types of networks within their digital signage deployment. ©2009 Zoom Media Networks.

Figure 2.13 Digital jukeboxes take advantage of people who seek them out and spend time in front of them by delivering advertising. ©2009 TouchTunes.

connected to local information, and, of course, the viewer is exposed to advertising that is local, regional, and national. Ripple TV CEO John McMenamin briefs us about his network and the dwell time. "We're a dwell time network and our core business is what we call a lifestyle network, which is in about 650 locations. The content we bring to those viewers is local relevant community content. The network also covers regional content and then goes to national content. It's sort of real-time content because it's updated throughout the day [Figure 2.14]." This is a case where there are two purposes for a network: one is wait time while people are in line for coffee or a bagel, and the other is dwell time while a customer eats or drinks coffee.

Lines for Service

In service-oriented environments where patrons wait in line (for example, banks and movie theaters), digital signage plays a somewhat different but important role. First and foremost, it can be an important element in reducing perceived wait times by providing a combination of information, entertainment, and branding to queuing customers. Disney has long understood this effect in their theme parks and has designed their lines to be attractions in themselves, entertaining customers while distracting them from considering the passing time. Nearly all service businesses with customer queues can employ this strategy for improved customer satisfaction and to present dynamic brand content to those customers. The content can be changed based on the expected wait time of that moment and typically allows for longer content segments than other types of signs.

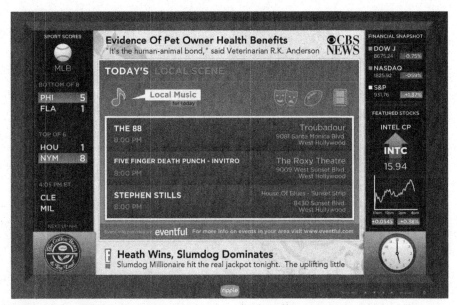

Figure 2.14 While a customer sits down to drink coffee or eat a bagel, the customer encounters content that is relevant to his or her neighborhood. ©2009 Ripple TV.

Waiting times for a bank teller, DMV clerk, or supermarket cashier are almost always shorter than for health networks, but people are generally focused on completing the transaction as quickly as possible instead of the reason for the visit. In health networks, the consumer has significant expectations of the service provider, but line networks represent commodity transactions where a positive experience usually translates to the least amount of time spent in line. A combination of content here is key; there is an opportunity to market additional products or services to create potential up-sell opportunities while engaging the viewer with informational and entertainment content.

Consider the experience of American Digital Signage, which maintains screens at the checkout lane in more than 250 locations and uses a number of methods to determine how to program relevant content for each installation. "Front-end items [things in the rack] at checkout account for 1.2 percent of grocery sales. If they do want to promote a product specifically at the front end, it will most likely be something that they sell at the front end, such as concessionary magazines," explains Jill Ruttenberg, managing member. A grocer is unlikely to want to use these register locations to promote specific items that are not available at the front end because that would mean the customer would have to get out of line and go back into the store—something that's not likely to happen. Instead, "What the grocer likes to do is promote something generic such as visit our floral department, visit our deli, remember that we can take care of your Super Bowl party tray...to remind people about what's going on [Figure 2.15]."

Figure 2.15   The perception of time while waiting in line at checkout in a grocery store can be altered with digital signage that promotes front-end items.
©2009 American Digital Signage.

But beyond the promotion of items and departments in the store itself, the network is an opportunity to generate revenue by promoting other local businesses that value the captive audience of local residents waiting in line.

"We enable local sponsors in the area to convey their message about their business in the grocery store," says American Digital Signage Executive Vice President, Sales and Marketing Drew Bernstein. The opportunity appeals to "real estate agents, auto dealers, small businesses in the local area that want to get their message across and sponsor the other messages." Community-based programming can also help to leverage the store's brand and community connection.

Stuart Jacob, VP of programming and Creative Services at CBS Outernet, has a similar view: "If I'm behind the deli counter and you're picking a number and you're in line to be served, I have an artificial queuing aid that's helping me get the consumers to want to watch my screen because at that point all I'm trying to overcome is potentially boredom [Figure 2.16]. The other place where we are, where there's traffic flow like in the produce area, there's not wait time. I know I have to engage with the consumer while they're shopping and making decisions. So our loop dynamics change based on where we are."

Shorter segments and fairly frequent changing of content, as well as multiple content selections on different parts of the screen, will be most effective in both marketing and reducing perceived wait time.

Figure 2.16 Taking advantage of shoppers' dwell time near the deli.
©2009 CBS Outernet.

Elevators and Office Networks

Elevator networks are familiar to many people who work in or visit large office buildings. These screens can very easily capture the attention of the small number of captive viewers for the short time they are in the elevator because there is little competition and an almost primal urge to look at anything other than the other riders. Rapidly changing, short segments are the rule in this environment. Marketers can combine brief ads with information such as news headlines, weather reports, and building details. Mike DiFranza of Captivate Network understands this subcategory more than most. "The average person takes about six elevator trips per day. On average those trips last about 1 minute. It also takes about 15 seconds for an elevator to go up one floor and open the doors and let somebody out. So depending on the high rise building and the time of day in which you're traveling, that 1-minute ride can turn into a 5-minute ride depending on the building, if you're going to multiple floors and lots of people are getting on and off the elevator. So we basically assumed that in a 1-minute time frame we want to get four stories across to that consumer [Figure 2.17]. So each content piece is 15 seconds long. So even if you came into the elevator, went up one floor and got off, you got 15 seconds worth of content, which is about the time you were in that elevator."

The ads can be made relevant based on knowledge of a building's tenants, visitors, and time of day—advertising a local lunch special at noon, for example. DiFranza explains further: "We've gone out and done numerous surveys to

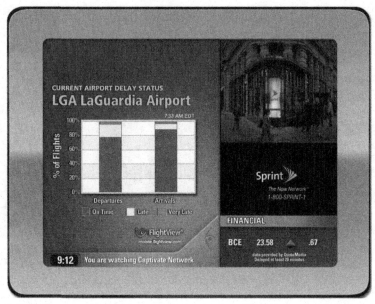

Figure 2.17 Captivate Network provides sports, weather, local news, and trivia content along with advertising in 15-second increments for dwell time viewers in elevators. ©2009 Captivate Network.

try to understand the composition of content that our audience wants. And what's interesting is that they don't want any one thing....Yes they're interested in business news, and in some cases they look at the elevator as being a break in their day. And so you really need to be sensitive to balancing things like sports and weather and local news and business news and trivia-type entertainment content."

To reinforce the point, he notes that the number one feature in popularity is the weather and the second is a feature called word of the day—it shows a vocabulary word, the pronunciation, and the use in a sentence. A variant on this is screens located in the passenger compartment of taxicabs, where the viewing time might be longer but unpredictable, so short advertising and information segments with local relevance are most effective.

A similar network is the Wall Street Journal Office Network. The biggest difference is they put the screens near the elevator, in lobbies, and inside the elevator. "We are in high dwell time, public areas of office buildings. Most often we're in elevator lobbies and by elevator lobbies [Figure 2.18]. Sometimes we're in the entry lobbies, if there's a central area where people will congregate. And we're often in elevators themselves as well," says Jim Harris, CEO. "The screens themselves take you through a 15-second segment progression of what's news, then 15 seconds of marketplace, etc. What you progress through

Figure 2.18 Wall Street Journal Office Network uses editorial from the *Wall Street Journal* to capture attention for the advertising to the right.
©2009 Wall Street Journal Office Network.

is the same way that you'd read the *Wall Street Journal*. So you've got the four sections of the journal essentially, but very current as live news breaks."

Internal Communications

Internal communications networks are a very different type of POW network. These are screens located in places where employees (and visitors) commonly gather, such as a lobby or lunchroom. Content here doesn't often seek to market particular products or services; instead, these networks are ideal for conveying positive brand attributes of the company as well as conveying important information to employees. The digital signage helps create a common experience that, over time, can impart corporate values and practices to employees. These are also ideal networks to provide training, particularly in situations where employees don't have access to company computers or intranets.

A prime example of this kind of network is one installed by Continental Airlines at its terminals in Houston, Texas and Newark, New Jersey. The primary purpose of the network is to provide employee communications and training about safety and efficiency, as well as passenger satisfaction. A series of screens directed specifically at employees are deployed in break rooms, the terminal ramp and aircraft maintenance areas, and in corporate training areas. The content reminds employees of everything from safety precautions and procedures for bag handling to how to handle hazardous materials. Additional screens in the gate areas communicate some of the same information to passengers and provides reminders to employees. Continental reported a 35 percent improvement in bag handling efficiency as well as a 30 percent decrease in unsafe incidents as a result of providing this information in places where all employees would encounter it on a routine basis.

Eli Lilly, a pharmaceutical manufacturer, also uses digital signage worldwide to put their employees on the same page. Digital signage can have a huge impact on employees who do not read the newsletters or corporate emails. Chris Bias, communications consultant and Lilly TV manager, underscores the importance of using digital signage to reach a diverse worldwide organization in many different languages and in 23 countries. "It's all internal communications that we need to reach out to employees with. So it's everything from benefits enrollment to breaking news that's available on all our drugs and on the up-and-coming drugs. We get content on to Lilly TV [Figure 2.19] so that people will see it there first versus hearing it on the 10 o'clock news. We coordinate information with our electronic newsletter that goes out Monday, Wednesday, and Friday and that goes along with the little bit of information I put on the screens. I'm trying to lead people to the content that's online through the content that's on our screens. We found that a high percentage, 68 percent of employees, said they saw something on the screens that caused them to go talk with someone or look something up online or find additional information elsewhere."

2.2   Digital Signage and Traditional Communications and Marketing Strategy

Although digital signage is a distinct new medium, it is not necessarily a stand-alone medium. Along with traditional media, it is part of the communication pathway to reach the consumer. To truly advance a company's business, digital signage needs to be integrated into the comprehensive digital landscape as well as the company's marketing, advertising, and communications campaigns.

Because of this, content created for digital signage needs to be reflective of the entire message tree that is delivered to audiences through all other forms

Figure 2.19 Lilly TV helps drive employees to seek out more information about something that was delivered on the network. ©2009 Eli Lilly.

of media. The specific content for digital signage may be different—as we will discuss later, mere reruns of TV commercials on digital signage is almost always a poor strategy—but it is vital to retain commonalities with the look, feel, and wording of the content on other screens. That is what will create the kind of continuity in an overall campaign that will multiply the effects of each screen to achieve the greatest overall results.

"The right hand needs to know what the left hand is doing," says Paul Flanigan, partner in The Preset Group, a consulting firm in North America. "The relationship between digital signage and the other screens is one of the things that has to be vetted out and executed with extreme care. You need to be cohesive with every other screen being utilized. This is where brands live and die. You can't say Coca-Cola in 57 ways."

This also applies across the various digital signage networks a company employs. As we've discussed, different networks have different purposes, yet are all linked in terms of communicating a brand's identity and value, and in many cases, companies will employ two or more types of digital signage networks. Ensuring they share commonalities with one another, as well as the larger messaging communicated through the other screens and traditional marketing, will give digital signage its greatest power and avoid the potential for it to work against a company rather than for it.

In the largest sense, this means that digital signage must be tied into the overall business strategy of the company or the venue where it is deployed. If the venue is a restaurant chain where the business goal is to sell desserts with every meal, then the content needs to reflect this strategy—showing the available desserts, promoting specials, even providing information on the history of desserts to create greater interest. This content would relate to other marketing that links the restaurant with great desserts or even public relations where the company's dessert chefs are featured in stories on food pages and TV shows.

"Every client we work with hopefully has a brand narrative, and if they don't, that's the first thing we work on when they come to us," says Jake Lambert, VP content director, of marketing communications agency Draftfcb. "That tells us what the consumer should feel whenever they see the brand. And that brand narrative really defines the kind of content we want to create."

When digital signage achieves widespread use in a large organization, then determining the relationships among national, regional, and local messages becomes part of ensuring the necessary degree of continuity.

Localization may be as simple as providing content in different languages to accommodate the demographics of the local customer base. Most of the time, however, it is more detailed. For example, a national POS network in the United States will almost certainly involve creating different messages tailored to basic geographic differences, as well as market priorities in those regions. The retailer's messages in Upstate New York in December might seek to drive sales of snow shovels or sidewalk deicer—messages with little relevance in San Diego, where garden spades and sunglasses are much more likely to sell. A retailer may also stock brands of a local nature or interest, and messages to support those products might need to be developed as part of the larger content set.

Likewise, when a corporation has a branding message that runs across all screens, regional nuances will also be established. This may consist of color palette changes, demographic changes based on ethnicity, or cultural nuances. At the local level, messages can be tied into the community to reach the real pulse of the viewer. It is this relationship that can drive better relevancy to create content that is absorbed wholly by the viewer.

2.3   Who's Involved in the Message and Why?

As you can see, the complexities surrounding network types and relevant content span the entire company, from top-level branding to regional and even store-level promotion. Thus, content decisions for digital signage will likely involve a number of decision makers and providers at various levels inside and even outside the organization. Ensuring their involvement is crucial to the effectiveness of any digital signage network. These can be considered in two categories: primary and secondary content contributors.

Primary content contributors are those who will be responsible for content on a frequent, even day-to-day basis. They will vary by type of network. For POS or even POW, these can be branding, marketing, and advertising departments; sales and promotions; customer service; and others who both develop content and oversee its strategic use. For POT and some POS and POW networks, these will include the key contacts at the brands that are being advertised on the screens. These contributors will be the source of original content from which those responsible for digital signage will create content that is most appropriate to the medium. These are really the primary stakeholders in the digital signage campaign; involving all these contributors early, and in concert, will ensure successful content and a successful network.

Secondary content contributors are those who provide either ancillary content (the information or entertainment content that's not specific to the brand) or who make occasional contributions (including executive management). In the case of an airport POT network, for example, this would include the entities that provide the flight and weather data that are either displayed directly on the digital signage or are used to help determine which other content should be displayed at a given time.

2.4   Digital Signage Networks Beyond Sales

Although it should be clear that a significant benefit of digital signage is directly boosting sales, it's important to remember that digital signage networks can direct content at three other major areas: consumer experience, brand equity, and training.

2.4.1 Consumer Experience

For years, retailers and business alike have rebuilt their thinking around the consumer experience. The consumer experience is measured by how the consumer reacts to the environment, interaction, and service. This is where POW networks shine, such as when they reduce perceived waiting time in a bank, for example. Consumers who are educated and entertained with digital signage while they are waiting in line are less agitated when they reach the teller. Giving the consumer a new positive experience changes the attitude of the consumer. Using digital signage helps retain customer loyalty by making an emotional connection. This helps beyond sales—it intensifies the bank's personal relationship with the customer. Digital signage has the power to create an emotional connection and make it personal.

2.4.2 Brand Equity

Creating brand equity is all about building brand loyalty. This is partially driven by the experience and creating community. Content that tells the viewer what a brand is doing for customers, their individual lives, and their community will create a greater bond with the consumer than the basic transaction. That relationship creates brand equity that translates to customer retention. Here is where content that's aimed higher than a specific offer pays off in the long run. Does it help the customer to know what the business is doing in the community? Does the content answer the customer's most basic question, What are you doing for me? Is it about the product or service, or is it about how the product or service affects the customer's life? How does the brand fit in this equation? Getting a brand positioned to be involved in the customer's life helps create brand equity.

DOOH really works when the content takes advantage of the ability for the medium to be up close and personal. Digital signage is a powerful emotional driver and, when used professionally, connects the customer with the brand.

2.4.3 Training

Training and experience are two very often overlooked keys to great content results. How does a company get everyone chainwide on the same page consistently? Via email? Via newsletters? Introducing digital signage to the communication mix is a very effective way to improve employee training, experience, and knowledge of your product. In many cases, the same screen can drive all three at different times of the day.

First, the associate experience is affected by customers and by customers' attitudes. Digital signage directly affects customers' attitudes while they wait in line. In turn, this affects your associates' attitude on a daily basis. Next, the associate passively learns by being constantly exposed to the messages on digital signs. The associate absorbs the messages and becomes more knowl-edgeable about the products you are promoting.

The decision of whether or not to use audio in these installations hinges in part on the effect it will have on the associate who must listen to the sound-track hour after hour. In most cases, audio will drive the associate nuts, and the system will be unplugged in no time at all. Also, as we will discuss further in Chapter 3, the refresh and loop times can also affect the associate, depending on where the screen is placed in proximity to the associate's post.

Finally, specific messaging and training for associates can be held before opening and after closing once or twice weekly. Back to our bank example, most tellers do not have access to company laptops or email. Digital signage is a powerful tool for corporate to communicate with employees about pro-ducts, news, events, brand values, community philosophy, and special offer-ings. Some of the same consumer content assets can be used to create these messages for associates.

Digital signage is not designed to replace the training classroom across cor-porate culture, but it can have a significant impact on day-to-day operations. As noted earlier, Continental Airlines uses digital signage in key areas where employees take breaks or pass by screens. Digital signage as a corporate com-munication tool has proven itself to be an incremental tool that benefits discon-nected (not online) employees in the workplace and helps put everyone on the same page companywide.

2.5 Summary

Understanding and determining the kind of network to be deployed is a rela-tively complex undertaking. As we have seen, there are many subnetworks, nuances that distinguish them, and even some degree of crossover among them. We will see in coming chapters, however, that this determination is the founda-tion of identifying and developing the right content. Taking the time to learn to distinguish network types and match them to their purpose will save time and money during the content development process and in fact make the difference between an effective network and a lost investment.

3 Creating Content Relevance

In the previous chapter, we often discussed the idea of making the content on a digital signage network relevant. Simply put, that means constructing content to carry a company's messages in a manner that has meaning to the specific audience whose behavior the company is seeking to influence.

Even before companies decide to make DOOH part of their marketing and communications strategy, they usually have a good idea of who the most likely buyers of their products or services will be. The choice of network depends in part on the habits of those buyers—digital signage needs to reach them in places they are most likely to be, at the times they are most likely to be there.

But it is the content itself that takes its cue most directly from the intended audience. As with any type of marketing, a solid understanding of the audience is what will provide the keys to creating compelling content. Further, because digital signage allows marketers to take advantage of so many variables—from the length of a content segment to the time of day it appears—it is vital for marketers to understand their specific audiences at a high level of detail.

"Digital signage has a very specific purpose, and it works best where context meets content—where the consumer is ready to receive the message," says Jake Lambert, VP content director of Draftfcb. "A billboard is just out there; maybe it matters to you, maybe not. Digital signage content can be tailored to the demographic you want to reach [Figure 3.1]. We day part our digital signage because we know who is shopping in the store at any time of day, and we can change our content to reach that demographic."

Delivering the right message at the right place and time to the right audience is the Holy Grail for every medium. But DOOH is perhaps the first medium that can actually deliver all those things together. In fact, for digital signage, delivering messages with that precision is not only expected, it is required for success—and it can be measured.

By combining audience understanding with the remarkable attributes of digital signage, marketers can begin to map out the content that will make their digital signage investment pay off.

3.1 Basic Demographics

Sometimes even the simplest truths can be forgotten when there's a new technology to deploy. It's no different with digital signage. People sometimes opt for the easier route of simply using any existing content they have to get their

Figure 3.1 Changing content based on seasons keeps it relevant to the shopper's mind-set and moms' calendar.
©2009 Qwest/Draftfcb.

networks up quickly. Instead, everyone needs to start with the basic question, Who is going to buy (or who do I hope will buy) what I'm selling? Even if the answer is everyone, it's still important to create different pieces of content that speak to broad demographic groups. Although an 18-year-old and an 80-year-old may both be targets for a company's soft drink or credit card, those products will represent completely different things to people in those age groups, and the marketing messages will be just as different. The challenge of creating content for diverse demographic groups is also an opportunity to deliver a product offering in several different ways and often requires just slight changes to some elements that can speak to events or ideas of significance for those groups, as illustrated in Figure 3.2.

These are, of course, generalities. Each group comprises millions of Americans, and within each group are a multitude of differences relating to gender, ethnicity, and sexual orientation; income, education, and occupation; region, neighborhood, and home ownership status; religious and political beliefs; marital status, parental status, and even pet ownership. It is vital to know which segments of these broad groups a piece of content will target and to be aware of the latest research on how those segments make purchase decisions.

For example, a recent baby boom along with the growth of women in the workforce has propelled the mommy segment to some prominence with marketers. Mothers of children younger than age 18 years (primarily spanning Generations X and Y) control enormous levels of disposable income and often are the main decision makers about a family's spending—and they are motivated by that family orientation. It is estimated that about 75 percent of American mothers in this category have primary responsibility for the purchasing decisions about groceries and basic household supplies, and their opinions are overwhelmingly what determines the outcome of all family economic decisions.

Likewise, pet owners (who span all age groups) spend increasingly large percentages of their disposable income on their pets and consider them to be family members, making spending decisions accordingly. Gay, lesbian, bisexual, and transgender (GLBT) individuals have also emerged in the last several years as a powerful spending cohort—with $610 billion in purchasing power—marked by significant loyalty to brands they perceive as supportive of their larger social and political issues.

Demographic	Memorable Events	Key Characteristics
World War II **(born from 1928 to 1945)**	Sustained economic growth, general social tranquility, the Cold War, McCarthyism	Conformity, conservatism, traditional family values
Baby Boomer 1 **(born from 1946 to 1954)**	Kennedy and King assassinations, Vietnam and political unrest, moon landing, social experimentation and sexual freedom, civil rights, environmental and women's movements.	Experimental, individualistic, free spirited, social cause oriented
Baby Boomer 2 **(born from 1955 to 1964)**	Nixon and Watergate, oil embargo and gasoline shortages, Middle East unrest, inflation and stagnant economy	Less optimistic, distrust of government, general cynicism
Generation X **(born from 1965 to 1979)**	Challenger explosion, Iran-Contra, social malaise, Reaganomics, AIDS, safe sex, single parent families	Quest for emotional security, independent, informality, entrepreneurial
Generation Y (N Generation) **(born from 1980 to 2001)**	Rise of the Internet, September 11 attacks, cultural diversity, two wars in Iraq	Quest for physical security and safety, patriotism, heightened fears, acceptance of change, technically savvy, environmental issues

Figure 3.2 Demographic chart.

Nielsen has recently introduced a fascinating method of slicing up demographics called PRIZM. It is based on Lifestage groups and income levels. Nielsen has divided the Lifestage groups into Younger Years, Family Life and Mature Years. The Younger Years are predominantly under age 45, comprised of singles and couples mostly without children. The Family Life group is predominantly middle aged families with children at home. The last group, Mature Years, is predominantly age 55 and over and empty-nest couples and mature singles. Based on those three groups and income levels, Nielsen then divides each group into 3 to 4 major segments. If one looks at the Younger Years group, it is divided into 3 segments: the high income Midlife Success group, medium income Young Achievers, and low income Striving Singles. This is done for each of the other groups. The Family Life group is divided by 4 categories: high income, Accumulated Wealth; medium high income, Young Accumulators; medium low income, Mainstream Families; and low income, Sustaining Families. For Mature Years Nielson again divides them into 4 categories: high income, Affluent Empty Nesters; high medium income, Conservative Classics; low medium income, Cautious Couples; and low income, Sustaining Seniors. Within each of these segmented categories are between 3 and 8 specific social groups. For example Mainstream Families has 8 social groups in it including: New Homesteaders, Big Sky Families, White Picket Fences, Blue-Chips Blues, etc. White Picket Fences social segment is predominantly made up of upscale middle age w/kids, age 35-45, mixed home owners, white-collar, service mixture of employment, some college, and race is made up of White, Black, Asian, and Hispanic. Their buying habits are classified as ordering from walmart.com, rent/buy kids dvd's, read people and Espanol magazine, watch Toon Disney, and own a Nissan Frontier. These are very finely defined demographics and are based on real data collected. Nielsen has also taken the same segmented groups and positioned them as social groups ranging from Urban, Suburban, Second City and Town, and Rural, and further breaking this up into high density population centers to small town and rural areas. This system allows one to profile a customer, locate them geographically, understand their buying habits, and understand their behavioral profile.

These are only some examples of the complexities to be considered in demographics. But to create effective content, marketers need to take the time to determine the common characteristics of the specific groups of individuals they plan to reach.

It's also important to understand how each of these different groups respond to technology in general and to digital signage in particular. Those most comfortable with technology and rapid message delivery tend to be those who have grown up with things like the VCR and the computer—that is, age 40 years and younger. Generation Y is particularly comfortable with technology and in general would see digital signage as normal and expected; late-stage baby boomers and the World War II generation might be somewhat less comfortable being surrounded by screens and messages.

The level of interactivity of a given screen is also a factor when considering the potential audience. Some older consumers, or those who are less accustomed to using personal electronic devices on a daily basis, might be uncomfortable or struggle with touch-screen interaction or other kinds of user feedback or control. But these are generalizations, not universal facts, says Lyle Bunn, president of BUNN Co. "There isn't one demographic that I have not seen extraordinary impact numbers coming back from, even in the elderly. There was a recent entry for the Digi Awards, where a seniors' residence had digital signage, and the perception through audit of the residents was extraordinary. I think it's going to be equally effective across age groups, gender, and ethnicity."

3.2 Behavioral Attitudes

In addition to general group characteristics, content should also take into account specific behavioral attitudes that will affect how a viewer will perceive a message. This is a complex area that is the subject of considerable expert research and highly sophisticated studies. But even without the budget or specific background in this area, marketers can still use some common sense and knowledge of their own businesses to impart a behavioral component to their digital signage content.

Let's consider content about the purchase of a car and consider three factors that are potential messages to deliver about the car. The first is that this car will cost the buyer $300 per month. The second is that people perceive drivers of this car as being more attractive. The third is that this is a reliable car that gets good gas mileage.

The cost is (generally) a negative—the buyer will have considerably less money each month if he or she makes this purchase. The perception of attractiveness is (generally) a positive—the buyer will gain a desirable intangible if he or she makes the same purchase. Reliability is (generally) a positive factor—the buyer's operational costs will be relatively low if he or she buys this particular car. All of these messages will affect the decision by a particular potential buyer. The question is how.

Here is where knowledge of the audience is crucial. For some groups, the air of attractiveness will outweigh all other considerations; their behavior is motivated by a desire for status or by the reactions of others. One can make a reasonable assumption that these people will be members of groups with a reasonable level of income, who are perhaps unmarried and don't have children to support, and live in a more urban area where they have a good chance to be seen by a lot of people. The content directed toward them might emphasize that this great attractiveness can be had for a sum they can easily afford.

On the other hand, a buyer concerned with finances may also want to appear attractive, but he or she will be far more motivated by the cost. One can make a reasonable assumption that these buyers would be younger or have families and mortgages tugging at their purses. To accommodate their behavior, the content would emphasize the way in which reliability offsets the purchase cost and therefore makes it possible for the buyer to gain the status of the car.

Finally, a buyer who needs a car for everyday use may not care about attractiveness at all. His or her behavior is motivated by the need to get from point A to point B reliably. Here we are most likely talking about someone who commutes many miles to work or takes the kids to school and has few practical alternatives, such as an urban subway system. People in these groups are most likely to respond to content that preaches reliability and its moderation of the car's cost; they probably will not respond as much to status.

As one can see, predicting behavior and measuring attitudes requires more in-depth understanding of an audience. The more strongly held a personal attitude, the more predictable the behavior and therefore the outcome of a particular message delivery. Paying attention to lifestyle, daily life patterns, and other aspects of groups of individuals that can uncover these attitudes will be particularly useful in shaping content.

3.3   Shaping Content Relevance

Creating content that is powerful and relevant will always involve good strategy and research. The creative marketer still needs to bring it home to the viewer by holding to the core of the idea, creating an experience that brings in an emotion, surprising the viewer, and being authentic and believable. The right story is one that we can relate to and see ourselves in. Creating relevance brings it home.

With audience research as well as marketing strategy and objectives in hand, the next step in content development is determining what other factors will make it most relevant. Understanding that the demographic makeup of the audience may change according to the time of day will almost certainly drive several decisions about what type of content is delivered at that particular time. A coffee bar during the 2 hours before the workday begins will probably attract a large number of people on their way to the office; they will be in a hurry and looking for a morning jolt. They will respond to product messages with an air of energy about them, perhaps mixed with information of immediate use (stock market prices, headlines, weather). Later in the morning, the audience might change to mothers with strollers who respond to lower-key product messages to promote lingering, mixed with softer information or entertainment content. After school, the audience might again change to teens and a different mix of content. This also, of course, depends on the location of this particular coffee bar; if it is in a downtown business district, the audience will probably be less dynamic than one that is in a suburban center near a commuter rail station.

Another factor that can help determine content relevance is a feed from an external data source. This can be as simple as a temperature or weather feed. If it is cold or snowing outside, the product content in our coffee bar is about the special flavored hot chocolate; if it is sunny and warm outside, the same content time slot may be used to promote iced tea. This creates more relevance to the experience that the viewer is having at that time of day. Diane Williams, senior media research analyst for Arbitron, has measured viewership when these types of feeds or even a simple clock is added. "Most people have a watch or something with time on it. People look at a sign more often if it has the time on it. Transit hubs were big. And it's not like people know what time the train's coming, and they're all excited about it. People just tend to look at it almost as a nervous habit. We actually did that with traditional billboards in New York where they just added a clock, a digital clock onto a traditional billboard and we saw an increase in viewership. So that is a very simple piece of content, but that's one that we frequently look at just because it does seem to drive viewership and it doesn't really cost anything."

To a large degree, relevance can be determined by the state of mind of a viewer at a particular place and time. That is, no matter the demographic or other fixed characteristics of an individual, one can't think of the person as somehow unchanging. The same individual who is in a hurry on the way to work on a Tuesday morning may be very relaxed at the same time and place on a Sunday morning.

3.3.1 Types of Viewers

One way to understand this important concept is to consider the difference between a consumer and a shopper. We can look at most individuals as consumers, that is, they have the potential to purchase products and services aimed at individuals or families. But one is a consumer at home, at work, and at play. In each of those circumstances, an individual may be thinking more or less about purchasing something or making any kind of decision surrounding a potential purchase. One can reach this consumer with certain messages—branding, for example—but making a direct offer is more difficult.

When in front of a POS network, though, the consumer has become a shopper. The mind-set of a person who has deliberately entered a store is much more attuned to cues and opportunities related to their needs and the wares on sale at the particular store. They are now reachable with more direct offers about products, particularly offers that now take into account their gender, age, and income, for example. Putting all these together creates real relevance for the content of POS signage because it can create an emotional response that drives desired behavior.

Looking at things from another angle, we can consider another two types of viewers: the dweller and the on-the-go consumer. Dwellers are in situations where they are either patient or have little choice but to remain passively in the area of the screen, or they may be in a situation where they are relaxed in an out-of-home situation like a food court in a mall. A dweller can be in an elevator or a doctor's office but in either case is stuck with a wait. They all have dwell time but for entirely different reasons, and it is those reasons that need to be considered when creating content that is relevant.

On the other side of this are the consumers who are on the go—people who are walking or driving and are in transit. These are people in circumstances where their mind-set is firmly fixed on reaching a destination or taking a journey, usually in areas where point of transit networks dominate. They are on a mission to get somewhere, and that's the key to relevance. Where are they headed and why? This is a very complex question with a range of answers. It certainly depends upon the subcategory of the POT network and time of day. This is the first place to start to understand the mind-set of the on-the-go viewer. During morning commute traffic you can guess that most on-the-go viewers are heading to work. On a subway it will also apply. What is on their minds? More than likely, it will be something involving work or coffee. They are also thinking about where they came from, such as home and related family issues or things they may need to find time to deal with during a busy work day. Conversely, on their way home they are recapping their day and looking forward to home, friends, family, and dinner. These examples are, of course, basic thinking about the mind-set of the shopper, dweller, and on-the-go viewer, and depending upon the subcategory of network, this can be fine-tuned to match relevancy.

When you think about content and categorize by type of network and the mind-set of the shopper, on-the-go viewer, or dweller, it immediately helps to organize your thinking about content.

3.3.2 Emotional Relevance

In POS networks, the psychology behind understanding the shopper's mind-set really rests in the experience that the shopper is going to have. Christopher Grey, PsyD, of Saatchi & Saatchi X, tells us, "The experience is categorized in four areas: The physical perceptions that influence the experience (what they see), the emotional reaction to the content and the environment (what they feel), the thoughts and attitudes they form about the environment and the interaction within the store (what they think), and the shopping behavior that results from the experience (what they do)."

The mind-set of the consumer definitely changes while in-store. The consumer becomes a shopper. As a shopper, the consumer's actions are dictated by his or her intentions, and it can be difficult to grab the consumer's attention to insert a brand into that mind-set that isn't already there. Shoppers are largely task oriented; they have a shopping list in their mind or in their hand. In turn that means most shoppers are focused on certain products and certain brands to the exclusion of other products and competing brands, a phenomenon known as deselection. In other words, the consumer blocks out other items while focused on the task and the list—the consumer regards them as background noise to be disregarded. Deselection is a brand's worst nightmare.

Great content delivered through digital signage can help break through the consumer's mental blocking. When implemented properly, digital signage exists above the general noise level of the location, which enables the brand to grab a consumer's attention and get a chance to be included in the selection process. But, says Grey, this means being judicious with how digital signage is used in-store. "Imagine if a horde of digital signage was lined up and down the aisle. There would be so much digital signage noise that the shopper would be overwhelmed and one message or brand is not going to stand out from the crowd. This is where digital signage done correctly and in the right amount will have great impact."

The second step in the process, he notes, is to bring the value proposition or the offer to the consumer while his or her attention is focused on the digital sign. In doing so one needs to create an emotion that will help to drive an action. Reason leads to conclusions, emotion leads to action.[1] "There is no such thing as a neutral environment," continues Grey. "There are either positive emotions or negative emotions created within the environment." With positive emotions the shopper stays longer, increases the basket size, and perhaps even spends more than he or she had budgeted before entering the store. And as Christopher notes, there is a direct link to impulse purchases and increased loyalty.

3.3.3 Working with the Eight Positive Emotions

For content to address the emotional equation, it must be created to trigger a positive emotion. So what emotions does one consider when creating this content? There are essentially eight psychological drivers that represent an emotion that the shopper is seeking: self-creation, mastery, dreaming, security, playtime, sport, sanctuary, and connection.

Self-creation is an emotion that reveals itself through creating, enhancing, and expressing one's identity by stimulating self-reflection, status, bragging rights, and values. For example, certain brands that may be environmentally friendly will evoke emotions about values (I'm a person who wants to save the planet), whereas the Rolls-Royce brand evokes status and bragging rights (I'm a successful, wealthy individual). Saatchi & Saatchi worked with Head and Shoulders to create a digital signage project that involved a camera above the shopper in front of a display. The shopper could walk up to the display and see the top of his or her head and look for dandruff. "This was very effective manner that allowed one to reflect on themselves and examine their physical identity," notes Dr. Grey.

Another emotional driving factor is mastery. Mastery can be evoked by learning, performance, and sharing. Consumer electronics is one area where

---

[1]Neurologist Donald Calne, *Within Reason.*

knowledge is given by the seller to create a feeling in the buyer of mastering complex products. Look inside any Apple Store and you will find the Genius Bar, a specific place with specially-identified experts set aside to provide expertise in a helpful manner where one can master the latest Macor iPhone. BMW takes each driver who purchases a car through a 45-minute training before the driver leaves the lot, providing a feeling of mastery even after the purchase and a positive emotional counterpoint to the potential of buyer's remorse.

Dreaming is hope, inspiration, ambition, and looking at the possibilities. To evoke this emotion one must create content that is relevant to these aspirations. Department stores that carry kitchen products and bedding and home improvement stores (Figure 3.3) are great examples of locations where digital signage content can be created to inspire shoppers and encourage them to buy products that lead to their dream home, patio, or deck.

Preparedness, replenishment, and nesting are key factors that evoke the emotion of security. Content about caring for and preparing the home, self, and family resonates with many shoppers. Dog food is one product that is easily identified through this emotion—so is cold and flu medicine. Surprisingly, fresh food is another. Creating content that is relevant to these emotions will be helpful to the shopper and ultimately create more sales.

Figure 3.3 Home Depot produced a promo called "Build the Deck of Your Dreams," which inspired the shopper with beautiful finished decks.
©2009 Home Depot.

One of my favorites is playtime. This emotion is engaging in childlike fun, expression, and amusement. The content to trigger this emotion needs to be entertaining and include aspects of creativity and stimulation. Although this can apply to many different types of products and services, certain products are very good fits—like amusement parks, cruise lines, and other recreational vacation packages. This can also be combined with some of the other emotions. Take the previous dog food example and combine its security emotion with playtime, and the content could now be shifted to children playing with a dog and the dog jumping up on the counter to get some of the food. This creates multiple avenues of appeal from a single piece of content.

Similar to playtime is sport, which drives the emotion of adventure, being on the hunt, competitive contests, and strategy. Sport is pursuing a goal with enthusiasm and then completing that goal with a sense of personal achievement. As one can imagine, this emotion is appropriate to sports and products for sports and outdoor activities.

Although all of these emotions have immediate associations with closely related products, they can also apply to many other nonrelated products as long as that emotion is aligned with both the product and the brand. In the same vein, although certain emotional triggers are more prominent in attracting female shoppers and other triggers are slanted toward eliciting a response in male shoppers, all these emotions can serve to evoke action in both genders if the product and other factors are appropriate (many women enjoy competing and will respond to the sport emotion, and many men with young children may well respond to the nesting aspects of security).

At the opposite end of the spectrum, sanctuary represents a safe, calming escape and relaxed emotions. When a shopper is rushing to achieve the task of shopping, one can create content to evoke this emotion, which can slow down the shopper's pace and provide an opportunity to introduce the brand message. Scenes of beautiful, calming footage of a running stream that is paced in such a way to let the shopper relax and spend a few seconds of reprieve from the pressure of the shopping experience can have a positive effect on the shopper's perception of the brand and the product. "Offering products like Dole's Apples and Crème as 'delicious, indulgent and guilt-free!' can offer an emotional feeling toward a safe product that one will not gain weight from eating," notes Grey.

Using the emotion of connection by developing, maintaining, and deepening relationships will help the shopper feel like he or she has bonded or belongs to a special group. "Costco Wholesale Club does a great job of making one feel like they belong. After all you join a club with a membership card and on that card is your picture. To get in you must show your ID membership card," Grey observes. "Deepening the relationship through continual bonding with the members is done even by offering free samples of food products. In this way the shopper feels the connection and gets something instantly out the experience." These emotional connections are powerful and drive loyalty to new heights.

When considering these emotional drivers, one must focus on matching content concepts with the product that provides the emotional relevance. This ultimately provides the consumer with a positive experience and encourages the consumer to purchase the product.

3.4   Adding Relevance to Any Network

Any team that is operating a digital signage network or is planning a network has a unique opportunity to bring excellence to this emerging industry and set some precedents. We can already see this in the work of some network professionals who have focused on research. Their innovative approaches use content as the source and cause for relevant messaging that is useful, helpful, and provides a positive experience for the viewer. Aligning consumer mind-set with network type is a large part of this exploration that brings success to some of the most prominent networks in the United States and abroad.

One such network is Adspace, with more than 1400 screens in some 110 shopping malls. Since 2005, Adspace has taken research, including learnings from focus groups, to inform content that reaches new levels of success, explains Chairman and CEO Dominick Porco. "You need to assume their frame of mind. What we are selling is an environment that engages the consumer. We recognize who we are targeting and we understand their mind-set and why they are there."

The Adspace audience in made up of women and teenage girls, and, according to Porco, "They are really there to escape—and recognizing that mind-set is critical to matching effective content to the network. We create content that reflects our specific audience in ways that are more relevant to them. It has been research that got us there."

The Adspace network was built based on several epiphany moments about content. The first was understanding the type of network that Adspace represents. Although the mall might appear to be a POT network with people rushing past the signage in common areas, it is, in reality, a POS network. Here Porco explains, "We have three types of shoppers: the mission shopper, who has their list and is fast-paced on their way to buy a blue shirt; they are in and out. We also have the browsing shopper, who is spending time in the mall as an escape, seeing what is new. And of course we do have the waiting men and shoppers in the food court. Through many surveys and focus groups we designed our content to be relevant to these groups, that each has different mind-sets, to make them feel like smart shoppers."

The content created for this network comes in three different forms, with a distinction between editorial content and ad content, he explains. "Today's Top Ten is a unique digital editorial environment [Figure 3.4]. Each week, we feature special deals on products from various retailers (which is free to them) to engage and drive them to specific products within retailers. We also have a

Figure 3.4 Adspace Networks used numerous studies over the years to arrive at relevant content like Today's Top Ten. ©2009 Adspace Networks.

program called Essentials; this is content which is about new unique products. The other content that we show is centered on mall events from puppet shows to concerts. And of course we show ads."

Keep in mind that Adspace has 110-plus malls, and each is unique, so the content has to be different for every mall simply because the retailers and events vary. Therefore, the featured products must also vary.

International networks require special attention to relevance. Neo Advertising is one such network that sees a future where the global advertiser can reach a relevant audience around the world and in different languages. Christian Vaglio-Giors, founder and CEO, is already booking ads across diverse networks. "It's a trend now to have a global launch for a product for a movie, for everything, so we see more and more that brands and agencies want to go for a central booking of international campaigns. We have some cross sales across the network with Canadian clients advertising on European screens. With movies, it's the same content for every country except the language. So in most cases this is provided directly by the agency, including the local language." Challenges also are based on the traditional sense of media that viewers are used to. "For example what we see as a difference is when we design the infotainment, the news, from one country to another it's very different. For example in the Netherlands ... the content used is video footage. While in Switzerland or in France, all content is based on Flash animation graphics [Figure 3.5]. No video," says Vaglio-Giors. "I think it's just the taste of the viewer. And the market adapts to the taste of the people. In the Netherlands, when they see a screen, even in the supermarket, they really expect traditional TV content on the screen. While in Switzerland or in France or even in Spain, the people they expect content which is similar to Internet banners like Flash. So you see the culture from one market to another is extremely different."

Shoppers come and go, but how do you keep corporate communications networks relevant when viewers tend to remain the same from day to day? Tom Hunter from McKee Foods believes the key is to involve lots of different individuals within the corporate structure to spread the work—and the focus—among many administrators at various levels. "I think that's been key in

Figure 3.5 Neo Advertising runs TV-like spots in the Netherlands and Flash-based spots in France to keep them more in line with viewers' expectations and agency requests. ©2009 Neo Advertising.

keeping the pertinence for the local areas," he says. "Generally there's an administrator and a backup at each plant facility or wherever there is a player. And then they have the option of assigning even lower-level contributors [Figure 3.6]. Those are generally the folks we figure have access to the most current content and we try to draw off them to bait our templates with the information that's coming across their desks."

Airport informational networks bring relevancy to viewers every day with exact flight arrival and departure times every few minutes. If one starts to think about relevant, useful information, these networks top the chart. If one strives to expand this same thinking to other networks, the innovation and creative juices will begin to kick in.

Consider what's appropriate (or inappropriate) for the mind-set of the viewers in that venue at a particular time. If the viewer is in a doctor's office, the display is central to the waiting area, and the content is specific to the viewer's reason for being there, then there is a win–win. In a sports medicine practice, for example, content and advertising about joint and muscle health, exercise, and performance will have more relevance and garner more attention than information on heart disease and how to quit smoking.

"If the purpose of the screen is to take the consumer's mind off waiting, the message needs to be something that puts your mind in a different place," says Paul Flanigan, partner of The Preset Group. For example, "If you're in line in the unemployment office you don't want to see something about how bad the job market is."

Localized content steeped in local information, based on network type, mind-set, culture, language, and even the right colors will create a high relevance factor, which in turn will create helpful and useful content that is not

Figure 3.6 Tying into the department contributors on corporate networks keeps content fresh and relevant to the employees.
©2009 McKee Foods.

only watched but will score high with viewers, creating more business for your network. Digital signage networks can be helpful, useful, and watched when one applies the logic and the power of relevance.

3.4.1 Location

As we noted in the previous chapter, the physical location of a screen is very important in determining its effectiveness. Similarly, location is a significant factor to consider when determining what will be the most relevant content.

In the largest sense, the type of network determines one aspect of screen location. A point of transit network is going to be located in a crowded public space, mounted on a wall or on a central kiosk in most cases, or even on the platform next to the schedule of incoming and outgoing trains or subways.

Even at Adspace, locating the screens in and around the food courts, escalators, and seating areas provides many opportunities for the content not only to be seen but actually watched. Adspace also positions its screens in portrait mode rather than in a landscape position, causing a unique live poster effect.

The Out-of-Home Video Advertising Bureau (OVAB) considers placement to be a key ingredient in measurement. One of the qualifying characteristics is that "A person must be present in a location from which the vehicle (display) is both visible and, where appropriate, audible. Out-of-Home networks are unlike traditional television in that there is not always an intention to view as a person encounters the screen. To account for this difference, an additional characteristic is required evidence that the screen has at least been noticed."

At the same time, because of their locations, in most POT networks the cost of the network will be underwritten by advertisers who pay to have a message displayed. They are paying for access to the eyeballs on a subway platform or in the airport concourse. Therefore, the content that the transit operator places within the playlist around those ads is critical to drawing those eyeballs to the screens and keeping them there to justify the advertising revenue. In most cases, some other relevant information will help to keep viewers watching.

With an on-campus TV network in high-traffic gathering areas of recreational sports facilities and student unions, The University Network reaches the college audience. Peter Corrigan, president, has many exclusive programming partners and a short-format approach to content. "The locations are in key areas to ensure the displays are watched … so the content has to be compelling for this age group [Figure 3.7]."

Even though in a doctor's office it is hard to miss a display, other considerations, including the receptionist, have to be taken into account. If the display is out of view from the reception desk and potentially out of extreme volume range, it helps keep the sanity of the employee, which keeps the screen turned on.

According to Target's Mark Bennett, group manager, Media Production, "We developed relevancy guidelines right off the bat, learning from other networks. You should only see content relevant to the particular area by store

Figure 3.7 Locating a digital sign in the right place so that it is noticed is critical for reaching the audience.
©2009 The University Network.

products. For example in the TV zone, DVD and CD sales area, or kids' entertainment and game area, the content that plays in these areas is directly relevant to the location of the display and the product."

3.4.2 Wait Time, Dwell Time, and Loop Length

One of the strongest aspects of digital signage in connecting with viewers is its ability to present an ever-changing mix of content. That, in turn, adds a level of complexity to the content decision that doesn't exist in paper forms, such as determining how long each piece of content needs to be on the screen and how frequently the entire set of content pieces—the playlist—will be repeated or replaced by a different playlist. The wait time and length of the playlist loop are directly connected. One needs to track both to ensure the messages are being absorbed by viewers and that viewers are being presented with the right number of messages while they are within range of the on-screen content.

The type of network immediately gives a clue to how much content can be employed and how long it needs to (or can) play on-screen. For most POT networks, the available time is very short because the viewer has only a few seconds, in some cases, to see the screen. So the content is brand oriented, relies more heavily on images than a lot of words, and has eye-catching action. At a convenience store, the average consumer spends just 3 minutes inside—more time than with a POT, but still enough time for the digital signage to make an impression that has an impact on purchasing. So the playlist will consist of short content segments of 10 to 15 seconds each.

Of course, each venue is specific, and geography and local issues may figure into this calculus. Take a bank, for example. In Malaysia the wait time to interact with a teller may be 40 minutes, whereas in the United States, the average wait time is about 6 minutes. A playlist that works in the U.S. bank would have segments lasting perhaps 15 to 30 seconds at most, and the entire loop would replay every 5 minutes or so. This approach would not be effective with Malaysian customers, who would wind up being exposed to the same content loop eight times while waiting. There, a longer playlist and potentially longer content segments are appropriate, with a playlist that could last a half hour.

"I remember being in a cell phone retailer, where I saw the same content over and over," says David Drain, executive director of the Digital Signage Association. "It seems the retailer didn't think how long people would be there, and hearing the same sound over and over annoyed me. There's no telling how much it annoyed the employees."

Marsha Morton, content producer for McKee's corporate communications network, looks closely at the loop length based on their employees' activities. "We try to keep the cycle, the amount of time before the slides start to repeat within about 7 or 8 minutes. Because for our audience—production employees—their breaks are like 12 minutes. So we want to make sure that all the content in our main window, that that information cycles. So the employees have an opportunity to see everything."

Brian Hirsh, president of Retail Entertainment Design (RED), which produces finished content for 12,000 retail locations, has a slightly different take on loop length. "We spend the time to understand our shopper profile, how long they're going to be in the store, how we can make a positive impression during that time, and how can we either direct them to products in the store, highlight a new feature or a promotion or an activity. Or just entertain them in that store environment. So a lot of times our programming wheels will be based on the average dwell time in that shopping experience. We're building up a lot of our shows to be about 8 to 10 hours of unique assets and then play-list them to be a 20 to 24 hour long show. Like a radio model, if it's more important, if it's more relevant and it's tied to a new release of an album, that may play more often in a store environment."

No matter what the length of stay within the venue, content must grab the attention of the viewer and keep it. Providing high-quality content will always apply no matter how long the screen is watched.

3.4.3 Visit Frequency

The third component that directly affects how many times a piece of content plays on any one screen is determined by frequency of visits at the venue, which is a huge consideration that will keep the content fresh and watched. This is more or less difficult based on the type of network. In a POS network in a department store, content can be changed once a month because most people are unlikely to visit more frequently and therefore have less chance to become overexposed. In a convenience store, where the average visitor may come in for coffee three mornings a week—or even every day—it's vital to refresh the content on an almost daily basis.

Internal communication networks have a significant challenge with this, more so than any other network, simply because the viewer is there every day of the workweek for 8 to 10 hours a day. At McKee Foods, Tom Hunter has addressed this issue by using more zones on-screen to keep the viewer engaged (Figure 3.8). "We just think having motion and multiple areas for the viewer's eyes to dance around helps."

3.4.4 Day Parting

Changing content based on what time of day it is and what day of the week it is can critically affect the impact of digital signage content on customers and associates. The same loop that is effective for the demographics of morning customers or midweek customers will not necessarily appeal to customers who frequent the business at other times. In addition, the employees of the business can easily become annoyed or bored with an overly repetitive loop of content. The danger is that associates may communicate that feeling—even unconsciously—to customers, negating some of the value of the screens. Or they may simply tune it out altogether, eliminating the screens' usefulness as training or employee information tools.

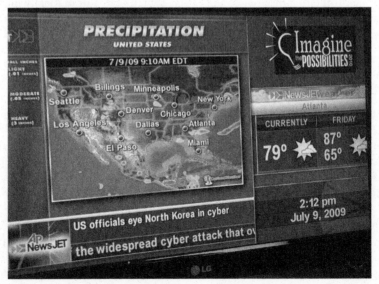

Figure 3.8 Using a number of on-screen zones in internal communications keeps the screen watched and the content fresh in the mind of the viewer. ©2009 McKee Foods.

A simple approach is to change the loop of content three times a day: morning, midday, and afternoon. This will keep associates happy and also creates programming that is diverse to the customer. It's also important to think about changing the order of the content within each playlist as it is repeated. The content can still be delivered in an overall pattern that is effective for the marketer in reaching different customers, but that doesn't appear to be overly patterned to either customers or associates.

A more sophisticated approach is to add and delete pieces of content throughout the day and week to keep playlists fresh. Like a radio station playing popular music, hit songs are repeated often, but not at the same time every hour, and new songs are brought into the mix as others are taken out to create variety and interest and keep people listening. The same idea applies here; continuous small changes to the overall content, plus shuffling its order, will prevent customers and associates from tuning out.

Although this may sound like a lot of work, the process can be automated through the use of cloning tools for playlists that are built into some software. These tools take one playlist, create a clone, and then change the order of the content according to certain rules. In effect, one now has two interchangeable playlists. This can be done several times depending on the length of the playlist and the length of the day segment for which that particular content is intended.

Software can also greatly help in delivering relevant content at the right time, right place, and right target. One can profile day parts with the demographic information, and that profile can be applied to each screen. Then, if one applies that same profile to a piece of content, that content can automatically match up to that screen. As networks become larger, automation is a must have to apply maximum relevant content to the right audience at the right time.

3.4.5 Speed and Length of Message

Along with the dwell time is also the speed at which the message is delivered. This resonates directly with the type of network.

Here's the way Paul Flanigan, formerly the producer for the Best Buy network, sees it: "If you're at POT, the messaging has to be very simple and very effective, 5 seconds of five words of copy, and it needs to be provocative and enabling. It's very fast, very simple messaging. But when you get to the POS, this is where you may change the content to say, 'You're here to buy something to drink, how would you like this?' It's much more targeted toward purchase."

In a POS network, delivering the attraction message (what will draw the viewer to the screen) in the first 2½ seconds is critical to getting the required attention. Next the value proposition (why do I want this) needs to be delivered within 3 to 10 seconds, followed immediately by the call to action within 15 seconds. The result is that within 15 seconds, the viewer has a complete story that can affect a behavior change.

This is true for many types of POS networks, but it is not always the case. A spa store is going to have a completely different speed of message than a grocery store. The speed of message at the spa and hot tub store is slower and more relaxing based on the atmosphere of the venue and type of products. But, again, if the message is compelling and useful (not just about price), the speed of delivery can be slowed down to become the antithesis of a very busy shopping experience, such as the grocery store. A message that slows the consumer down with useful tips about healthy food can be a reprieve in the din of a grocery shopping experience.

Dominick Porco of Adspace uses a unique approach to address the issue of a moving audience. "What we're noticing is you've got to have a blend of video, audio, and static. And the reason for the static is remember these consumers are in motion while watching screens. Be it very slow motion. You can't assume they're paying attention from second 1 to second 15 of the 15-second spot. So, as soon as the shoppers glance, the logo and copy has to be on that screen and static the entire 15 seconds. Then in-between the static is where they can run video. They certainly have to adapt or repurpose their regular commercial as long as they have one."

Vaglio-Giors agrees with Porco. "First of all we have to make sure as we are not using sound that the people can understand the message. In many cases we have to add some text inserts to replace the sound. We try to use more I would say dynamic objects because with the motion of some graphic elements you can attract the attention of the consumer, like using Flash effects. And we try to make it shorter when possible. The 30-second format is definitely too long for this kind of contact, 15 seconds is better."

Brain Hirsh of RED looks at the trends driving his media production and notes that what in other places might be considered short form—like a music video, movie trailer, or game trailer—is actually "starting to feel more like long form. I think that the other element that's added here is the, kind of the micro form or something like that, to coin a new term. You're actually starting to see a whole other trend of broadcasters that are pushing web-based media right into this same size. So, take an entire 24-minute broadcast spot and cut it down to 3 to 5 minutes and that quite honestly works really good. So you're seeing people like CBS and Discovery Channel leverage their existing broadcast programs for digital signage."

Messaging in any environment can be very effective given the right ingredients of the story and product. These concepts can be categorized from simple and basic products to complex and luxury products. Considering these two very different product attributes will help create the right content for the right product. Layering the brand attributes of the product can also affect the speed with which the message is delivered. The venue's atmosphere can also directly gauge the speed and length of the message. Combining these ingredients requires the correct strategy and methodology, as described in Chapter 2.

3.5 Summary

The effectiveness of content is directly related to its relevance to the viewer in demographic, behavioral, and emotional terms. The relevance of content is further determined by its relationship to important factors related to the way in which viewers encounter the network. The time of day, the activities in which the viewer is engaged, and even the weather can be important considerations in developing content. Combining the viewer's profile with the network's environment will help the programmer make important decisions about how to assemble individual content elements into complete programming loops and how to determine the length and frequency of change of each element and loop. Ensuring the content is relevant in the eye of the viewer is what will get it noticed and lead to it having the intended effect.

4 Keeping the Content Flowing

So far, we've considered the value of the 5th Screen, the three major kinds of digital signage networks, and some of the significant factors that one needs to understand when setting out to create content. It's clear that two things are most important: ensuring the content is relevant to the viewer and ensuring that it is kept fresh to attract and maintain interest.

Regardless of the type of network or the frequency of content refresh, keeping the content machine churning is a potentially daunting task. When the network is switched on, content needs to be produced and delivered in a constant stream. This is a problem familiar to people who put out content for many of the other four screens, such as the manager of a television station or the webmaster of an Internet news site. One of their main tasks every day is finding new content or determining what they have in their content library that can be re-presented to viewers.

In this chapter we will look at the process of determining how much content a network needs, ways to organize that content, and some sources for content that will help to fill in the gaps. Anyone setting out to launch a digital signage network should think of it as a journey, one that, if carefully planned and considered, will prevent an unpleasant encounter with the insatiable monster aspect of the network's personality. Approached correctly, the monster can be tamed into a domesticated animal with content that is fresh in the eyes of the viewers.

4.1 Keeping it Fresh

Keeping viewers interested in the content is a primary challenge of a digital signage network. For some networks, it's a greater challenge than others. For example, keeping a corporate communications network fresh can be especially daunting because content is presented to the same viewers day after day. To keep up with that need, many managers of corporate communications networks make a crucial mistake and display all their content assets in the first month of operation and leave themselves with nothing new for the rest of the quarter or even longer, not to mention that their audience becomes bored and is likely to lose interest rapidly. In all networks, and here in particular, pacing the delivery of existing assets is a key to success.

At McKee Foods, the corporate communications network rotates several categories in the main window: corporate content, policies, benefits, financials, and safety tips. They have a number of pieces ready to be placed into the loop at any time, aimed at varying the specific message while maintaining the integrity of the category flow. Tom Hunter, media productions administrator, tells us more: "The loop has a safety message, and as the loop plays through the entire playlist, the system advances to the next safety message in the queue. It resets the safety message up to the top each time it goes around. So you're always getting a new safety message that is different every time—just in case you did sit through the loop twice, you'd get another safety message."

Keeping ahead of content demands begins with the development of a significant pool of assets prior to launching the network. Think of these as basic building blocks that will be available for a relatively long period and can be mixed and matched in different ways. This is not stockpiling the content around a specific campaign, but rather it is about the overall look, feel, and identity of the site.

This involves creating key graphic elements and templates to develop a large library that can be manipulated as you create and present your content. It's crucial to know the current and upcoming campaign objectives (at least for the quarter, and preferably for the year) to be able to create the necessary content elements well in advance. This is an area that requires full attention, and procrastination is *not* an option. The more planning for content, the more successful a digital signage implementation will be.

Mark Bennett and his team at Target are always making sure the content from each vendor featured on their in-store network remains fresh for the consumer (whom Target calls a "guest"). "As far as the vendor content, we are more like consultants to help them understand how content gets stale so fast. We create multiple versions (of a segment) that are slightly different. We also try and mix up the content (in the loop). For the vendor we produce a number of templates that can meet the high standards of the network and also add to the network. This gives our vendors an easy way to get onto the network."

To ensure that the content adds to the experience of Target's guests, Bennett will watch an entire show on each of the store's channels—based on store department—each week. "Every network operator needs to take a step back and look ... from the guest's point of view."

Creating a multitude of assets that can be tapped into at any time will allow flexibility in most any campaign. Start with creating graphic elements that can be put together in a number of diverse ways. This enables one to change the look slightly by shifting the elements around on the screen.

These graphic elements span the gamut from logos and labels to photographs and icons. A network that will be selling coffee drinks will want to gather images of the coffee cups in use, the logo of the brand, and any logos of the drinks themselves. An in-store network at a consumer electronic retailer would want to gather images of its key products, manufacturer logos, and brand marks, such as Blu-ray. An internal communications network that will mix messages about safety with those about corporate policy might want to develop several sets of related designs to go on top of the relevant text—a red striped bar for a safety warning, a blue striped one for policy—that will carry consistent elements of the network's design across various content segments.

In some ways, this is similar to the idea behind designing a web site or a print publication. Although there will be a constant stream of shifting content, there are certain graphic elements that are used all the time and that let viewers know visually what site or publication they are looking at. These elements help create a sense of connection and comfort with viewers yet provide a great deal of flexibility in terms of how a particular piece of content can be presented. Because these elements are important to a network's identity and used so frequently, they are considered and developed ahead of any other content.

4.2 Templates

Another key to keeping the content presentation fresh is to create a series of templates that can easily be adapted for most situations based on the objectives and messaging desired. Templates, simply put, are predesigned arrangements of graphic elements, colors, and empty space for specific content to be added. Rather than taking on the task of designing a new layout for each content segment, network managers save time and more easily retain the network's identity by using templates.

It's not necessary to overdesign templates or make numerous complex changes for them to be effective. Think about designs where a simple change of color or one graphic element could take a template suitable for one use and turn it into another. For example, a template meant for financial news might have a green dollar sign in the upper left corner, a space for a headline, space for text below, and a block of space at lower right for a chart, all bordered in green. Change the dollar sign to a yellow sun, the chart to a thermometer, and the border to blue, and the template now can serve to show the weather report (Figure 4.1). (It should be clear now why assembling elements as discussed in the previous section is so important.)

When considering templates, don't be tempted to merely copy from one DOOH network to another. Every network has different needs, and the assets available and the type of templates created will be unique. If we are talking about a point-of-sale network—specifically an in-store network—the content will always have overarching brand messaging that appears along with product offerings. One can create brand elements and templates that will be used throughout the year to drive that brand messaging while leaving central locations for a product offering to appear. One can also create a layer within the brand messages for product offerings that will have their own brand. Creating elements to drive these

CTS Pharmacy

Rx Refills for In-store Pickup
Prescriptions Delivered to
Your Door
Refill Reminders
Health Resources
Medicare 2007
Easy Read Label
Extra Care for Caregivers

A

SPECIAL!

APPETIZERS		DESSERTS	
Cheese Balls.	0.00	Ice Cream.	0.00
Chips/Salsa.	0.00	Cheesecake.	0.00
Breadsticks.	0.00	Fudge Brownie.	0.00
PIZZAS		Fruit Salad.	0.00
		Pie.	0.00
Cheese.	0.00	Cookies.	0.00
Pepperoni.	0.00	Cake.	0.00
Supreme.	0.00	Ice Cream Sandwich.	0.00
SANDWICHES		**BEVERAGES**	
BLT.	0.00	Soft Drinks.	0.00
Grilled Cheese.	0.00	Lemonade.	0.00
Chicken.	0.00	Coffee.	0.00
BBQ Chicken.	0.00	Juice.	0.00
Tuna.	0.00	Iced Tea.	0.00
Club Sub.	0.00	Bottled Water	0.00
Pulled Pork.	0.00	Milk.	0.00

B

SAVE 50%

Save big on all our winter wear.
This week only all items are 50%
off the labeled price.

WINTER SALE 2007

C

Figure 4.1   (Continued)

Figure 4.1 Using template designs in which one can swap backgrounds or change text and pictures can help in refreshing a network.
©2009 MediaTile.

offers is just one example of a template that can be reused and changed slightly to keep the messaging fresh. Menu boards are another great example of how templates can be used to change the pricing, pictures, or specials that need to be updated from breakfast to lunch and dinner.

For any network, one needs to create a set of templates that are refreshed at least once a quarter. This isn't an exercise in rebranding the company or building an entirely new visual language for the network, but one should create variance that introduces new elements into the ones that have already enjoyed a 3-month run. For example, create a series of templates that have corporate branding elements for a specific purpose. You may have a series of compliance messages that you need to get out, so create a template that is designed for that type of message. The viewer will learn that when that particular template is up, the content pertains to workplace compliance. Creating templates with branding elements for other types of messages will also play well with viewers. If you use the same template for everything, the viewer will get tired of the same look all the time.

At Adspace, for example, CMO Bill Ketcham creates templates for POS networks that allow weekly content changes and a complete shift with each retail season. "We have a spring set of templates, a summer set of templates, a fall set of templates, and so on. Then within those templates we have different creative for holidays. In addition, we are following [the customer]: 'What is Mom thinking for back to school or the holidays?'"

Also consider a series of community messages and good old eye candy that can give retail employees a reprieve in the daily grind. Give them something to smile about, too. There are many methods to generate viewer interest on an internal communications network, and the digital signage communication offers power.

It is also important that the templates create an overall look for the entire network—something that gives graphic consistency across screens. This is where we can take a lesson from the 2nd Screen. TV stations create that kind of identity so that even catching a brief glimpse of local programming or a promo spot will visually tell viewers they are watching Channel 5. Network owned and operated stations take that a step further; one can tell they are part of a particular network by the consistent visual cues like typestyle, screen layout, and even the shape of the station's logo. Not only do digital signage networks benefit from this kind of continuity; the fact is that after many years of TV exposure, the viewer expects, even subconsciously, that certain standards of appearance and identity will be met. As Mark Bennett notes, "You know you are watching Target TV because a nice chunk of content playing is advertising an event or sale that is Target [Figure 4.2]."

Target's ID plays a huge role in establishing the network look and feel. "The station ID or brand is a breath of fresh air," Bennett says. "It's a bright shiny spot and they're fun. It really starts off to give the channel a Target branding moment. It gives it cool factor. It is designed to surprise and delight our guests. In production we go into a treatment that is part of an existing campaign with specific art. We can take those campaign elements and slice them up and add the motion. It's really cool and pushes the bounds of branding of how and what form the bull's-eye [Target logo] shows up in."

In addition, Target looks at all of the content that runs across their network. Target does not throw just any content up on the network simply because the vendor wants it there. The Target network is much more of a collaborative affair than a mere purchase of airtime by a vendor.

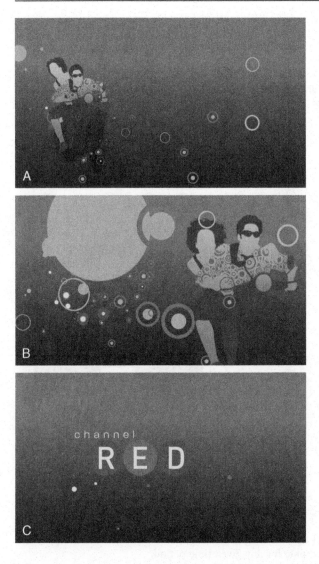

Figure 4.2 Target's ID establishes continuity of the network and surprises and delights the shoppers. ©2009 Target.

4.2.1 The Template Formula

To better understand how many templates one will need to keep a network fresh and relevant to the demographic, a simple formula can assist in creating the right number of templates: $D \times V = T$ or (day parts) $\times$ (visits) = (demographic templates). This is based on each demographic one takes into consideration, then one can take all the demographics and add them up for the TT (total number of templates) required using a message template similar to the

Refresh Optimization Formula

$$D \times V = T$$

$$T_{(1)} + T_{(2)} + T_{(3)} + \dots + T_{(n)} = TT$$

D = Dayparts
V = Average Monthly Visits
T = Demographic Templates
TT = Total Template Count
■ = Target Demographic #1
■ = Target Demographic #2

$D = 5$

$V = 3$

$5 \times 3 = 15\ T_{(1)}$

Target Demographic #1 Ave. Monthly Visits = 3

	Monday	Tuesday	Wednesday	Thursday	Friday	
8:00 - 10:00a						1
10:00 - 12:00p						
12:00 - 2:00p						2
2:00 - 5:00p						3
5:00 - 7:00p						4
7:00 - 10:00p						5

$D = 2$

$V = 6$

$2 \times 6 = 12\ T_{(2)}$

Target Demographic #2 Ave. Monthly Visits = 6

	Monday	Tuesday	Wednesday	Thursday	Friday	
8:00 - 10:00a						
10:00 - 12:00p						1
12:00 - 2:00p						2
2:00 - 5:00p						
5:00 - 7:00p						
7:00 - 10:00p						

$$15\ T_{(1)} + 12\ T_{(2)} = 27\ TT$$

Figure 4.3　This table and formula will help one create the desired number of content pieces for the right demographic for any given time period.

example (Figure 4.3). One can lay out in a spreadsheet the number of versions of the message one needs in a given month and understand what time of day the specific demographic is in the venue. This will tell one how many versions of the message one may need to keep it fresh and when to put the versions in the schedule. For this example the monthly visits (V) for demographic 1 is 3. So to create the right number of fresh templates for demographic 1, simply multiply the day parts (D) = 5 by visits (V) = 3, which totals 15 templates (T). One can do the same for demographic 2, where day parts (D) = 2 and visits (V) = 6, which totals 12 templates (T). And a grand total for all templates is 27 total templates

(TT). One then knows that during the week between 8 and 10 o'clock in the morning, one needs to play demographic 1 on Monday and Wednesday, and between 10 o'clock and noon one needs to play the ad targeted toward demographic 2. The target demographic ad versions can be altered slightly based on the templates. Keeping your content fresh and relevant to the demographics will keep your digital signage network watched!

4.3 Snack Size Versus Long Form

Whether it's a snack or a meal, a feature story or an item in a gossip column, things people want to consume come in dramatically different sizes. In most cases, the characteristics of a DOOH network—the message being displayed to a viewer for a short time, the message being inserted into the viewer's space rather than directly chosen by the individual, the value of being able to deliver multiple messages—call for feeding the viewers in small bite-size pieces that keep coming at them. Even if the network's goal is to communicate a complex message to the viewer, it will almost certainly be more effective to break that message into short, easy-to-digest bursts.

Remember that even in a point of sale network, the content is not a brochure. It is an enticement, an emotional plea to get the shopper to request more information or make that purchase.

For Retail Entertainment Design (RED), CEO Brian Hirsh goes to great lengths to create an experience in retail, particularly brand-name clothing retail. "You have lots of different ways to have a media play in that space. From a content perspective, obviously if it's in the front of the store, it's short, smaller. It could be some ambient footage, meaning quick edits of us being on site during a photo shoot where it's live product shots and merchandising shots. But generally it would be real fast. You know you have about a second to attract the consumer. The goal is to get them to walk inside the store."

Inside the clothing retail space, the game changes, and it is a much different game than in a grocery store. "It's no longer about a 15-second ad with one off-the-shelf piece of a fish in a fish bowl, and switching to a happy little customer. In our environment, it's more about let's see the fish swimming, let's see the fish do this, let's see the fish do that. So you end up kind of expanding on that same idea but understanding that at retail it's actually a little bit longer."

In any network, even point of wait (where loop times are longer), information should be presented in short bursts, which provides the network manager with the ability to shuffle content frequently. That will keep both customers and staff members more attuned to the screens and prevent boredom and aggravation on the part of the person who is at the desk day in, day out to greet clients. It also makes it possible to intermix shorter informational capsules that will likely help keep the messaging fresh and update advertising that supports the messaging.

Does long-form messaging work? Yes, there are a number of cases, especially in point of wait networks, that do require longer messages. For example, when one is at a hospital waiting for a patient or going into surgery, the person is highly interested and literally glued to every bit of information on the procedure and postop wellness steps that one may take. This content can be in longer form, provided it is divided up into shorter segments. The question to be posed to a network operator is, If you slice up the messaging, does this lead to greater flexibility when changes are needed? The same applies in a corporate communications network. Shuffling content within a loop in combination with a broad assortment of templates will always keep viewers on their toes.

4.4 Educational Content

Educational content is a foundation element of most digital signage networks. Telling the viewer something that is both useful and that they likely don't know will attract and maintain interest.

At The University Network (TUN), CEO Peter Corrigan explains how their network really replaced the traditional cork bulletin board in recreation centers and student gathering places on college campuses around the nation (Figure 4.4). "Our screens are partly informational—they give information to the students on events and special circumstances relating to the logistics or campus issues and facilities. And then we combine that with other content and advertising. This keeps our screens watched because we have useful

Figure 4.4 Digital signage keeps college students up to date on events and other information and replaces the old bulletin board.
©2009 The University Network.

information, entertainment, and advertising. And our advertisers benefit from association with the reliable campus information and entertainment."

This is particularly effective when the educational content relates to a particular product in a point of sale network. Useful, factual information about a product is very high on the list of attributes that consumers use when they make purchase decisions.

Take a store's pet food aisle with a POS display at the shelf next to a client's dog vitamin product. Besides merely reflecting the product's other advertising and a discount for that day, consider adding an educational component to the mix. Rather than the advertising that conveys the message that giving vitamins to one's dog is good for the animal, tell the viewer specifically how the addition of vitamins to the diet creates increased energy and playfulness, which in turn makes spending time with one's pet more rewarding. Now add to that information about the specific recommended vitamin programs. How would the product be used for a large dog? An older pet? A puppy? When and how should the vitamins be given for best results? With food? In the morning?

This is an example of how the addition of interactive technology, which we discuss in more detail later, can play an important role in the success of the network. Instead of simply rolling through all the available information about a vitamin regimen for a dog, allowing the viewer to select from different options would maximize interest and allow the viewer to make a connection with the material. Chihuahua owners aren't interested in the program for Great Danes; others may want to know how convenient the product is first.

If this network combines a product sales pitch and interactive educational content, and if it relates the content visually to a happy family experience, then the sales success is almost certainly going to be higher than without the educational component.

In some point of wait subcategory networks, like banking, educational messaging of a similar sort works very well. For example, if the network seeks to sell new savings accounts, then the offer will be more effective if it is interspersed with instructions on effective ways to build up savings. How much should one save? Is it based on income level, age, life goals, or all three? What are the options— direct deposit, automatic transfers, bringing in the week's change every Saturday? Based on current interest rates, how much will the viewer accumulate over a year? Five years? Relate this to the viewers' future and give them hope.

With educational material, it is still important to be concise for most network types. The exception to this rule is a healthcare network, a subcategory of point of wait networks. With viewers waiting an average of 30 minutes in a doctor's office, for example, one has the opportunity to add depth to the programming, and health care is an example of extremely motivated viewers eager for informational content. A note of caution, however: longer content does not necessarily equate to a better viewing experience. Don't ramble on, but make every second count. Treat the viewers with respect for their time by providing shorter content segments; the viewers' experience will likely be better if they see good content twice rather than bad content once.

In the United States, the Ad Council is a great resource for educational content in the form of public service announcements (PSAs). These are high-quality spots that focus on community, education, health, and safety. These typically 30-second spots are also free. According to their web site (http://www.adcouncil. org/default.aspx?id=68), "The Ad Council has endeavored to improve the lives of all Americans since first creating the category of public service advertising in 1942. From our earliest efforts including 'Loose Lips Sink Ships' to the more recent 'I am an American,' Ad Council PSAs have been raising awareness, inspiring action and saving lives for more than 65 years. Based on our long history of effecting positive change, it's fair to say that Ad Council campaigns have inspired several generations of Americans. Our ultimate goal is to ensure that future generations will reap the benefits of our efforts to date, and continue to be inspired by our public service campaigns in the future."

PSACasting is the Ad Council's entry into the digital signage realm, providing royalty-free access to a rich library of PSAs that were previously available only to traditional media networks. They are formatted for digital signage and are available at www.PSAcasting.org (Figure 4.5).

Figure 4.5 PSACasting.org is the clearinghouse for all digital signage public service announcements.
©2009 Ad Council.

4.5 Advertising

With few exceptions, paid advertising is the key element that pays for the network. Whether this takes the form of a specific offer at the shelf in a POS network or a brand message on a highway point of transit digital billboard, advertising in a new and effective way is one of the key benefits of digital signage. The major difference is each type of network will require a unique approach to give the advertiser the best advantage and create a connection with the viewer.

The most important rule is that a product advertisement on digital signage is not the same as an advertisement on television. It is a completely different medium with completely different goals and viewer experiences. Sharing the messages from a TV ad campaign with content displayed on digital signage is both important and effective; it makes the most of the investment in both media. But the ad on digital signage needs to come in a different form that is in context of the mind-set of the viewer.

Let's consider why TV ads do not normally work in digital signage in retail. The most important difference is in the objectives of the two screens. Retail-oriented commercial content on TV has as its primary mission driving customers to the retail store—persuading them to change their frame of mind from consumer to shopper. The TV ad is competing with other ads as well as other distractions in the home environment. And finally, TV ads cannot, by themselves, create sales. Consumers need to leave their homes and travel to the retail location to complete a purchase.

There still must be continuity between the campaigns that are seen on TV and those that are seen in-store. Paul Flanigan, partner in The Preset Group and formerly the producer for the Best Buy network, agrees that having alignment among campaigns across screens is absolutely one of the most crucial things that must be discussed, ferreted out, and executed with extreme care. Here's how he sees it. An advertiser—a retailer or a brand of product in the store—can create an amazing and powerful campaign that is shaped by attributes from a slogan to colors. But if those attributes are not the same on the in-store digital signage, then there are significant problems.

First, he says "you have a major disconnect there. The customer outside the store has an expectation. If they have seen it on a billboard or they see it on their computer, and they want to go to the store and purchase, when they walk into the store and they do not get that same visual emotional feeling that you've tried so hard to present outside of the store the buyer becomes confused."

This buyer confusion is compounded by the fact that the typical employee experience with the campaign will be heavily weighted toward the in-store visuals. So the employee involved in guiding the sale can actually exaggerate that disconnection because he or she lacks awareness of the customer's expectations. Flanigan continues, "The customer comes in saying, 'I've got this great feeling about this toaster. And I really want to buy it.' And they walk in and the employee says, 'I don't know what you're talking about. And I don't know what that toaster is and I don't know where it is, but we have a beautiful blender over here.' Wow. It's a huge miss all around."

In the store, to illustrate Flanigan's point, the POS network is engaging with a motivated shopper, not a consumer. The work of the TV spot has been done. Now the advertising needs to persuade the shopper to choose the advertiser's product. Clearly, it's valuable for the in-store advertising to include graphics, templates, and tag lines the viewer has already seen and associates with the product. But it's also important at this stage to show something that the consumer has not seen. For example, Best Buy uses a very effective technique to sell DVD titles in the chain's stores. Instead of the POS network running the same trailer the consumer has seen on TV already, it shows an intact clip from the movie. The results are an uplift in sales. In-store digital signage has multiple diverse purposes, and in-store content can create a lasting emotional connection to retain existing customers.

Point of transit networks are typically all about the advertising. Subway stations and airports have proven to be very effective locations for brands to engage with viewers. Again, what won't work is simply running last week's TV spot on screens in the airport terminal—consumers will ignore it. But they will pay attention to a thought-provoking ad designed for the environment of the location, sharing some of the same elements from the TV campaign for continuity and brand recognition. The fundamental issue in the terminal or station is attracting the attention of a busy traveler (a mover in most cases). Like television ads, point of transit networks are meant to build mind muscle through sending repetitive messaging that makes a lasting impression on the viewer. But, like exercise in the gym, repeating the same routine over and over gets boring, and in the case of digital signage, repetition leads to viewers not paying attention. Consider, for example, that the average commuter riding the same subway line to and from work passes a given POT screen in their home station 10 times a week. So the network operator will not only want to day part the screen to account for the mind-sets of inbound commuters going to work, midday nonworkers, and homebound commuters, but the operator also should rotate ads on the screen every 10 to 15 seconds and from day to day. Creating variations on the same ad while varying the presentation to the same audience every day helps to prolong the life of the campaign on digital signage and helps to keep the viewer's attention.

Another key to consider about advertising is that no matter how good the ad and how often it is varied, it may not be effective if it is out of context with the network and location. Don't believe that merely building a network and selling some advertising on it makes a successful business. With digital signage, the business is about more than just eyeballs—it's about being able to deliver messages that are extremely well matched to a large number of characteristics about the viewers and even interacts with them. Even in a POT network, where it can be more difficult to narrow down the interests or characteristics of the large number of passing viewers, context for ads is just as important as the context of educational or informational content. News about the destination, weather, and community events draws the viewer in, and ads related to those transit topics will have greater punch on the platform.

Getting advertisers to understand the details of using DOOH can be difficult, particularly if they or their ad agency are focused on traditional metrics, such as reach and frequency. That is a mind-set that works for TV and other traditional media because the greatest effect comes from reaching as many viewers as possible with one ad and repeating that impression as often as possible. What DOOH provides is something totally different: the ability to deliver a higher-quality message in a relevant contextual setting. This is the key to capturing the mind of the viewer. Whether it is a POS, POT, or POW network, understanding the uniqueness to each type of network and specifically the subcategory of network will provide the most relevant and effective advertising results for the advertiser. The content choice for the ad, based on the network, will drive results well beyond what might be expected for TV or other media.

4.6 Informational Content

Weather, news, sports, and stock feeds via an RSS ticker, or even full screen with visuals, are another way to keep fresh content coming across the network (Figures 4.6 and 4.7). This is information of general interest that changes with considerable frequency because of the nature of the information and its source. Viewers have also come to expect this kind of information delivery on the other screens they encounter every day—for example, headline crawls along the bottom of cable news programs and weather displays along the edge of their computer web browser. The feeds are widely used, and providing this utility content to viewers will give them a comfortable entry point to the digital signage they encounter and serve as another way to capture and maintain attention. A number of companies provide the XML data and then add the customized images and graphics.

Media RSS (MRSS), designed by Yahoo!, is an extension to the RSS format that enables content providers to easily syndicate multimedia files with a simple XML-based feed. The data format has many current uses on the web and is quickly becoming the standard method for delivering dynamic, relevant, web-based content and now digital signage (Figure 4.8). MRSS allows for multiple media files to be delivered with a story, whereas nonextended RSS can deliver only one. Video, Flash, and other rich media content can also be delivered via MRSS. Building in MRSS has significant advantages because a great deal of metadata for each asset can be included, such as file size, media type, duration, description, and author.

Captivate Network employs an editorial staff to keep relevant news content refreshed via an RSS feed. The difference is Captivate's network is designed to provide just that: informational content mixed with weather, news, and of

Figure 4.6 Weather is a common RSS feed. Customized graphics use XML data from AccuWeather.
©2009 Image courtesy of MediaTile.

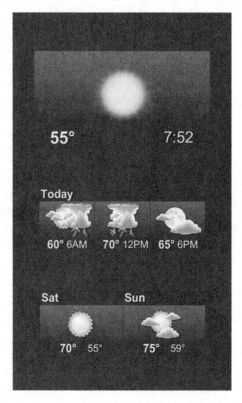

course advertising (Figure 4.9). Their screens are primarily seen in elevators. Mike DiFranza, CEO of Captivate Networks, points out, "We aggregate and editorialize content every day and continuously and keep the screen refreshed with editorial content that we edit."

Jim Harris, CEO of the Wall Street Journal Office Network, notes that one of the reasons their content strategy has been so successful with property owners is that they give them time on the network to inform. "We give them time to present tenant welcome announcements, building news, any sort of thing that they want communicated [Figure 4.10]. And if you've spent much time in many of these buildings, you'd typically see a lot of easels and printed boards and things like that, which is what they mostly use to communicate with tenants. And now they can use this digital network. In fact we've even created templates for them, which they can customize."

Again, one needs to consider the type of network and what type of feed will be relevant to the viewer when choosing which informational content to present and how to present it. The most significant thing to consider is whether the approach to presentation will capture attention or prove to be a distraction. For example, in a POT network, having a ticker along the bottom of the screen can be counterproductive. Knowing there is limited time to capture the viewer, an advertiser naturally wants the viewer's full attention when an ad is on the

Figure 4.7 Stock quotes is another RSS feed that is in demand.
©2009 Image courtesy of MediaTile.

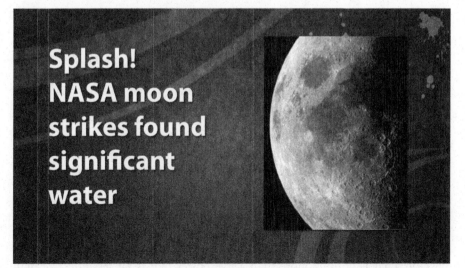

Figure 4.8 A Media RSS feed provides multiple media files that can be delivered with each story.
©2009 Associated Press. Image courtesy of MediaTile.

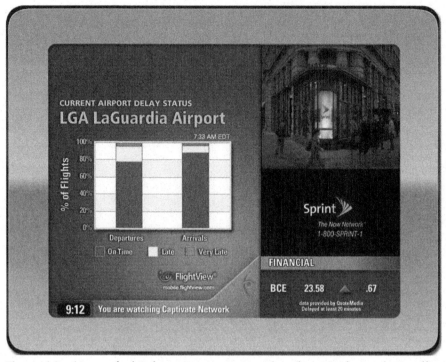

Figure 4.9 Airport feed information is automated to keep professionals in office buildings up to date on flights.
©2009 Captivate Networks.

screen and is going to want command of the entire screen area to get it. Presenting a ticker will create competing motion and draw the viewers' eyes to that area of the screen and away from the ad. In fact, given the challenge to viewers to keep watching the ticker crawl to not miss part of the information it contains, they will be reluctant to even glance at the ad. This distraction means the ad will not create the number of impressions that are desired and therefore may be less effective.

Instead, in this situation network operators should consider giving the informational content the same full-screen treatment as the ads and alternating ad segments and informational content. This ensures variety without forcing each segment to compete with others.

It's also tempting to consider not using informational content at all, particularly in a POT network. This can already be seen at many airports where the digital signage, in many cases, delivers only national brand advertising. In effect, the network operators have spent considerable time and money to develop what is nothing more than a live poster that is far less effective than mixing in informational content to capture the greatest attention possible among passing viewers. A top-flight, compelling, and thought-provoking ad

Figure 4.10 Along with *Wall Street Journal* information, the Wall Street Journal Office Network provides tenant messages.
©2009 Wall Street Journal Office Networks.

helps, but given many people's mental resistance to ads, having content they will watch interspersed with ads means they will be exposed to the ad message while waiting for the next bit of information to come on.

Pointing to The University Network, the content is zoned and mixed with ads. Why? Peter Corrigan explains, "There is some controversy on advertising dilution. I've experienced this enough with the advertisers to explain to them that the reason we would add more content zones is to attract the viewers more. To have them spend more time in front of the screen. To have them come back to the screen more frequently for the campus information, to increase the frequency and to increase the reach. So that's why we've added zones. I think most advertisers get that now."

4.7 Eye Candy

Eye candy provides a reprieve in the customers' daily lives and lightens them up. A moment in a network's playlist with beautiful images that may be local, seasonal, or holiday related takes the consumers' minds to another realm, if only for a moment. Examples include a Valentine's Day message filled with images of flowers and wishes or beautiful autumn photos of swirling leaves and harvest scenes. High-definition monitors can have a mesmerizing effect on viewers. Viewers consider them to be windows rather than pictures on a wall. This engages them more strongly on an emotional level, so lighten them up and relax them when you have a chance. Some content companies are creating high-quality HD footage just for this purpose in health care. Providing a change in the ambience of the medical office, and therefore calming the mind of the patient, is the primary goal. Just like having the fish tank in the office has a positive effect at the POW network, high-quality images will do the same. The advantage of the digital version is that one can layer messages in a very tasteful, integrated manner that is not interruptive to the desired experience.

These techniques work well on almost any type of network. For point of wait networks, like a bank or hospital network, adding this kind of content works well to grab the attention of viewers simply because it is relevant to their lives. Providing high-quality holiday or event content on a monthly basis has proven that the viewer looks forward to the next holiday or event for any given month, especially on networks that have high-frequency visits.

In a number of restaurants in the MGM Grand in Las Vegas, great content is created to simply soothe the mind and help in creating the atmosphere. In particular, Shibuya, a sushi restaurant, has a fantastic video wall that runs across the entire side of the restaurant and plays animations of fish swimming in a very calming, visually appealing manner (Figure 4.11). Using visuals to drive a desired effect in a restaurant or healthcare facility can have a great impact. Creating or buying this type of content will help to create brand loyalty simply because one is providing useful information in an entertaining manner.

Figure 4.11 MGM Grand's Shibuya restaurant and its digital signage mood wall. ©2009 Kenneth Kelsen.

4.8   User Generated Content

User Generated Content (UGC) refers to people creating content, usually while online, either with their PC or mobile phone. The content the user has created is then uploaded to a network to be displayed on a screen. Some examples of user generated content can be seen in the form of personal pictures and stories posted on Facebook or Myspace, reviews posted to Amazon.com, videos posted to YouTube, and photos posted to Flickr. Other dialog posts of UGC include Blogging using WordPress or Tweeting on Twitter. One may ask how does digital signage work with user generated content and to what end? In 2009 Razorfish released a Digital Brand Study. Razorfish reported that digital brand experiences create customers, and in fact 65% of consumers reported that "a digital brand experience has changed their opinion of the brand". Moreover, 97% of the consumers in the study stated that the digital experience influenced purchase decisions. These types of experiences can also bridge on-line and mobile experiences with DOOH. Primarily the interaction is integrated using dynamic flash, a media player, and one of the user sites like Flickr, YouTube, or Twitter, but one can also use a mobile phone with SMS or even voice commands. Verizon Wireless recently incorporated Times Square to promote their new DROID's built-in location-based voice-search feature by giving passersby control of two digital out billboards; Thomson Reuters and Nasdaq. Passersby could call a toll-free number that connects them to a user prompted application and it tells them what to expect when interacting with the signs, along with instructions that they will receive a call back. After the callback, the participant can do one of two things: Speak a search term for info on New York City stores, restaurants, movies or plays and watch as the result is displayed on a Google map on the Nasdaq sign, or speak a secret code that displays a spectacular animation on the signs. Once a call was completed, users received an SMS message directing them to the nearest Verizon Wireless store, where DROIDs can be bought.

Typically the UGC is first auto moderated for key words that one does not want to show in the middle of Times Square on a 50' Digital Billboard and then also actively moderated by a person to exclude content that is not intended to be shown by the advertiser. Another example of using UGC is RMG networks (formally Danoo). They provide the facilities for users to post local events to their screens through an online tool and mobile tool. These hyper local events like a "block party" for instance can be posted and RMG will distribute mes-sage to the local screen. Other examples include polling from a mobile phone using SMS and influencing the results on screen or uploading a photo or image to be displayed on a large screen, at a predetermined time and place.

UGC is a mobile trend that will influence DOOH. Digital signage can also embrace this new social experience which can engage the user in new and novel ways and ultimately influence purchase decisions. Keep your eyes on this one for future interactions.

4.9   Buy or Create Content

The level of expectation that the viewer has for digital signage is high. The continually increasing quality of the images and content on other screens—whether it's Flash and video on the Internet, HDTV, or IMAX movies—creates an expectation in the mind of viewers for any content they see on a screen. One has to create content whose quality is high enough that the viewer is engaged and doesn't develop an impression that the image (and message) is cheap. Creating PowerPoint slides with text is a sure way to let down viewers, and frankly it will affect the viewers' perception of the company, retailer, hospital, or hotel that is hosting the network.

Just as one creates any other marketing effort, this medium is no exception. When creating a brochure or newsletter, one creates something that is professional and reflects the best visual impact, brand, or product information that one can afford. DOOH is no different. The visual impact of digital signage is a feature that makes this medium so compelling. The idea that network managers can simply put up text or a company logo and leave it at that will find them trying to justify the screens to others simply because the content is not compelling. Digital signage is a powerful medium, and, when used correctly, it is a compelling tool to further any marketing need. Conversely, when it is abused by putting substandard content on-screen, it will surely fail.

So what are some ways to prevent the network from failing due to issues with the content? One good way is to purchase outside content or services created at a level of quality that will enhance the professionalism of the network. There are a number of services that are provided, including stock photo, video, or Flash companies that specialize in unique content that can help convey concepts. Using great visual images to help convey great ideas will go a long way toward the success of any network.

Some content companies are now specializing in creating content for point of transit networks, that is, billboards. These companies are usually agencies. Others creating content for point of sale networks, like retail clothing stores, have a lot of licensed and self-created content that is ready to be integrated with the brand. Some content providers for these types of POS networks are even creating episodic short burst program series that have story and brand integrated.

Retail Entertainment Design (RED) is a company that does exactly this. CEO Brian Hirsh explains his philosophy: "I think the stock houses have historically been content aggregators. So they've collected a mass of video and quite honestly I feel like they're trying to do business with the digital signage market the same they would with an agency. And they don't necessarily understand that there aren't big budgets in this business for creating a lot of content. In most cases it's about a scalable media platform that will work across multiple locations. In some cases the stock houses are trying to apply the traditional model of $500 a millisecond or whatever they can come up with. And when you're building a traditional broadcast spot, that may work out fine. When you're building point of sale media or on site media, you need a ton of that. We look at content strategies differently and really where we would source content differently. I have HD networks that are up and running today and the entire goal is to get that TV to look the best it possibly can first and foremost."

Budgets vary depending on the scope and breadth of the network. Typically, RED's clients pay to produce the show on an ongoing basis. They allocate 10 to 15 percent of the total show costs to new media content acquisition, and in some cases that direct cost is where RED is actually sourcing content and paying for it. They have a content acquisitions team that goes out and sources the best possible content and the best price.

The other 85 to 90 percent of the budget is really the cost of getting the show produced, created, and wrapped accordingly. "Producers, editors, graphic designers, and technology partners are how we get the content actually playing within the way the show is designed to, with its ultimate goal ... to increase sales. We haven't been historically building advertising-based networks. We've historically been building entertainment-based networks that are sometimes ad supported," Hirsh explains.

A number of television and cable networks are licensing content to DOOH networks. What makes it work depends on the DOOH network and how relevant the content is to the venue. Short clips that help brand a show or the TV network itself are common in some POW networks. Anything from CBS and NBC Sports to Comedy Central and the Speed Channel are licensing re-edited versions of shows into bite size content that plays well in high dwell time areas. One such network is Indoordirect, which has screens in quick serve restaurants across the nation. They have created a TV like atmosphere in the eating area of the restaurant and then place advertising in between the bite size licensed content. This is unique to this type of POW network and is a very qualified approach.

Even point of wait networks like hospitals have specific content that is health related, even targeted toward a type of surgery, for example. This approach to buying ready-made content with slight modifications is a great way to get a lot of content quickly. It is important that you qualify the creative team that you are going to work with. There are a number of companies that claim they create content for digital signage. Buyers beware. Make sure that the company is not just trying to jump into DOOH just because the industry is hot. Make sure that they have a dedicated team and an in-depth understanding of content for digital signage. Ask for examples and client references. As with any new medium, there are a limited number of companies that really understand digital signage. This book is designed to help more people get up to speed on content and broaden the understanding of the medium. The level of understanding will vary from company to company. After reading this book, you will know a lot more than most. Use the knowledge to help you find the right partner to work with.

4.10   Data-Driven Content

A number of services will provide data-driven content that will help keep the content fresh. They include RSS feeds for sports, weather, stocks, flight information, news headlines, and traffic, to name a few. Even the TV and cable networks will provide RSS feeds to digital signage networks. These are feeds for which at least permission, and more likely a contract and fees, is required because the data are to be used in a commercial application.

These types of data can be customized using Flash and graphics to create a high-quality look and feel. The data can also be customized by using specific portions of the feed. For example, the network operator may want only a particular result from one or two NASDAQ stocks and accompanying graphics to go along with it.

One can also drive content with these RSS feeds. If a particular sports team wins, the product-related content can change in automated ways to present the relevant products based on the winning team. This can also be applied to products that are weather sensitive—for example, promoting umbrellas when it is raining.

Delivering content in a localized and customized manner can be challenging in many ways. To help drive content that is more relevant, companies are employing customized software to deliver the right content to the right place at the right time. Some of this is even data driven. For TouchTunes, programming for localized content is based on which type of music needs to be in which type of bar—and it can be a complicated scenario. Ron Greenberg, CMO, explains: "I would say we try to make it look easy, but it is pretty complex because essentially you're programming some customized content to every individual location out of 40,000. We have historical data for almost every individual location. Because we have the records of what's being played, we're using it primarily now for sending out music. So we make sure that based on what's being played in a particular location, they get the right genre of music. So we don't necessarily push out country music to a hard rock location. It all depends on what is actually being played. So we've got an algorithm that's set up to recognize that. But it also gives us the ability to localize advertising content. So, for example, we may not run a promotion across the entire network. We may actually profile it and say, ok, so if it's a music promotion, it's going to be for this artist and we're only going to run in locations where this artist or artists of this type have a strong play history. This can also be used for psychographic targeting."

Data can also help drive localization based on where the screen is located to pull the right content for the right location. For example, advertisements for an airline that flies out of New York City and San Francisco may have brand messages that are the same, but the flight destination from New York City may be different than when leaving from San Francisco. For example, if I am going on holiday from New York City, I may go to the Caribbean, but if

I am leaving from San Francisco, I may be going to Hawaii. The ad can automatically assemble content based on the location of the screen, thereby providing more relevant content to the viewer.

Using data to help drive content in automated ways and on many new levels will keep viewers watching and informed, and it will keep your network relevant to viewers' daily lives and mind-set.

4.11 Summary

Feeding the monster—keeping fresh and relevant content flowing to a digital signage network—is a big challenge, but we've seen that there is a wide variety of types and sources of content. Although not all of them are appropriate for a given network, the proper mixing and matching of content types will create and maintain interest among a network's viewers. Content types serve to inform, entertain, or simply attract attention, and they serve to support the main messages of a screen and fill in the gaps around the core messaging. Organizing it correctly will also ensure that this content mixture amplifies the value of the network and doesn't become clutter or noise that distracts rather than informs or motivates a viewer. Remember, keeping ahead of the game of content is a challenge that every network operator must overcome. If you are starting behind the curve, try a few of the tools discussed in this chapter and tame that wild beast!

5 Process for Creating Great Content

Even if it is heavily reliant on outside source content, every digital signage network requires the actual creation of the final content for its screens. This can be as easy as assembling the external feeds within templates, as discussed in the previous chapter, reusing and recombining existing content elements from internal sources, or creating entirely new content just for digital signage. For most networks, some combination of all three methods will be necessary to produce all the content for the playlist.

In previous chapters we examined how to look at methodology and process and how research and relevance directly affects the messaging. This is all in preparation for creating the blueprint and design guidelines from which content will be created. This chapter will examine the process for creating the content from that blueprint—analyzing existing assets and creating new concepts as well as the tools that can be used to create the final content. We also examine the question of when sound is and isn't an appropriate element.

For many network operators, this is where the work of building a digital signage network becomes fun. In smaller networks, where only a handful of individuals are involved in creating content, the process lets people take on multiple roles: producer, director, art director, cinematographer, screenwriter, animator, or technical director. In larger networks, these roles are dispersed to people with the appropriate backgrounds and skills. In either case, like putting together a TV show or movie, this is the time when creative juices flow best.

5.1 Analyzing Current Traditional Media

Most digital signage will be deployed as an additive component to existing marketing and advertising campaigns. As we've discussed in previous chapters, it's important to keep campaigns on digital signage aligned with the images and messages of the overall campaign. Operators should closely examine all the raw assets available for each of the other screens—TV and computer, primarily—for material that can be pooled and then reused or repurposed in digital signage content (Figure 5.1). Doing this not only ensures compliance with the look and feel of the existing campaign but also is an extremely cost-effective way of obtaining raw material for content. Creating content from scratch, which is often necessary, can also be much more expensive.

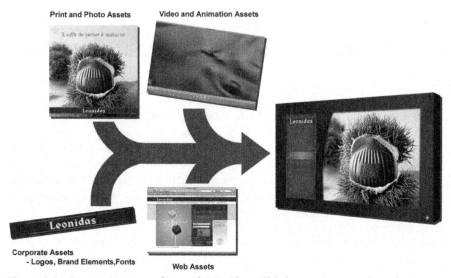

Figure 5.1 Leveraging assets from other media will help continuity and production. Images courtesy of MediaTile.

Existing content can consist of both finished and raw advertising footage, still photography and graphic images, animations, sounds, and voice-overs, in addition to the basic graphic elements and building blocks identified in Chapter 4. Understand that if one obtains finished production work, such as 30-second TV spots, they should be considered as compilations of individual shots and segments that can be taken out of the spot and reused in other ways that are more appropriate to the digital signage network.

In addition to considering the screen-based assets that are available, don't neglect the potentially large volume of assets intended for use in printed materials. Because print preproduction today is almost entirely digital, the photography, illustrations, and even text are likely to already exist in computer files that are immediately useable on a digital signage screen; images are almost certainly in sufficiently high resolution to take advantage of even the highest of high-definition screens.

There are several places within typical companies where one can seek the existing collection of assets. The company's internal marketing department is the most logical place to start because they are charged with the job of creating and maintaining the brand image and messaging. They will likely have many of the raw assets, and if they don't have them directly, they will know how to obtain them. Having them involved and cooperating in the development of the network is crucial to its success.

There are other internal sources for materials, sometimes depending on the type of network involved. Human resources or other functions involved in internal communications will have both printed and digital materials from which to draw for point of wait networks in corporate settings.

Investor relations groups will also have materials related to the financial side of a company if its shares are traded on the public market, which may be appropriate to point of wait networks in corporate lobbies or other areas where customers and others might want to be reminded of the company's performance and stability. Community relations departments will have information on philanthropic and other community outreach programs that can help create content that will highlight the good citizenship of the brand.

Finally, the group responsible for maintaining and programming the company's web site is likely to be an excellent source of raw material. In addition, this group will already have the material in the same formats that are used in digital signage and will likely have significant familiarity with the same creative tools—hardware and software—that will be used to create the final content for digital signage. In most cases, they will store these files in organized databases that will make it easier for the digital signage team to take and maintain an inventory of the available raw materials. Once again, synergy, consultation, and cooperation with these individuals, in addition to merely obtaining material, will help drive a successful network.

Dan Grant and his small media production team at McKee Foods have assembled the necessary resources to create digital signage content, and they leverage those resources from a number of departments across the company. "That's one thing we've been successful with the LDTV [Little Debbie TV] is that we have a department, instead of a secretary trying to manage some big thing." Even though the company has a more traditional media department, Grant's team maintains full control over the content. "We care how it looks. We care about the content. We care about the image. We care about professionalism. Having the staff supports making good LDTV."

The advent of digital signage means that Grant and his team think about gathering assets far differently than before they implemented a digital signage network. "Even how we think about doing video is different. It used to be we had a very production company style, where we would follow the script and shoot exactly what the script dictated. Now in the back of our minds, we're thinking: 'Can we use any of this for LDTV? Can I get the guy to give me a real quick quote that I can use for LDTV? What if I got some extra footage and then we can put together a little something for LDTV?' So that's always kind of in the back of our minds in almost every project we do now. We really had to change the way we ran our business to some degree. It really represents the migration of the industry."

Most companies doing outside communication to the public do not create all their own materials, however. There are a number of external consultants and service providers who will have created materials and thus have access to files and raw materials that make up, for example, ad spots. The company's external advertising agency, if it has one, is certainly deeply involved in the creative decisions and production of material. They can also be a source of creative and technical expertise for network operators who do not have sufficient skills in those areas.

Companies and their agencies may also use an independent production house to shoot, edit, and produce the final form of ads, marketing videos, and other moving visual images. Once again, not only can these consultants provide material, they are also sources of expertise, particularly on the technical side of production.

It's important not only to collect the available assets but also to take a complete inventory and analyze what's on hand. There are two reasons for this. The first is that one will need to understand what's available before deciding on what the most relevant and useful pieces of content are and how they might be reused. This will save considerable time when creating the final digital signage content. In addition, network operators will be able to identify any holes in the inventory and thus ascertain the amount of creative material that will need to be applied to the network on an ongoing basis.

One should pay careful attention to the organization of the assets as they begin to accumulate. The materials and categories can be organized by quarter for refreshing content and by campaign within that quarter. It may also be useful to create categories based on the type of network one is operating. In a POW network, like corporate communications, one can organize assets based on the type of message and perhaps by the department that may be contributing to the message. Categories may include safety, human resources, sales goals and information, employees, company events, community projects, marketing campaigns, and by-products. It is critical to understand the resources that will be dedicated to the creative material for the network. The volume of assets a company has will determine how much creative budget will be required. Creating templates from current assets by categories will go a long way in accomplishing this goal at a very cost-effective rate. Typically a few templates with new information will go a long way in satisfying the demand for fresh content.

If one is building a point of transit network, for example, one realizes that the kind of messaging that will play on this network is advertising and mostly branding, and one will work closely with the agency to track the campaigns and produce the right content for this medium.

As digital signage becomes part of the marketing mix, it will be included in the media's creative and marketing thinking, so it's vital to think cross platform. For McKee, it's gone from the traditional in-house production department (which is really rare to find anymore) to a production team that has migrated its thinking to really embrace and understand multimedia. Grant explains how the team thinks about the assets collected. "Let's make sure this can get up to our web folks. Let's make sure we get our main target project done of course. But we are always keeping the other…side of the media cycle [in mind], of which the signage production is a big part. We are integrating similarities into the web and through a newsletter that is [developed in] another department. But it changed our thinking from…straight photography or videography or video editing to [the idea that] it's in our best interest to keep all or as many shoots [as possible], it just adds value."

No matter which type of network one is operating and creating content for, assets need to be collected for the overall network look and feel, or as it is referred to in television, the station ID. The assets created and needed for continuity for any network are usually created fresh on a quarterly basis. These assets include seasonal assets (related to holidays, for example) and cultural events. Attention to quality of the content and assets created will ultimately make or break a network.

Over time, this process of asset collection for digital signage needs to shift to the creation of assets that serve all screens. The most cost-effective manner to create the assets for cross-platform media is to create basic media assets that can be used for TV, print, computer, mobile, and digital signage. When photographing a product, for example, one can shoot stills and video in 360 degrees to potentially create 3-D models of the product. These assets can then be used across all media, including digital signage.

Michael Chase, president of Alchemy, one of the leading digital signage agencies, is doing just that. "What we do is a lot of planning up front and consider how do you leverage your assets and how to get it out to all these mediums. We are creating that content for all mediums. It's really about saying, 'I'm going take a product like a KitchenAid blender or mixer and I'm going to shoot it in all the different ways possible when I've got it in my studio. So I'm going to take a really high definition shot of it. I'm also going to shoot it orthographically and shoot it 3-D. I'm going to take CAD drawings of it. I'm going to shoot it within a lifestyle. I'm going to shoot it with someone holding it. Since I've got it all lit and properly set up at the front it's an incremental cost for me to shoot it 10 different ways so that now I can take those assets and put them out to all different mediums.' If I don't do that what I always find is that it's coming back to the studio over and over and over for different uses. It might be the Internet, it might be digital. It might be a contest or promotion. It might be a flyer execution of direct mail."

If one thinks up front of all the different media one wants to supply with content, then one is going to realize that creating an incredibly dynamic asset management database is critical to accomplish a widening need of content for many platforms. It is from this asset database that one can pull and push the appropriate content to all the appropriate media and create a greater return on investment for the client and the network.

5.2 Considering Content on Two Levels

Previously we discussed the concept of how the network's ID can be incorporated into the overall look and feel of the network. Here again one must consider at least two levels of content that need to be created for most networks. First is the entire network look and feel; second is each individual piece of content, with attention to how it will be coordinated into the entire experience.

5.2.1   Network Identification with Consistent Guidelines

The next step in the process is establishing the blueprint or design guidelines and then producing a creative brief. Start with the most fundamental question, Why? Why are you doing it? What are your objectives? What follows is the message design, which is everything from colors that resonate, fonts that work, right through to the psychology and dwell times, imagery, and how to build content that's relevant for people.

Creating design guidelines for the network and the content is an import step in the process. This process starts with discussions with key stakeholders and ends with a formal design guideline document for everyone in the process to follow. The guidelines will include specifications on logotype and colors, logotype usage, fonts, ID design and usage, network design elements, and identity system and creative briefs. This document is vital even for a small-scale network; consistency is mandatory to maintain the effectiveness of the network's identity and messages, and much time will be lost establishing this consistency at the end of the process rather than in the beginning.

For example, some key design elements for the network may include photography, bright colors, endorsements, and quotations. The content designs may include directions like having a main photograph; clear headline; short copy; short, large, and legible words; bold colors; and high contrast, to name a few.

Taking the time to create a network guideline will save on time and money in the future. These are the minimum basic areas one can consider while creating the network design guideline for one's network:

- Color usage
  - Identify the brand colors of the company, product, etc.
    Colors are usually designed to work well together and live in harmony within compositions.
    Use color bracketing, which is using the colors' opacity to deliver gradient shades of each color.
    Use gradients, which is using gradient backgrounds to create a sense of space around products.
- Font usage
  - Utilize the brand's font guidelines to ensure continuity among other marketing materials. There will typically be only one or two fonts used on the network.
  - Vary the usage of the font to create visual texture in contrasting ways that are appealing and balanced. Combining bold and light weights will help keep the viewers' attention on the right words.
  - Select three or four font weights, such as light, regular, semibold, and bold.
- Showcasing products
  - Ensure that one is consistent in how products are photographed or videotaped so the look has continuity from one product to the next.

Maintain high quality and resolution of product shots to ensure high quality of all content on the network.

- Icons
    - Create a shorthand language for the network with icons to help guide the viewer around specific themes. Depending on the network, these can fall into a number of categories. They can be seasonal, departmental, contextual, or emotional.
    - Animate icons in specific ways to enhance network continuity.
    - Icons need to be consistent. For example, all icons may relate to a specific look and feel. They may be bold or soft, or bright or pastel, in nature.
- Transitions
    - Transitions add movement to the screen and can direct the viewer's attention to one place or another on the screen.
    - Transitions need to be seamless within a piece of content and among other pieces of content.
- Screens
    - Determine which screens within an environment are designed to serve a specific purpose. For example, one may have screens on an aisle end (end cap) or at the cash register. Each type of screen may be treated differently to accomplish one's goals.
    - Determine what on-screen zone layout may be appropriate for each type of screen to help serve the intended purpose.
- Zones
    - Structure the zones on the screen. In some networks one may want to have an on-screen zone with main content, another zone with secondary content, and potentially a third zone with informational content.

The main zone is usually the product or the main advertisement.

The secondary zone typically relates to the main zone in context and tells the viewer what to do next.

The informational zone could provide weather, news, the date, or the time.

- Themed messages
    - Themed messaging can be useful according to the type of network. For example, in a corporate communications network one may want to have themes based on the department so viewers understand the type of message being presented.
- Content specifications
    - Determine the content specifications. Setting the standards for acceptable deliverables will save a lot of headaches. Determine what formats, codecs, and sizes are acceptable and whether the deliverables will be high definition, standard definition, or both.

Michael Chase is much attuned to the blueprinting process before any creative material is in production. He asks his clients, "How are you going to use it? Why is it significant? We go through every single piece of that thought process from traditional media to what campaigns are running, to is it relevant to people now that they've seen mixed messaging out in the marketplace. Are they getting the same message when they get into your location? And it really spells out a course or a blueprint for them."

Network branding creates a personality and identification (network ID) to which the viewer can relate. It creates an emotional response based on colors, images, and the speed of the message. While contemplating the overall network image, remember to bring its purpose and usefulness to the viewer.

An example of network ID can also be taken from the Internet. Google creates a new version of its logo on almost a daily basis to focus attention on something special, memorable, or evocative about that day—it could be a holiday theme, historic event, or current event. At the same time, the logo is unmistakably Google; it conforms to an established identity (color scheme, typography, alignment) that instantly, visually communicates the Google brand. Creating, organizing, and utilizing these types of assets for digital signage can help one's network live up to the media-savvy public that expects high standards for content. Expectations and the overall look and feel of the network can directly affect its success.

One can create templates that act as containers for content that have an overall look and feel. This works well when creating local community networks. Branding a community network gives a sense of togetherness. These networks usually offer a community events calendar and local information that is branded with the network IDs and logos. The viewer finds this information to be useful and helpful and, in turn, identifies the network brand with that feeling. This emotional connection is very high on the list of network aspirations.

5.2.2 Concept Creation and Storyboards

The creation of a complete piece of content for a playlist will always involve what advertising or marketing professionals call a concept. This is, in essence, the overall idea for the piece—the setting, the product or service, the characters involved, and the who and how of delivering the message. Think of a situation comedy on TV. The creators came up with a concept that included where the show would take place; the main characters, their personalities, and their relationships to one another; and the general kind of plots that would make sense with those characters and places. There has to be a sense of believability in the way the entire concept hangs together; a show about the daily travails of New York City cab drivers will probably not have a plot where the drivers argue the finer points of nuclear physics.

Adspace Networks recently played some great creative content that speaks to unleashing the power of digital signage. In the *Paul Blart: Mall Cop* spot, Kevin James is standing still as if it is a static ad and then he turns to his radio and speaks into it and says, "Is anyone going to the food court…can I get a little something…" then he turns and is still again (Figure 5.2). In the *Step Brothers* spot with Will Ferrell and John C. Reilly, Ferrell tries to pick a fight with a viewer while Reilly holds him back (Figure 5.3). It takes a little thinking outside the screen to really capitalize on the medium. Bill Ketcham, CMO of Adspace Networks, explains: "To the studios' credit they figured this out. The creative guys at Sony Pictures went to a mall with us. They go up to the screens and suddenly they realized that the best way to advertise is to engage

Figure 5.2 Kevin James in a *Mall Cop* ad tries to get someone to bring him something from the food court.
©2009 Sony Pictures. Image courtesy of Adspace Networks.

the consumer in that environment because it lends itself to that. So they figured why don't we have the actors talking to the viewers. Literally like they're having a conversation with them. And that was the genesis of the Will Ferrell spot and the *Mall Cop* spot."

People tend to approach the process of concept creation in one of two ways: the low-budget approach and the medium- to high-budget approach. Both approaches follow the guidelines for successful content creation that were laid down in the previous chapters of this book; the difference is in how the final message is crafted.

For lower-end budgets on local networks, the process of acquiring assets is absolutely critical. The general approach is to analyze the existing material to see what concepts are suggested and then create templates that will deliver the assets to match the concept. This is a relatively quick and cost-effective method for smaller networks. Minimal new content will be created when budgets are tight, and the content will have to be simple. Low cost and high

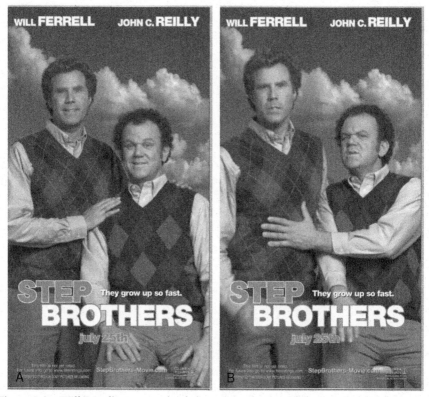

Figure 5.3   Will Ferrell tries to pick a fight with a viewer as John C. Reilly holds him back. ©2009 Sony Pictures. Image courtesy of Adspace Networks.

production values are at odds with each other, so being too ambitious on the concept will likely produce less than compelling results.

Budgets vary depending on the scope and breadth of the network and each individual campaign. This accounts for producers, editors, and graphic designers. Even when budget is an issue, a most important element that cannot be skipped is to storyboard the concept or script prior to creating the content. Storyboarding is a standard procedure in the production of films, TV shows, and commercials; in fact, some of the best-known directors in history, such as Alfred Hitchcock, were famous for their meticulous storyboarding his scripts.

Storyboarding is the process of sketching, in advance, the sequence of events, images, and effects that will make up the final product. These can range from a handful of simple pencil sketches, with a sentence or two on each describing the action, to a detailed layout of every angle, shot, and image (Figure 5.4). In effect, what a storyboard does is create both a proof of concept for whoever must approve the content and a set of instructions for those who will actually produce the content. The longer a piece of content, or the more complex the action, the more detailed a storyboard must be to do these two jobs. But even

Figure 5.4 Storyboarding helps get everyone on the same visual page.
©2009 Qwest. Image courtesy of Draftfcb.

a simple piece of content benefits greatly from the use of the storyboard process. This storyboarding process helps to get everyone on the same page. It is a very visual medium that takes the script one step closer to production. When everyone agrees on the look and feel that the production is going for, then one can take it to the next level.

Although this may be a tough concept for many people who have not worked with storyboards, skipping this step will cost more time and money in the long run. At the other end of the spectrum, agencies always create concepts and storyboards for each message that is produced. Creating the necessary storyboards will get the concept across to the client in a clear and visual manner that the client can sign off on.

After the concept and storyboards are approved, the creative production process is well on its way (Figure 5.5)

5.3 Building Great Content

From storyboard to final production piece requires only three things: time, tools, and talent.

The tools for building great visual content are limitless. Some of the most popular tools for building digital signage content include Photoshop, After Effects, Maya 3D, Flash, Final Cut Pro, and Illustrator. Each of these programs has a different purpose—Photoshop is for manipulating still images, Flash is used to assemble and then display video or animated images, and Final Cut Pro is used to edit video.

The tools you choose will depend, in large part, on the complexity of the content you are creating for your network. Tools to produce simple signage, with perhaps a little movement in some elements, won't take the same tools as an environment where you will be producing full-blown 3-D models. This becomes a very specialized world with tools that span a wide range of capabilities depending on the level of complexity and desired effect. One can use an extreme 3-D program like Houdini that uses incredible 3-D depth and movement, such as was used for effects in films like *Spider-Man 3* and *The Incredible Hulk*. The middle ground is to employ a software effects program like Maya 3D, which can produce visuals approaching the Hollywood standard but is far less complex to use. The simpler solution is creating motion with graphics that were created in Photoshop or Illustrator.

There are all kinds of ways to approach tool selection, and there are all kinds of great software that can get you to a simple Flash output. Although some of these tools are expensive, as software goes, it's important here—as in any kind of work—to invest in good quality tools. It's also important to understand that these tools are what will allow you to produce the content in a digital format that can be used by the software that operates the digital signage network.

Building great content requires great talent. One can scale talent according to the needs of the network. Some networks require a full team of production personnel, including an executive producer, creative director, Illustrator artist, production artist, 3-D model maker, Flash production artist, and technical Flash animator. The list can be longer—or shorter.

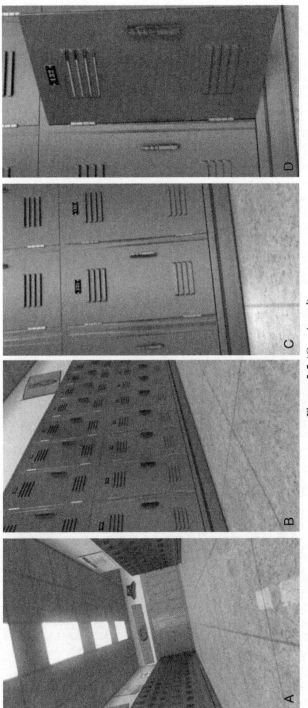

Figure 5.5 (Continued)

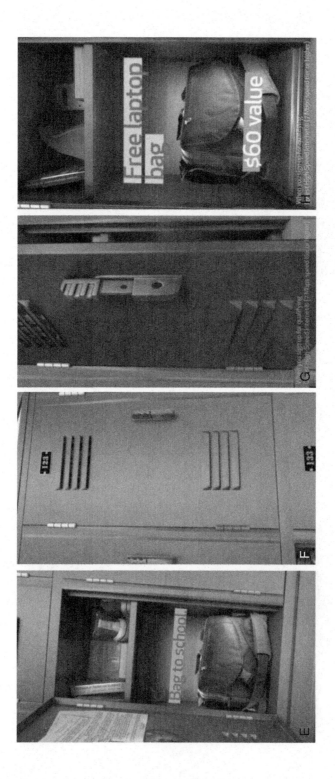

Figure 5.5 (Continued)

Figure 5.5   Final animation sequence.
©2009 Qwest. Image courtesy of Draftfcb.

It is important, even in a small team, to have an artist and technical Flash animator. A person with Flash experience is highly recommended for this media. The capabilities of Flash are very powerful. Having this talent on board will allow the network operator to use specialized data feeds and create custom Flash templates that ultimately save time and money in the long run. A number of examples in this book were created using Flash. Refer to the real Flash and video animations, along with other updates, on www.5thScreen.org the companion web site for this book.

I am a huge advocate of high quality content. When one has the ingredients of talent and the right tools to create great content, one must also allocate the right amount of time. The time to produce quality content of course varies based on the project, anywhere from an hour to create a still image to months to create a full motion 3D animation spot. Once one includes an animated sequence the time and budget invariably go up. Simple movement requires less time and can add a positive component. Keep in mind that to run a network and keep it watched requires a balance of these three elements, time, tools, and talent.

The process one goes through, no matter how big or small the team or the project, is really three steps: preproduction, production, and postproduction.

5.3.1 Preproduction

Planning is essential to create the content that is desired as well as to ensure the best use of resources and budget. In addition to developing concepts and creating the necessary script and storyboards, one needs to take several other planning steps before beginning to shoot. A budget needs to be created. The logistics for video shoots need to be laid out—securing the use of locations, scheduling crews and other participants, arranging necessary transportation, and the like. Similar logistics planning is needed in the case of graphics and animations—arranging for designers, technical experts, and any use of special equipment or studios that may be required. Make sure to account for time dependencies during the planning of logistics. Many a shoot has had to be postponed at considerable expense because a prop, set, or other item wasn't available.

5.3.2 Production

Production is the actual shooting of film or video footage, the creation of graphics and animations, and preparing any special effects that are to be added into the final process. Depending upon the complexity of the content, this may require less time than the preproduction and postproduction phases. In effect, this is where the last of the raw material for the final content is developed, not where the raw materials are assembled into the end product. Production can, however, be the costliest aspect of the process, which is why storyboarding and logistics planning in preproduction are so important.

For video, new footage is shot that follows the storyboards and may be integrated into the final piece. For animation, the production team can see what the piece is doing when it's moving. As with any digital animation, one can start to make changes at certain points during the animation process. Rendering time is a major factor when making changes to animations. It's important to make changes earlier in the process with rough animations rather than later in the process after full rendering has been done.

5.3.3 Postproduction

Postproduction is where one takes the assets that have been collected and begins to integrate them into the final content message. This includes selecting and editing the footage and then incorporating Flash, animations, 3-D, and special effects into the production as described in the storyboards and script.

5.4 Sound or No Sound?

Sound can be part of digital signage content, and where it is appropriate to employ, it in fact enhances the viewer's experience. In some cases, it will be an absolutely necessary component of a successful network. There are a number of instances where it won't work, of course; the network type will usually dictate if sound can be considered at all.

Of the three types of networks, point of transit is least likely to have sound—a talking highway billboard makes little sense. Point of sale networks can have sound at the shelf, but it is not likely in other areas, depending largely upon the location of the screens. Point of wait networks are most likely candidates for sound. For some healthcare networks, it's difficult to imagine presenting 30 minutes of silent content and in others sound will drive the staff to turn off the display because of their proximity to the screen.

In a point of transit network, there is really no time to take in an audio portion of the message. It is all about the visual experience. Even in transit terminals, the sound of the network may have too much competition from the frequent public address announcements of departing flights or arriving trains to convey any message. In fact, the acoustics of many such locations are not at all conducive to audio, as people straining to hear announcements about their delayed flights will attest.

In a point of sale network, the use of sound will vary according to the venue type and where the screen is placed. Even within a store, audio may be appropriate on an end cap (aisle end); for example, in consumer electronics stores audio works very well, especially for complex products. The vendor likes the audio simply because it enhances the sales personnel's education and is effective in getting a passing shopper to stop and watch. The sales personnel even use digital signage with audio to their advantage to park a customer for a moment while taking care of another customer. One must consider cashiers in checkout lines and their experience with audio. Listening to a short loop over and over again will drive anyone crazy enough to unplug the unit or otherwise cause it to not function. Using audio in a cashier line is a sure way to cause problems for the employee and ultimately the customer.

In other venues, like an apparel store, audio drives an experience. Brian Hirsh of RED tells us how the company uses audio to drive that experience in retail environments. "We are creating compelling, engaging experiences and audio plays a huge role in the shopper experience in most of our retail environments. The content is short form with high-energy music that drives the beat of the feet of our shoppers." The amount of programming and refresh plays a critical role when using audio. Brian's programming team creates many hours of programming to quell employee content fatigue. "Generally what we'll do is we're building up a lot of our shows to be about 8 to 10 hours of unique assets and then playlist them to be a 20 to 24 hour long show."

Within a point of wait network, audio is more than likely to be used simply because audio is almost always part of the message. The messages are usually more complex and more in-depth, educational, and more like TV. It's important to note, however, that there are exceptions to this. For example, waiting in line at the DMV or for a passport are two areas where audio is not appropriate; instead you must provide all of your information with visual cues in the form of text and images.

"In our case it's the entertainment for the gym," says Francois Beaubien, CEO of Zoom Media. "So walking in and hearing that music and seeing that music video up on the screens, that's what we do. And of course we're selling ads around that, [from] which the venue benefits. So it's entertainment, music videos with advertising."

Caution is the word when considering sound. Technology is sometimes the answer. One needs to carefully consider the placement of the screen in relationship to the associate that may spend an 8-hour shift in the presence of the display's sound.

"Say it's in a break room right around the corner from where somebody is sitting," Chris Bias, communications consultant and Lilly TV manager, points out. "While I can control the sound and raise and lower it, it's just a beast to know what level to have it on in each of those locations. I tried running a video during the lunch hour in the cafeteria but I couldn't get the TVs loud enough for people to hear them from where they were sitting. And then when there's nobody in the cafeteria, it's entirely too loud. It's blasting you out. I have certain screens in certain buildings that would be good for sound, to show the latest commercial about a drug or the latest PSA."

Technology can assist in minimizing the direct affect that DOOH has on the environment. There are several companies that provide targeted speakers. The speaker can direct sound to a 1-square-foot space across the room. This is really quite amazing technology. The sound can be directed from across the room to a person passing through a 1-square-foot sound zone. The person will hear the sound only from that display while in the zone. If the person steps out of the zone, the sound from that source cannot be heard.

An attenuator with ambient feedback can also be employed to adjust according to the level of sound in the venue. It can raise the sound when a crowd is present and lower it when only a few people are present.

Ambient sound can add to the consumer experience. In some cases the display can play a continuous set of music tracks while the visual information is independently running. But when the visual information has synchronized sound, the music track will end, and the combined audio and video segment will play, and then the music track will pick up again.

Sound is an enhancement to visual content. Specialized companies supply sound to enhance the experience in a venue, whether it is a corporate communications or retail environment. Imagine providing digital signage with beautiful images in conjunction with beautiful sound, a combination that works very well in restaurants.

When designing content, ask if it requires sound. If so, research the type of network and subcategory of network to understand if sound is really appropriate.

5.5   Summary

Creating content is best achieved by following a process that begins at the highest level of your network's identity and works down. Networks that are successful have a consistent set of guidelines that dictate the styles, tone, and other characteristics that will make it instantly identifiable to viewers. The individual content segments are also best created through a process, in this case one familiar to movie and TV producers, of mapping out the project on a storyboard beforehand. When the planning process and guidelines are complete, it will be easier to determine the tools required to produce the content in all three phases of production and allow you to make key decisions about whether to enhance your content with audio.

6 Specifications For Content

In the previous chapters we covered a number of subjects about types of networks, strategy, relevance, and audience. These subjects are designed to help you build a knowledge base to make great decisions about building great content. In the next few chapters we will get to the practical specifications and the mechanics of creating content for digital signage.

Although the network operator need not be concerned about all the technical aspects of the network, there are several such issues that are important to recognize, from the varying shapes of screens to the digital formats in which the content will be created and stored. There are also some basics of design, ranging from type and color choices to how to divide the available screen real estate, that are crucial to consider. This chapter will examine all these issues.

6.1 Aspect Ratios: How Content Shapes Up

If digital signage were real estate, then the aspect ratio would be the overall shape of the lot—in the case of screens, its width divided by its height. Many people are already familiar with this general concept thanks to the development of HDTV and its widescreen images. For digital signage, this is more than about the sheer size of the screen, though—it's about getting the shape of the content, particularly video content, to match up with the screen.

The aspect ratio of the traditional television screen prior to HDTV was developed from the movie screen, built to display the 35 mm film that had been developed in Edison's time. It is not quite square; the aspect ratio is 4:3 (Figure 6.1), also known as 1.33 (what you get when you divide 4 by 3). Until recently, most computer screens were also built on a 4:3 aspect ratio. Almost all films prior to the 1950s, the vast majority of TV programs until very recently, and TV ads were all shot in this aspect ratio and hence fill up the full frame of such a screen.

In the 1950s, in an attempt to stave off competition from television, the movie industry developed a collection of widescreen formats, and today film-goers are accustomed to seeing movies that are almost twice as wide as they are tall—and in some cases, even wider. The development of HDTV involved the adoption of the most common of these newer aspect ratios, 16:9, also commonly called 1.78 (Figure 6.2). Many films since the 1950s, significant prime time and sports programming on TV, and some TV ads are in this aspect ratio. Almost all computer screens being sold today are in this format, and as HDTV

Figure 6.1   4:3 ratio screen.

Figure 6.2   16:9 ratio screen.

becomes more widespread, more video will be available from the TV world in this format as well. If one is installing a new digital signage network, chances are it will consist solely of 16:9 screens, whether they are small shelf-mounted POS screens or large outdoor digital billboards.

These are the most commonly encountered aspect ratios, but there are others, notably the 2.35:1 format used by some movies, typically high-budget productions. (It is extremely rare to find digital signage in this format, but it is available from a few manufacturers.) Some screens in custom form may have unique ratios, or they may be taller than they are wide to accommodate the location (the large exterior digital signs in Times Square are an example of the latter).

The reason these ratios matter is because content created in one aspect ratio must be modified in some way to be displayed in another. This can create a number of problems for a network operator. If a digital signage network consists of screens of different aspect ratios, the same content will look different on each type without special treatment. Even for a network comprising a single screen format—and 4:3 is being phased out in existing networks as hardware is updated—any content created in another aspect ratio poses the same display issue. (This is another reason for carefully considering the direct use of TV commercials in digital signage networks; almost all ads today are still in 4:3.) Know what type of network the content will be deployed on; ask for the specifications.

It's quite likely, unless a network is of single aspect ratio and all the content for the network can be built from scratch or acquired in that same ratio, that the network operator will need to decide how to place content of one ratio onto the screen of another ratio. There are two basic methods for taking 16:9 content and presenting it on 4:3 screens, methods that might be familiar to buyers of widescreen movies on DVD who watch them on older TVs.

The first is known as letterboxing (Figure 6.3). In this approach, the 16:9 image is allowed to fill the horizontal width of the screen. Because of the difference in aspect ratios, this means the content will not extend the full height of the screen. Instead, it is centered vertically on the screen and two black stripes are displayed as borders on the top and bottom of the image. Letterboxing has the advantage of retaining the full image of the original content, although it leaves some significant screen real estate unused. If the screen is not sufficiently large, then some individual objects in the image might become less distinct.

A second approach is to allow the 16:9 image to fill the full vertical height of the 4:3 screen (Figure 6.4). By necessity, this means that the full width cannot be presented, and some of the original image will not be visible. This can be accommodated by cropping out both the left and right sides of the original image and displaying the 4:3 section at the center or by a more laborious process called pan and scan, in which the cropping may be more pronounced on one side or the other to keep important parts of the image centered. This typically requires an editor or technician to view the original content and determine which part of each frame to crop and then create a 4:3 version of the original according to those decisions. In either case, the content takes up all the available screen space but at the loss of a considerable amount of the image.

Figure 6.3 Letterboxing; One method of fitting a16:9 HDTV video in a 4:3 screen.

Figure 6.4 Pan and Scan by cropping a 16:9 image onto a 4:3 screen.

Because of the prevalence of 16:9 screens in digital signage, the more common problem in most networks involves displaying 4:3 content on wider HDTV-style screens. Most TV content production is converting to HDTV 16:9, but some production is still done in 4:3, so this issue is most common when acquiring assets from commercial TV. One option is to display 4:3 materials in their correct aspect ratio using the full height of the middle of the screen. One ends up with black columns on each side of the content that fills the space between the image and the sides of the screen. This is effectively the opposite of letterboxing and is known as pillarboxing (Figure 6.5). It has the same pros and cons as letterboxing, although without the potential problem of individual objects appearing to be less distinct.

Another option is to stretch the 4:3 content horizontally but not vertically so that the resulting image fills the 16:9 frame. This is how widescreen movies are actually projected, using a special lens that expands the 35 mm film image horizontally, but the image itself was created with a special widescreen lens that compresses the image. Stretching a standard 4:3 image significantly distorts the appearance of objects in the frame—people appear to gain weight, ordinary cars become long and low to the ground, doors and windows appear unnaturally wide, and any words on the screen appear out of proportion (Figure 6.6). Because of this distortion, stretching the 4:3 content horizontally is not recommended.

A third option is to zoom into the 4:3 content and let it fill the width of the screen. As with cropping the sides of 16:9 content on a smaller screen, this results in loss of image but at the top and bottom (Figure 6.7). When choosing to display the middle section of the content in full frame 16:9 in this way, recognize the danger it poses with any close-ups in the original—faces will lose the top of the head and the chin. Although the viewer's mind will complete the picture, it can be a little disconcerting to see such an image. This choice will depend a great deal upon the shooting style of the original.

Figure 6.5 Pillarboxing is placing the 4:3 video on a 16:9 screen without cropping.

Figure 6.6 A 4:3 image stretched horizontally to fill a 16:9 screen.

Figure 6.7 4:3 image is zoomed in to fill the width of a 16:9 screen.

6.2 Screen Zones: To Subdivide or Not?

One fundamental question about displaying content on the screen goes back to the real estate analogy. Should there be a single structure taking up the whole display property, or is it better to subdivide and put something in two, three, or even more distinct areas? In digital signage, these screen areas are called zones.

One typical approach is to take the full area of a 16:9 screen and split it up into three areas: one that retains the 16:9 format, another next to it in the 4:3 format, and a short, wide zone along the bottom of the 16:9 area (Figure 6.8).

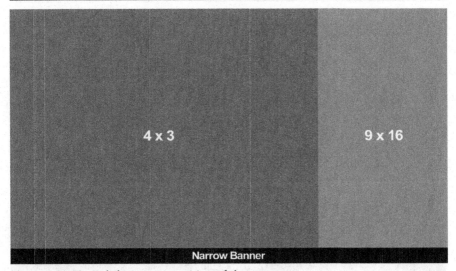

Figure 6.8 Typical three-zone partition of the screen.

One could use the first zone for branding content, the second for informational or secondary ad content, and the third as a ticker. When using zones, one may want to flip the entire image zones horizontally to prevent a latent image burn on LCDs. This is when the pixel gets stuck or locked into a particular color. It is best to flip the layout as your playlist is rotated throughout the day. Should a latent image or stuck pixels be on-screen, it can be fixed in most cases by creating a full-screen Flash graphic that alternates between black and white frame by frame. If this does not work, then one can create a flash file that alternates between red, green, and blue all full screen frame by frame, along with 2 minutes of red, then green and then blue. This can help unstick the pixels. *Warning*: This can cause seizures in people with epilepsy. *It is extremely important to do this fix when the screen is not being viewed.*

Indeed, the question of how many zones to use—or whether to use any at all—often arises when a network will use data-driven content, such as news headlines, weather forecasts, or stock prices. Although at first the zone approach appears to deal with a number of issues—from providing a way to display the full images of content in multiple ratios to creating variety for the viewer—there is a fundamental question to ask (Figure 6.9). Is it preferable to display this content at all times or does that create a distraction that confuses the viewer or prevents the viewer from focusing on the revenue-generating content?

This conundrum is not an easy one to solve, and the answer often depends on the type of network involved. So let's look at a few types of networks that have zones and some that do not to understand why the given choices are appropriate.

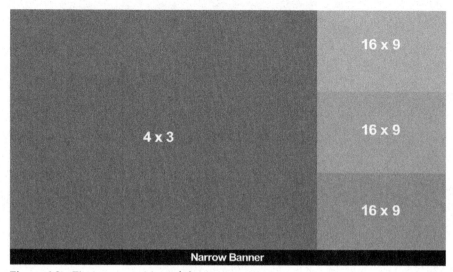

Figure 6.9 Five-zone partition of the screen.

As a rule, most POT networks do not employ zones. Why not? Because the function of these screens as something akin to a live poster, combined with the limited time the viewer is exposed to them, means that a powerful message needs to be conveyed in just a few seconds. Advertisers understandably want full command of the screen so there is no interference with their message. Although the message on the screen will change periodically, at any given time there should probably not be any competition for the viewer's attention from secondary zones.

There are occasions, however, where even a POT network can be more effective with zones, provided they are used in a creative manner. Keep in mind the issue of viewer relevancy. At an airport, weather and other information about a destination is of great interest to a viewer, and having such information displayed in a zone on the screen could attract and hold a viewer's attention for a somewhat longer period of time, exposing the viewer to ads in the main zone. At the same time, the weather information could also be displayed full screen as part of a loop that also contains advertising. Care needs to be taken with such choices given the existence of several studies that suggest zones in transit networks do not work and detract from the message the advertiser is trying to get across.

This may change as people become more accustomed to the visual cues of digital signage as it proliferates and plays more of a role in our daily lives. With changes in both content and technology, the perception of the viewer is becoming altered as well. We no longer see mobile phones as oddities, and laptops are part of the tool kit of high school students. Digital signage is well on its way to becoming exactly that ubiquitous, and viewers may soon be more accustomed to them and pay more attention to all their zones. Continual evaluation is the only thing that will clarify how this element of digital signage will be perceived.

One subset of POW networks that is amenable to the use of zones is an elevator network. Although there is still a limited amount of time to get a message across and a relatively small amount of screen real estate to do it, the fact is that the average person in an office building rides the elevator six times a day, and each ride lasts an average of 1 minute. This sort of network is ideal for presenting short bursts of content (15 seconds or so) in a few different zones on the screen. The viewer who chooses to focus on one zone during one ride may well choose another zone on the next ride, maintaining interest in the screen and making this approach a viable option for this type of network.

Mike DiFranza, cofounder and CEO of Captivate Network, tells us about the four-zone approach they use in their network (Figure 6.10), the world's most widespread in elevators. "The main zones are about editorial content that is aggregated and [condensed] by our staff. That is placed on the left side of the screen. The ad zone is placed on the right side of the screen. We positioned the ad zone to the right simply because people read left to right and that way, they see the ads in the ad content zone. On the bottom of the screen under the editorial zone, we provide time and date, and under the ad zone we provide stock and weather information, etc. We also provide a ticker along the bottom that will come in with important breaking news from time to time."

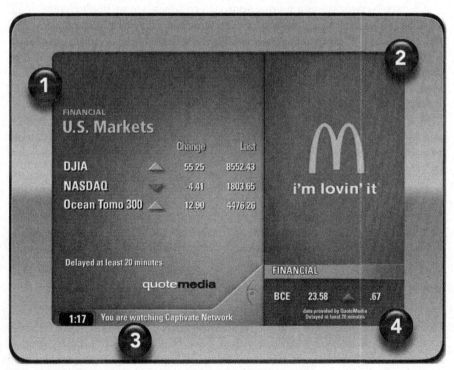

Figure 6.10 Using four zones in an elevator POW network.
©2009 Captivate Networks.

In other networks, zones are very useful precisely because eliminating the chance for boredom is an important concern. Especially in a POW network like i communications, zones help keep the messaging fresh, simply because the viewer sees the displays many times during the day and week. Providing zones of information lets viewers focus on different parts of the screen because they are engaged frequently over a longer period of a week.

One other company that has changed its thinking about zones is The University Network (TUN). CEO Peter Corrigan helps us understand why they made the change. "There is one zone that will play the content that is the main media. And then there is another zone that is treated as a print text column at the bottom or in a box to the right. But we let the colleges go up to three or four zones."

Corrigan explains that savvy ad buyers understand this strategy. "They get it. They say, 'Yeah we know why you have multiple applications running. We understand that you want them to come to the screen.' And they're going to see your ad when they come to the screen to look at the other stuff that's there."

Corrigan notes that although advertising buyers and content providers who are used to the broadcast model have difficulty understanding this approach, those that come from the Internet side "get it because that's what they do there as well. They understand it's effective. I think again we're all kind of learning about this as we go along."

Adspace Networks has a unique approach to zones—some don't change at all. Bill Ketcham, senior vice president of marketing, says they base their ideas on well over 30 studies. "You've got to have a blend of video, audio, and static. And the reason for the static is, remember, these shoppers are in motion. So you can't assume they're paying attention from second 1 to second 15 of the 15-second spot. So as soon as the shopper notices the screen, the logo has to be on that screen and static for the entire 15 seconds. Then we run [the client's] regular commercial."

One example of how Adspace Networks sets up static zones is to put motion and video with an ad midscreen but have the top and bottom of the screen act as a static billboard. "We try to blend them because we definitely know that motion attracts the eye."

With zones, keep in mind that it is all relevant to the mind-set of the viewer and the type of network. If zones are part of your DNA and are effective means to capture attention, then by all means, use them. Viewers will ignore the screens if their mind-set and the type of network does not match the purpose of why the shopper, waiter, or mover is in the venue in the first place.

6.3   Text

On-screen text is always a great way to communicate product names, brand names, pricing, and very short messages. Few, if any, successful digital signage networks will function without text. But as designers of printed material and web sites have found, there are many considerations about text that play into how well the viewer can receive and absorb the information. When text gets too small, when a list of bullet points appear, when sentences and paragraphs become long and complex, text in digital signage usually goes awry. A text-heavy sign of any kind is visually overwhelming, and few people will stop to read it. No matter what the type of network, too much text is too much text. State your message in as few words as possible and balance the text and graphics.

Tickers are particularly troublesome because they are usually all text. The issue for network operators to consider is that moving text takes longer for a viewer to comprehend—2 to 10 times longer, in fact, than if it was stationary (Figure 6.11). And the faster the ticker scrolls to allow more information to be displayed, the result is, ironically, a lower comprehension rate. The preferred alternative is to display a full line or two of text at a time and then fade or flip to the next line(s). Consider that scrolling text has a 10 to 22 percent lower recall rate than text that is faded in and faded out, even when the text is on-screen for the same amount of time. Be careful to not overload the viewer with too much information or too much motion in text.

Size is also an important consideration, something most people understand from personal experience. Network operators need to balance the use of screen real estate with the location of the viewer to determine how big to make the text. It is commonly thought that letters displayed 2 inches high can be seen clearly from about 20 to 25 feet away. After testing this on a 42-inch

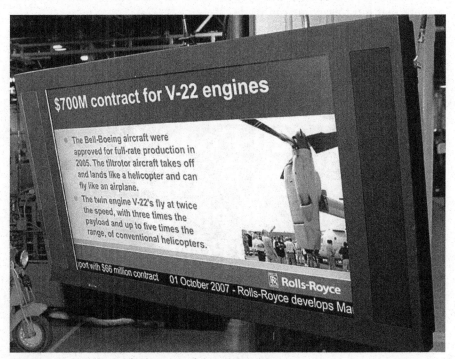

Figure 6.11 Ticker at the bottom of digital signage.
©2009 Rolls-Royce. Image courtesy of MediaTile.

high-definition 720p monitor, I found that with digital signage the font size can be slightly smaller. In fact, at a glance with white lettering on black, one can comfortably see 1-inch lettering at a distance of 20 feet. At 50 feet one can easily comprehend 2-inch lettering that is white on black, and at 100 feet one can effortlessly read 2½-inch fonts. Although most digital signs are not used at those kinds of distances, except for highway POT billboards, this rule of thumb can certainly save time and money when conveying a message to viewers (Figure 6.12). At the other end, at 10 feet one can easily see a ½-inch to ¾-inch font that is white on black.

But consider three variables that are equally as important: contrast, color, and yes, age. First, the obvious is the higher the contrast, the more legible the text. The less contrast, the less comprehension. Color also plays an important role (this is discussed in the next section). What about age? The number of adults aged 65 years and older will reach 71.5 million by 2030, twice the number in 2000, and they will represent nearly 20 percent of the total U.S. population, according to estimates by the Federal Interagency Forum on Aging Related Statistics. Along with age, peoples' eyesight begins to fail, and the lenses of the eyes actually become yellow. This has a direct affect on contrast and color, let alone 20/20 vision. Realizing that these trends are currently occurring in 10 percent of the population, one has the opportunity to make adjustments to text content that targets these demographics. Why not create content that most everyone can read?

What about font styles? In the print world it is understood that in most cases a serif font—one that has small extensions at the edge of most letter strokes—is easier to read than a sans-serif font. Unfortunately, this same rule does not always apply to digital signage. The reason for this is technical; to blend colors effectively between adjacent sets of pixels on an LCD screen, the screen usually

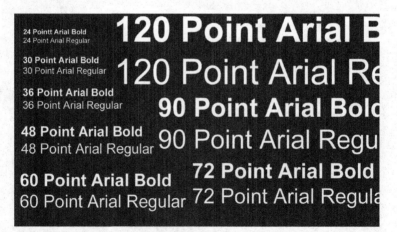

Figure 6.12   One can download this example from 5thScreen.info and apply it to a 42-inch monitor to see the results for ½-inch to 2½-inch fonts at variable distances.

employs what is called an antialiasing algorithm to make subtle alterations in some pixels. But the same technology that blends colors tends to blur serifs because it makes them less distinct (Figure 6.13). The exception is if a network

Figure 6.13 (Continued)

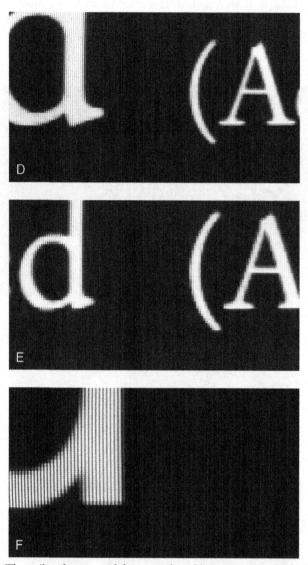

Figure 6.13 The tails of sans-serif fonts tend to blur, except on high-definition monitors and in larger font sizes. One can download this example from www.5thScreen.info and apply it to a 42-inch monitor to see the results. *B,* Looking closely at a 2-inch Times New Roman font, one can see the blurring effect. *C,* At 1 inch, Times New Roman has significant loss of its tail. *D,* Adobe Caslon Pro has less of a tail and holds up at 2 inches very well. *E,* Adobe Caslon Pro has less of a tail and seems to hold up even at 1 inch. *F,* Arial, a sans-serif font, has no tail and no blur effect.

employs true high-definition content on commercial-grade monitors and uses larger text. This combination of higher pixel density and larger font size reduces the blur and allows serif fonts to be used. The style of serif font can also make a difference. Times New Roman has a thinner serif than Adobe Caslon Pro (Figure 6.13). It would be a dull world if everyone used 1- to 2-inch lettering and sans-serif fonts (Figure 6.14).

When it comes to upper- and lowercase type, ALL UPPERCASE TYPE IS MORE DIFFICULT TO READ. Using Upper- and Lowercase Type Takes Less Time to Comprehend. Use bold and italics for emphasis only. There are exceptions to this rule. What will really determine the final look of the text after application of the basic rules is to take a step back and look at the final presentation on a screen and at a distance similar to the circumstances in the field. If the result isn't readable, then it's time to break the rules.

Text should be on a contrasting background (dark text on a light background, or light text on a dark background). Take care that there is a sufficient degree of contrast between the text and background colors. In the print world most people have more difficulty comprehending light text against a darker background, but in digital signage light text on a dark background is easily comprehended simply because a digital sign is an emitting light source. An excessively bright background color may also create difficulties for viewers—what's great for a graphic doesn't necessarily work for text.

Figure 6.14   The world would be dull if we limited ourselves only to sans-serif fonts. ©2009 Zion National Bank. Image courtesy of MediaTile.

In addition one can make the visual presentation of text as bite size as possible. Compare the two options in Figure 6.15. The list version on the right is easier to read and comprehend faster than the paragraph on the left.

Another technique to make sure the viewer can get the information quickly and easily is to cluster text on the screen, use a different font size for emphasis, and use caps as opposed to just writing all the text in lines across the screen, as shown in Figure 6.16.

The order in which one puts a list or introduces a series of scenes is guided by the simple rule of memory. Humans typically remember the first thing they see or hear and the last thing they see or hear. This is a phenomenon known as the serial position effect (Figure 6.17). One can maximize the recall of the message by placing the important information first or last. This same concept applies in deciding the overall order and delivery of each piece of content within an advertisement or even a playlist.

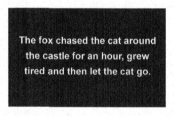

Figure 6.15   Bite-size text is easier to read and comprehend.

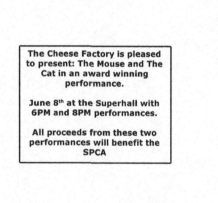

Figure 6.16   The use of spacing, different font sizes, and caps can provide a hierarchy for the information, making it easier for viewers to digest.

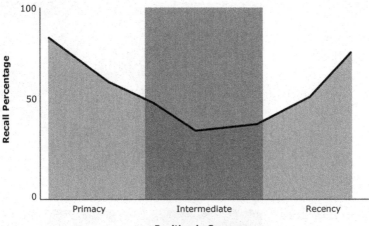

Figure 6.17 The serial position effect tells us that the order in which we see something has a direct effect on recall.

Memorable slogans are a great way to encourage high recall. According to Ad Age, the top 10 ad slogans of the century are as follows:

Diamonds are forever (De Beers)
Just do it (Nike)
The pause that refreshes (Coca-Cola)
Tastes great, less filling (Miller Lite)
We try harder (Avis)
Good to the last drop (Maxwell House)
Breakfast of champions (Wheaties)
Does she…or doesn't she? (Clairol)
When it rains it pours (Morton Salt)
Where's the beef? (Wendy's)

What about copy for digital signage? It would be grand if one could come up with great slogans all the time. Instead, here are some copywriting tips:

Define up front the action you want your viewers to take.
Tell them the specific benefits.
Use curiosity as a motivator to the solution.
Headline the most compelling benefit.
Call for viewers to take action.

Remember that digital signage is a moving, living medium. Using motion to emphasize and bring attention to one's message, even in text, can be an elegant method to help recall.

Another issue to avoid in general is the use of text over pictures (Figure 6.18). This tends to make the message very difficult to read, especially when the picture has shadows, dark colors, or sunny areas with light colors.

Figure 6.18 Text
overlaid onto pictures
makes it difficult to read.
©2009 Associated Press.

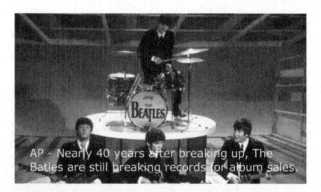

Figure 6.19 Placing text
next to the picture makes
it readable and frames the
visual.
©2009 Associated Press.

Placing the picture in a box and shrinking it within the screen area, then putting the text underneath or above it will make your signage pop (Figure 6.19).

6.4 Color

The basics of color can be summed up by saying there is a rainbow out there, so use it. But use your rainbow sensibly. Some color combinations are pleasant to view; others are jarring, even ugly; while still others send messages based on our common cultural background (in the United States, red and green means Christmas; red, white, and blue implies the flag, patriotism, and the Fourth of July). Some combinations simply make it too difficult to present text in a readable and comprehensive way.

First, let's look at the typical color wheel that is most familiar when choosing colors while working in PowerPoint or Word (Figure 6.20). By looking closely at the color wheel, one notices that the outer edge of the color wheel displays the darker colors and the center displays the lighter colors. This is based on the 32-bit color standards of RGB (red, green, and blue, where values of zero for each color creates black, and R 255, G 255, and B 255 creates white).

A value of R 255, G 0, and B 0 is pure red, and so on. Setting different values for R, G, and B within this range of 0–255 gives several million possible color choices, although a very slight change in a single value rarely produces a color that the human eye can distinguish from the original.

When selecting colors from the wheel one can use the combination of inner wheel colors and outer wheel colors to set a contrast to any presentation that uses text. Figure 6.21 shows how choosing contrasting values—such as white on black and gray on black—directly affects how well the content will be comprehended and the speed at which one can comprehend the message.

Similar thinking can be applied to color in practical ways while choosing contrasting colors that work. First and foremost, choosing a dark color for

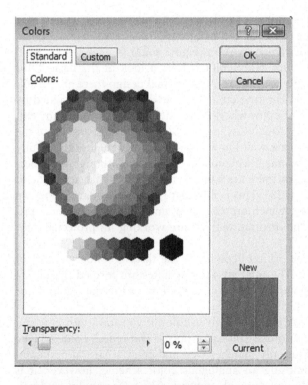

Figure 6.20 Common type of RGB color wheel chooser (see the color version at www.5thScreen.info).

Figure 6.21 Using white on black rather than gray on black creates more contrast and makes text easier for the viewer to read.

Figure 6.22   Use contrast when choosing text against backgrounds (see the color version at www.5thScreen.info).

the background and a light color for the foreground or vice versa will have a direct impact on the ease of comprehension (Figure 6.22).

Which colors work best with other colors? Take a look at the basic color wheel in Figure 6.23; you will notice that in its original design there are 12 colors that make up the wheel. The first circular color diagram was designed by Sir Isaac Newton in 1666. The color wheel is designed so that virtually any colors you pick from it will look good together. Although important aspects of the color wheel and color theory are well-known to artists, they might not be fully appreciated by someone who has a technical background. Although the wheel is made of 12 shades of colors, there are basic primary colors that are made of red, green, and blue (Figure 6.23). This is different from the primary colors we learned at a very young age, which are red, blue, and yellow. These new primary colors are based on the medium that we are working in: projected light rather than reflected light.

The colors adjacent to the primary colors are the three secondary colors of cyan, magenta, and yellow. The final six intermediates are formed by mixing a primary color with a secondary color and are known as tertiary colors, for a total of 12 main divisions.

Analogous colors are directly next to a given color. If you start with blue and you want its two analogous colors, you select purple and red. A color scheme that uses analogous colors usually matches well and creates natural and comfortable designs. When choosing an analogous color scheme, however, it is important to make sure you have enough contrast. Choose one color to dominate, a second to support. The third color is used (along with black, white, or gray) as an accent.

Complementary colors are opposite each other on the color wheel (for example, red and green). The high contrast of complementary colors creates a vibrant look that is undesirable for digital signage, especially when used at full saturation. Complementary colors are best used as accents or when you want something to stand out, but they are particularly inappropriate for text (Figure 6.24).

12 Point RGB Color Wheel

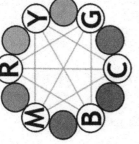

Color Wheel

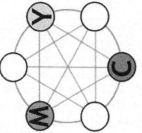

Primary Colors

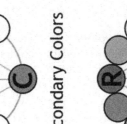

Secondary Colors

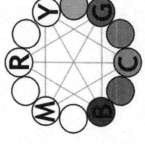

Tertiary Colors

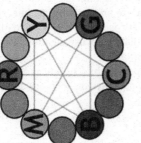

Analogos Colors

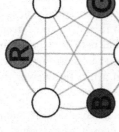

Complimentary Colors

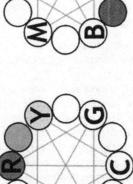

Warm Colors

Cool Colors

Figure 6.23 Building blocks of the RGB color wheel (see the color version at www.5thScreen.info).

Figure 6.24 Tertiary
complementary color
combinations are
difficult to read
(see the color version at
www.5thScreen.info).

Warm colors and cool colors are on opposite sides of the color wheel (Figure 6.23). One can use this basic warm or cool color scheme as a guiding palette.

As with any media there are colors that work together well and combinations of colors that collide. When choosing colors that work well together, one can reference the color wheel and remember to look at the contrasts (light over dark) even within the same color. For the RGB scheme of colors, yellow and blue work well together, as do red and yellow. The opposite is true for colors that fight each other or vibrate on the screen (Figure 6.24). Color combinations to avoid are typically the tertiary complimentary colors.

Working with brands and company colors, one can use the color wheel to create tasteful backgrounds and other graphics that will work well with the company's color scheme. In creating any message, choosing the right color combination can make or break the comprehension of the message.

Color trends can be fickle and are always changing. Seasonal colors are also considerations. Even for political or environmental issues, color trends will change. With America as the melting pot and global networks becoming reality, cultural color influences have some interesting twists. In Figure 6.25, one can see some cultural references for how color can affect the viewer.

Of course, colors also have attributes unto themselves:

- Blue is considered to be the favorite color. It is seen as honest, loyal, and devoted. Blue also affects us physically and mentally, provides a calm feeling, and aids intuition.
- Green is the most visible color in the spectrum to the human eye and is also selected as a favorite color. Green is everywhere in nature and is soothing and relaxing.
- Red is a very personal color, and the intensity is directly related to the level of energy. Red draws attention and can immediately focus attention. Red can also increase enthusiasm and can encourage an action.
- Yellow is a color that brings a feeling of happiness and optimism. Golden shades bring the promise of a positive future. Yellow activates the memory and encourages communication.
- White is considered to be pure and clean. White also helps mental clarity and purification of thoughts or actions.
- Gray stands the test of time and is a practical and solid color. A longstanding favorite, gray can mix well with any color.

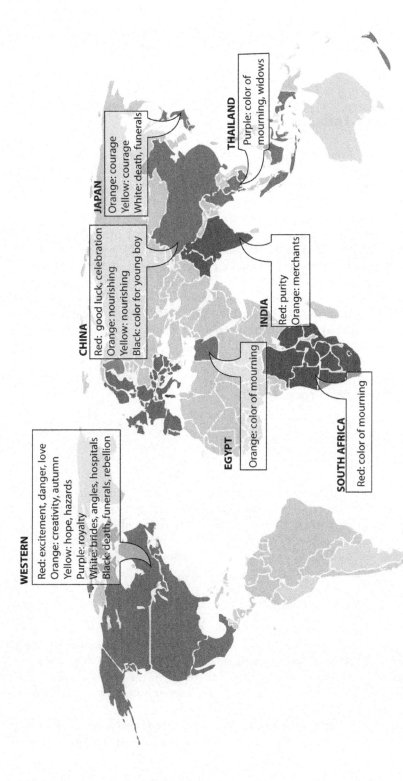

WESTERN

Red: excitement, danger, love
Orange: creativity, autumn
Yellow: hope, hazards
Purple: royalty
White: brides, angles, hospitals
Black: death, funerals, rebellion

CHINA

Red: good luck, celebration
Orange: nourishing
Yellow: nourishing
Black: color for young boy

JAPAN

Orange: courage
Yellow: courage
White: death, funerals

THAILAND

Purple: color of mourning, widows

EGYPT

Orange: color of mourning

INDIA

Red: purity
Orange: merchants

SOUTH AFRICA

Red: color of mourning

Figure 6.25 Cultural references affect the use of color.

- Black is powerful and commanding. It is great as a background for white text on digital signage. It is also mysterious and brings a sense of potential and possibility.

6.5 Content Formats

You can't put a cassette tape into a CD player; the songs may be the same, but the format in which the content is stored is entirely different. Digital signage networks are the same way. Although there aren't the same obvious physical differences, there are a number of distinct ways in which the data are stored for different types of content. Network operators need to pay attention to the formats their networks can accommodate and ensure that these same formats are specified when working with the content's creators. The wrong format will either not display correctly or will require extra steps and resources to translate it into a format that is compatible with the network. In addition, certain formats have advantages over others when it comes to the amount of data that must be stored or transmitted to the network to display a certain length of content at a certain quality level. Operators need to balance quality, size, and the rate at which the network can transfer data when considering different formats.

6.5.1 Common Video Formats

The most common formats for video are H.264 and MPEG-2. Most networks can accept one of these formats.

AVI

AVI is an acronym for audio video interlace, a format introduced by Microsoft in 1992 and widely used on PCs and the Internet. It can store synchronized audio and video in a single file. It can accommodate video whose raw size has been reduced through a number of different types of compression technology. Compression—found in most video formats—is important because of the enormous size of even a few seconds of video in full high-definition form.

MPEG formats: MPEG-1, MPEG-2, MP3, and H.264 (MPEG-4 Part 10)

MPEG (pronounced M-peg) stands for the Moving Picture Experts Group, a standards body that has developed a number of different formats for storing moving images and audio using increasingly sophisticated and effective compression techniques. Besides being a global standard, the major advantage of using MPEG formats is that the files are much smaller for the same quality than with most other formats.

MPEG-1 was developed to encode compressed, progressive scanned audio–video data for use with earlier PCs, for example, as CD-I (compact disc interactive) formats. MPEG-2 was created for broadcast use and works at higher data rates than MPEG-1; it works well with interlaced video, which is what most TV sets display. MP3 (properly known as MPEG Audio Layer 3) is an audio-only format that is the most common way for music to be compressed and encoded in digital form online. All three formats achieve acceptable levels of high-quality reproduction while substantially reducing file sizes by eliminating parts of the original data that the algorithm considers to be more or less extraneous to most needs.

H.264, or MPEG-4 Part 10, is the most advanced form of the MPEG audio–video standard to date and is included as part of the Blu-ray Disc format. Increasing amounts of video will be produced using this format.

WMV

Windows Media Video (WMV) is another widely used compressed video format developed by Microsoft. It was originally intended for streaming video delivery over the Internet but has since been standardized for use in Blu-ray discs as well.

6.5.2   Animated Graphics

Adobe Flash format is very widely used for digital data today, particularly on web sites. Originally meant for showing fairly simple motion graphics, the current version can display H.264 video as well as numerous other types of video, audio, and graphics. As such, it is one of the most powerful tools for digital signage.

6.5.3   Still Images

As with video, still image formats generally provide high-resolution images while compressing what would otherwise be files of ungainly size to transmit on a network. It is possible, when necessary, to use uncompressed still images for maximum realism, but the trade-off is storage space and transfer speed.

BMP

The simplest file format is BMP, or the bitmap. As the name implies, it stores an image as a map or grid of pixels. For each pixel in the image, the file contains as many as 32 bits that define the pixel's color (32 bits allows for an image to contain millions of different colors). Uncompressed BMP images can be extremely large, and most of the time some form of compression will be used to make the file more manageable.

PNG

Portable Network Graphics (PNG) is another bitmapped image format that employs a kind of compression scheme known as lossless—that is, the full original data can be obtained from the compressed file if desired—whereas in other compression schemes (lossy compression), some of the original information is permanently lost. The advantage of lossless compression is the degree of faithfulness to the original, but the drawback is that only modest levels of file size reduction are possible.

JPEG

JPEG is an acronym for the Joint Photographic Experts Group, the standards body that developed a series of compressed formats for still images that are used in photography, including digital cameras and on websites. JPEG files can use varying degrees of lossy compression to create files that have different size-to-quality characteristics. Because of its ability to compress with minimal loss of quality at some levels, JPEG can be a better choice than PNG for many images. The exceptions are images that contain line art or text where sharp edges is important. In this case, JPEG compression can create an unacceptable degree of fuzziness depending on the degree of compression.

PNG is, however, a better choice than JPEG for storing images that contain text, line art, or other images with sharp transitions. Where an image contains both sharp transitions and photographic parts, a choice must be made between the large but sharp PNG and a small JPEG with artifacts around sharp transitions. JPEG also does not support transparency.

PDF

Adobe PDF (or Portable Document Format) was developed as a way to exchange documents among computers that could not otherwise process one another's file formats. It also presents the files using the same format, layout, and fonts as the original, even if the receiving computer doesn't have the needed fonts installed. PDF files can contain text, graphics, images, or all three mixed together. Because it has been around since 1992 and is ubiquitous online, there is substantial content of various kinds available in PDF, both documents generated by computers and scans of printed originals. It is not a common format for advertising content, and only a few digital signage network software platforms allow its display.

PowerPoint

Microsoft PowerPoint format is used to store slide shows created with the program of the same name. It can mix a variety of content on each slide—images, text, even embedded video. Again, this format has been in wide use for some time and therefore it is commonly encountered. It is a fairly easy tool with which to create certain types of digital signage content.

6.6   High Definition Impact

On screen high definition (HD) content has a different impact on the viewer than standard definition. To maximize impact of DOOH one may want to consider producing content and displaying content in HD. When one watches standard definition content, the mind considers this a picture, similar to one that would hang on the wall. When one views HD content on a HDTV, the mind converts the idea of a picture into a window. This significant change in psychological perception happens for several reasons. First and foremost is the obvious, the resolution. The secondary has to do with the color range differences between standard definition and high definition. Standard definition displays to the viewer only 25% of the natural color one can see in the world. HD on the other hand brings forth 75% of the color spectrum that the viewer normally sees in the everyday world. This increase in color spectrum and resolution resonates with the memory and recall of images one sees. If the mind considers that it is looking out a window; this becomes a reality. And something the mind considers real will remain in memory longer and have higher recall.

HD also can have further impact on recall by bringing it up to life size. Large HDTV screens in portrait mode can accomplish a new level of physiologic impact. When one sees an image that is life size the mind will immediately decide whether it is friend or foe. It is our body's primitive, automatic, inborn response that prepares the body to "fight" or "flee" from perceived harm to our survival. This dates back to very early human development when one had to determine quickly whether to "fight or flight" or to run out of fear or embrace the encounter. This is a fundamental physiologic response that potentially DOOH can impact in a positive manner as life size images will temporarily heighten the senses and create an acute awareness even for just a few moments. It all adds up to better recall and acceptance of on screen content.

6.7   Summary

Behind the content the viewer sees or hears is a variety of technical and visual specifications that the producer and network operator must consider. Screen sizes, ratios, and resolutions vary widely, although there are certain standards. Each standard has a bearing on content produced for the network and, especially, adapted for it. Choosing whether or not to have different zones on the screen for categories of content also depends in part on these technical factors. Colors and typefaces also have a significant impact on the effectiveness of content. Colors can create an appropriate mood or be jarring; they can make content jump off the screen or render it impossible to see against the background. Subtle text choices can make the difference between content that is readable and digestible and information that perplexes the viewer or is ignored. Finally, the underlying digital format of the content will be determined by a combination of factors, from whether or not the content will have motion to the capabilities of the underlying network software and storage system. Understanding all these choices, and making appropriate selections, is a crucial step in preparing your content.

7 Programming the Network

So far, we've discussed many considerations about how to choose the right content for a digital signage network and how to create the various content building blocks. Now, with all the building blocks in hand, it's time to consider how to assemble all of them into an operating network. In this chapter we'll discuss how each network is programmed to maximize the viewership and balance the advertising to keep the network profitable and watched.

7.1 Making a Network a Network

One of the most significant problems of early digital signage networks stems from the fact that, technically, it isn't particularly difficult to install a screen and display content on it. As a result there have been many examples of networks that, for all their cost, end up displaying content that is not relevant and is poorly produced. In many cases, these networks are not merely ineffective; they are eyesores in their environments. Poor content makes a poor network, and even quality content poorly programmed reduces the value of the network and will create negative impressions among the very customers the network is seeking to reach. Thus, along with improving the content, we also must consider the programming techniques and technologies that might play a part in making the content more relevant and add continuity to the network itself.

Viewers have very high standards when it comes to content on any screen, not simply those screens that are more personal than digital signage, such as TV or mobile devices. Viewers have been conditioned to expect quality and consistent network identities on those screens, and this expectation carries over to screens that are in public places. As many network programmers have learned the hard way, the audience is tough and unforgiving. The right way to address the viewers is by creating great, relevant content that is programmed correctly with continuity across the network.

Why is that important? Think about the experience of watching an established, familiar network. It usually takes little time when watching television, for example, to know the network that's on the screen. Whether it is a logo bug, a promo for a show, a station ID, a familiar face, or some other characteristic, the identity of that network is quickly and regularly established with the viewer. When one sees—or even hears a reference to—a peacock on television, what comes to mind? The answer is a memorable brand: NBC. Because viewers have experience with the brand and understand its brand attributes, providing that kind of branding and continuity helps viewers both feel comfortable and know what to expect. It is what makes a network a network.

This is something that the largest and most sophisticated retailers understand when they are designing POS networks. Target's Mark Bennett, the Channel Red executive producer and group manager of media production, makes certain that the Target ID logo appears regularly, and in motion, on Target's networks to create what he calls the "surprise and delight" factor (Figure 7.1).

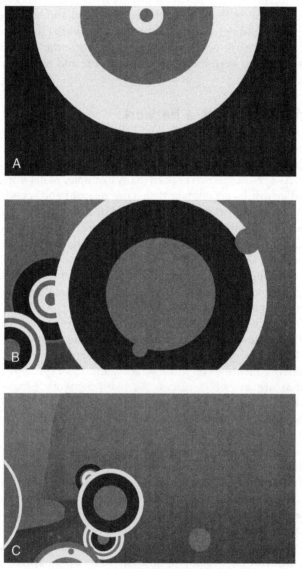

Figure 7.1   (Continued)

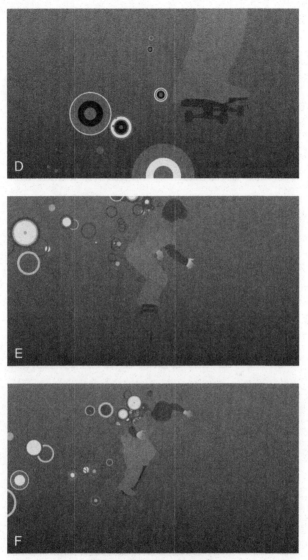

Figure 7.1 (Continued)

"It helps brand our network and shows that it is a network and not just a couple screens on the wall. It gives our guests a sense of largeness and comfort and it enhances our guest's shopper experience. Just like a station ID that you get in a network when you're watching a TV network, you get these Target station IDs and interstitials kind of throughout the network. So even though you're in a store, the [the network ID comes up and gives you] hopefully a bit of a

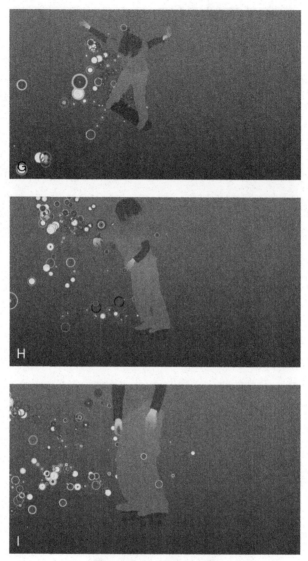

Figure 7.1 (Continued)

breath of fresh air and they're something like the bright shiny spot in your day. But it's a fun little thing to see. . .a surprise and delight."

On the Wall Street Journal Office Network, the power of the brand is foremost (Figure 7.2) and is on the screen 24/7. The content that is played on the network is *Wall Street Journal* editorial content in four news categories: What's News, Marketplace, Money and Investing, and Personal Journal. CEO Jim Harris

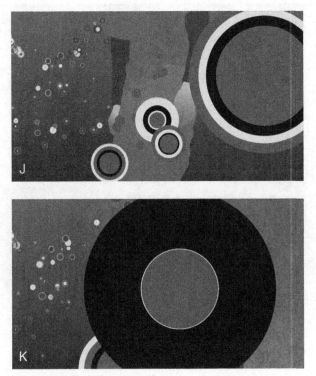

Figure 7.1 Target's ID called Skate Board.
©2009 Target.

talks about how import the *Wall Street Journal* brand is to the network. "We are located in premier office buildings across the country reaching an affluent decision maker. The same sections of news or headings that people are used [to] when they are reading the *Wall Street Journal* are playing on the screen. The content is more interesting to the viewer with [the] *WSJ* brand associated with it and the advertisers inherently are attracted to the brand because of what the brand means to the audience. The advertisers do receive some cachet from the brand itself."

Programming a digital billboard POT network usually does not have IDs or interstitials that apply. Tommy Teepell, chief marketing officer of Lamar Advertising, has just six advertisers running on the company's digital billboards at any one time. And there really isn't time or the need to run station IDs to create continuity within the network. The one characteristic among digital billboards that negates the need for IDs is the fact that they are stand-alone screens with no other relative continuity between the screens and a venue. Some POT networks located within airports occasionally brand the airport name itself or even the network that owns the screens to create a brand for the network operator to attract new advertisers.

Figure 7.2   Screen shot of Wall Street Journal Office Network.
©2009 Office Media Networks.

Chapter 5 discussed how creating guidelines will help to implement this continuity. Moving from the guidelines to practice involves programming. How that is accomplished depends on the network and where the screen is placed.

Stuart Jacob, vice president of programming and creative services for CBS Outernet, creates content for several networks owned by CBS. One of those networks is deployed in grocery stores, which consist of several microenvironments. In one part of the store, for example, the screen is located at the deli and meat section to be viewed while the shopper is waiting for counter service. The focus of that screen (Figure 7.3) is on meal ideas along with health and wellness. "We have four on-screen zones. In the main zone we are playing health and wellness messages, one of the zones (upper right) is dedicated to the grocers' logo and ID, and the zone just below that is dedicated to promotions and retailers' messages. This is always up on-screen and creates the continuity for the viewer." In the bottom zone, CBS places a ticker that includes CBS news, sports, and weather—ideal content for a part of the network that straddles the line between POS and POW.

In the same store another screen could be located in the produce section. Here customers are serving themselves rather than waiting on someone behind the counter, and the selection of items varies with the season and location compared to meat and deli departments, where the items being offered generally

Figure 7.3 CBS deli screen with health and wellness content along with deli promotions.
©2009 CBS.

remain constant. For this part of the network, the screens maintain a consistency of layout with those in the rest of the store, but the main screen area is programmed differently to target the different approach to shopping and the difference in merchandise. Jacob explains, "The weight of content changes. We have 'Michael Marks your Produce Man' who talks about the produce that's in season. We work with an editorial calendar predicated upon what the retailer is pushing and what's on mom's calendar." In this case, the content is programmed differently from screen to screen even in the same store, but the continuity of the network remains the same across the store.

The University Network (TUN) has its own take on programming. Peter Corrigan explains the different types of content they put in their playlists and on-screen zones. "There are really three sets of content. There's local content related to things that are happening at that school. The second part of the content is local and national content from our partners that is relevant to our audience of 18- to 24-year-olds. And then the third component is advertising, which pays for it. The advertising is also a combination of local and national content."

TUN creates relevance and viewer interest by providing content from their partners that interests or relates to their audience of college students. Some of the content they run comes from Jim Cramer's TheStreet.com, which has a big following on campuses, and eAsylum, which is a group that does red carpet interviews conducted by college students with Hollywood actors who are promoting upcoming movies that appeal to a college demographic. "They'll ask questions that are sometimes more relevant, more interesting to a college audience than what you'd see on television," says Corrigan. He explains that having high-caliber content can also help brand the network and provide

Figure 7.4 NBC on Campus segments are just one part of the programming lineup that are relevant to college students.
©2009 NBC. Image courtesy of TUN.

continuity. "We have content from NBC as part of NBC Everywhere that is branded as NBC on Campus [Figure 7.4]. NBC takes out some of their content that's relevant to the 18- to 24-year-old crowd and they bring it down to the shortness and the duration that we need."

7.2 Determining Segment Length

We've discussed the issue of timing in a number of ways in previous chapters, noting that some networks require shorter segments and some can contain longer ones. We've also noted that there are few instances in which an existing TV ad spot can be used unchanged on a digital signage network.

The same logic applies to the idea of using standard timing from TV for any content, including ads. Although TV ads appear in 10-, 15-, 30-, or 60-second segments, those are artifacts of a much different business model based on offering standardized breaks in standardized-length programming that can then be charged at some kind of per-second rate based on audience size and demographics. That business model isn't operative in digital signage, and neither is the need for standardized timing of content segments. They can be as long or short as they need to be given the characteristics of the network and specific screen.

At Best Buy, Paul Flanigan created an ad for the company's Insignia TV brand that was close to a minute and a half in length. Why? Flanigan defends his out-of-the-norm timing for the spot. "We created the Insignia LCD spot to tell a story, and the story that we told took a minute and a half. We were not concerned that it needed to fit into a 30- or 60-second timed spot because at Best Buy their customers are not normally on a timed mission."

Brian Hirsh, CEO of Retail Entertainment Design, echoes Flanigan's sentiment. "It's no longer about a 15-second ad and you're filling parts of it up with
one off-the-shelf piece of a fish in a fish bowl. In our environment it's more
about let's see the fish swimming, let's see the fish do this, let's see the fish do
that. We end up expanding on that same idea but understanding that at retail
it's actually a little bit longer. It's not about a 30-second spot. It's not about
[a] 15-second spot. It's about an experience."

This approach leads to the creation of shows that take 8 to 10 hours of
unique assets and mixes them into a playlist that lasts 20 to 24 hours, much
as a modern, semiautomated radio station might do. And, similar to radio,
something that's hot is assigned more frequent appearances in the playlist.
"If it's more important, if it's more relevant and it's tied to a new release of
an album that may play more often in a store environment," Hirsh says.

Most network operators like some kind of uniformity to their spots. The
CBS Outernet team comes specifically out of television; they do, however, have
an in-depth understanding of programming for digital signage. The lengths of
the loops are even different by zone, but typically they are running 30-second
spots. Jacob tells us, "In the main zone we are playing health and wellness messages in short form 30-second segments mixed with advertising and local community events. This zone is an 8- to 9-minute loop based on the dwell time,
whereas the grocer's promotion zone is a 3-minute loop with 18–20 slides."
So when programming the screens, even with different zones, there is a combination of loop length considerations, timing of each piece of content, and the
use of motion content versus stills. This is a critical balance between what
works well and what can be considered over the top and unwatchable.
For example, too much frenetic motion on the screen prevents viewers from
focusing and absorbing messages, or it creates an emotional response that is
out of character for a place like a produce aisle.

The opposite applies at another network that CBS Outernet runs at the video
game retailer GameStop. Here the network is programmed to tie in with current game releases, complement other forms of marketing by game producers,
and capture the interest of their target shoppers. As a result the network identity is more tuned to the social aspect of game play. Screens are located above
cash registers as well as the areas where gamers go to browse, yet the network
is completely different than CBS Outernet's grocery networks.

"We program widescreen and full screen with no zones. The content loop is
2 hours long and the length of ads and content are from 30 seconds to
4 minutes. We have such a long loop [because] we do not want the manager
to get bored with the content. The purpose of the content we create is to educate the manager and the shopper about what deals are on the table. We will
play a music video that ties in with Guitar Hero, and we communicate the
VH1 brand and in the specific game that the rock band is part of."

When a network is more ad based than product or education based, then uniformity of programming is more of a necessity. One typically needs to have spots
that are standardized to set pricing that is uniform. Roadside digital billboards,

for example, are a type of network that works on specific timing, but also regulation plays into how frequently the advertisement can change. Tommy Teepell of Lamar Advertising explains, "Typically, it's based upon what the local governmental restrictions are but what we have are six advertisers and their message is up from 8 to 10 seconds depending upon the regulations. And we worked with research folks who told us that the optimum time to read the message is 8 seconds. So that's how we came up with 8 seconds. We also rotated and tried different combinations, 10 advertisers, four advertisers, trying to figure out what is the maximum number of advertisers you can put on there and be effective. And a study we commissioned showed us that it was six. That's how we decided on six advertisers. So basically if you're one of those advertisers, your message will run anywhere from every 48 seconds to every minute 24 hours a day."

Another ad-based network, American Digital Signage, has screens in independent supermarket chains. The company takes a uniform approach to programming. Partner Jill Ruttenberg describes their approach, which is unconventional by television standards but works for digital signage in their environment. "The loop typically runs 4 minutes. [Based on experience] we try to limit the number of sponsors or advertisers. We limit the ads to 11 or 12 and each ad runs 13 seconds. That is a good time ratio and it allows enough time for a good Flash ad to be displayed."

The issue with timing here is different than the time of day considerations we looked at earlier that determine what type of viewers might be in front of the screen and what might motivate them. This is a consideration about how much time the content loop and its parts spend in front of the consumer, based on the mind-set and the speed at which a message can be absorbed. Given the variables in networks, there is no specific magic length of message across the board in every network; it is different for every subcategory of network.

Christian Vagilo-Giors, CEO of Neo Advertising, took a completely different approach to the programming, dividing content into information and advertising headings and feeding each to separate screens in each location (Figure 7.5). To do so, Neo's networks use two screens in landscape mode side by side. Vagilo-Giors explains how attention and advertising balance the viewers' interest and notice of the ads. "In Canada we are in the food court and the screen on the left is providing entertainment, what we call infotainment, which comprise news headlines, sports results, weather forecast, stock quotes, charts of movies and CD sales and on the screen on the right we show the advertising." The programmed mix they provide is 50 percent infotainment on screen one and 50 percent advertising on screen two. There is no information about mall events. With this approach, Neo combines the attention power of the infotainment screens and applies the advertising to that message. It is similar to what the TUN network has done with zones, except Neo uses two full screens.

One of the reasons for two full screens is the sheer size of the food courts and malls in Canada. Using this kind of mega real estate for the screens helps ensure they will be seen by significant numbers of diners.

Figure 7.5 Neo Advertising uses two screens to program their content and advertising. ©2009 Neo Advertising.

In Europe, Neo takes a similar approach but uses one screen. "In Europe, we have a different setup. First of all, in Europe the malls are smaller. That's easier to cover the common areas and it's less…intensive. We started by installing landscape 42-inch [screens] coming from the ceiling where people were passing by and transiting and some in waiting areas. We designed [a] program loop of 5 minutes, the same program on all the screens at the same time. The loop is made up of 50 percent advertising, 20 percent more information about the mall and 30 percent infotainment, again news headlines, stock quotes, weather forecast and so on."

In programming for international networks there are some specific challenges and expectations from stakeholders about what type of content format should be programmed. Vagilo-Giors enlightens us on these subtle but important differences. "I think it's just the taste of the viewer and the agency, who are used to TV formats. They continue with their history basically. In the Netherlands, when people see a screen, even in the supermarket, they really expect traditional TV content on the screen [Figure 7.6]. [While] in Switzerland or in France or even in Spain, the people they expect content which is Flash. So you see the culture change from one market to another is extreme."

Booking advertising and programming across countries and oceans can be challenging. Localization, continuity, and the right product are key to making this successful. With networks that span Europe and Canada, Vagilo-Giors

Figure 7.6 A Neo Advertising loop uses more video than Flash in certain parts of
Europe because of viewer acceptance.
©2009 Neo Advertising.

illustrates, "Our vision is that this media will become more and more global.
It's a trend now to have a global launch for a product for a movie, so we see
more and more brands and agencies that want to go for a central booking of
international campaigns. We do this already, especially from Canada to Europe,
where we have some cross sales across the network with Canadian clients
advertising on European screens."

Adspace Networks, one of the premier players in malls, looks at the programming from a completely integrated model. They have advertising and editorial
content that is custom created. Dominick Porco, CEO, tells us about one
approach to programming. "It's called Today's Top Ten. What we do is, we have
a staff of young people here in the office and we invite every retailer in the mall
every week to submit what they think is their very best deal. It is always free to
the retailer. We never charge them. What our folks here do is evaluate all of these
offers and typically will get 50 or 60 per mall and they'll all evaluate and say these
are the 10 best. This pair of shoes at this price is a great deal. At the end of the day
we're selling…what we think are the 10 best deals in the mall, and that's why the
viewers reference our screens" (Figure 7.7).

Bill Ketcham, vice president of Adspace, believes that the editorial content they create is why their screens are watched along with the advertising. "We also have two other pieces of content. We have a program called Essentials, and it's essentially cool stuff for cool shoppers to look out for new and interesting products that are being introduced. The other things they're most interested in, believe it or not, are just mall events. They want to know what's going on in the mall. Is there a puppet show for the kids this afternoon? Is there a band playing? And then in between all of those little nuggets is information we sell advertising preferably at 15-second intervals. Our number one category is Hollywood studios. Most every major studio uses us regularly for releases. Consumer package goods have also become a pretty steady category."

Ripple TV has more than 650 locations in mostly coffee-type locations reaching 9 million viewers monthly where the dwell time is as much as

Figure 7.7   (Continued)

Figure 7.7   Adspace has editorial content called Today's Top Ten that provides relevance to the viewer. (One can see the animated color version at 5thScreen.info). ©2009 Adspace Networks.

30 minutes (Figure 7.8). I spoke with John McMenamin, CEO, about how their programming is organized for this POW dwell time network. "We program national, regional and community content on-screen at any one time. We have a skin based on the venue the screens are in, so if we are in the Coffee Bean outlets, then it has the Coffee Bean genre and look. They also have some time to run some of their specials. On the left side of the screen we have national sports scores and sport schedules and on the right side of the screen we have stock information. Along the top we have CBS headlines and along the bottom we have the E! Entertainment headlines. In the center of the screen, we have video, which can be a mix of content and advertising plays and they are local events, concerts, movie times and weather."

Although it may seem like there is a lot happening on the screen that runs in the face of what some networks say consumers will ignore, Ripple TV is finding

Figure 7.8 Ripple TV fills the screen with ads and content. Viewers can choose to watch a number of different pieces of content that are on-screen at all times, depending on their interests.
©2009 Ripple TV.

that not to be true for their type of network. "There's always something on the screen for everyone. We kind of have a look that is a mix of TV and web." McMenamin continues, "Consumers are used to more than one message—it gives a greater sense of immediacy and I think advertisers know that other content that is on the screens is driving the viewer to watch and become more engaged around their interests."

The thinking about programming and what works for the specific networks also directly affects how the advertisers buy a network spot. From an agency point of view, one needs to address the question, What are the standard lengths to buy? And how do I create media that works across all the types of networks? One can address the programming of these networks by the type of network, and this, in turn, will drive the length of the advertisement. The question that the industry needs to ask is, Is it about the 10-, 15-, or 30-second spot, or is it about the message? Just as the Internet has standard banner-size ads that really have no duration at all, perhaps a flexible-length message is the answer. One can imagine how this might work, for example, by using Flash-based programming enhanced with video segments to help make the duration more flexible. All messages have attraction and brand, and some include a call to action. If these segments can be split into distinct assets, then perhaps they can be assembled in a cohesive manner that will work depending on the length that is required for the message. The industry will standardize advertising on digital signage networks to move the industry forward. This will directly affect programming and will apply to advertising-based networks.

7.3 Managing and Delivering the Content

At this point, a network operator has assembled the content needed for the network and determined how its programming should flow, the length of loops, the various zones, and almost everything else to get to the point of flipping the switch. But how do you actually go from a stack of content and a series of screens to a functioning network?

The mechanics of programming a network take into account all of the previous chapters plus good software. One key feature that must be addressed is ease of use. To do complex programming, operators need to have software that handles as many of the repetitive and complex tasks as possible that need to be done for digital signage. Some software was built from the ground up to serve this medium, and other software is television scheduling software. It is important to find software that serves your needs and size of network. Choosing software is an important consideration that has an impact on the total cost of operating the network along with the ease of setup and management.

The technology has a number of purposes. First, it functions as a central server on which the different content segments reside. It allows the use of a variety of different content types, including text, still graphics, photos, video, and streaming feeds. To do this job well, the system needs to provide the operator with an efficient and effective way to organize, label, and identify the content so that it can be readily located and integrated into the appropriate loop or feed to a given screen.

This technology will also provide tools with which operators can create the content loops themselves. Usually this is done by specifying a playlist of various content elements and instructing the system when to start each piece, how long to display it (if it is not a fixed-length content block), and what time of day to begin the loop. Clearly there must be a way to specify multiple playlists and loops for different times of day and different screens within each network. There also must be controls that allow operators to actually create the on-screen zones and direct the correct content to them.

When programming interactive screens, the operator follows a completely different method for adjusting what content is playing on the screen. In most cases there is a short loop that is playing as an attraction loop. This is usually changed based on average visits per month. The interactive portion of the experience is usually not changed that often, depending on what type of network is in place. One may change a segment of the interactive screen that may be a layer deep into the experience. This segment will be changed based on the unique benefits that interactive screens offer and the engagement and feedback from the user.

7.4 Top Features to Consider

If one has a relatively small network that runs mostly the same content on all screens, then a simpler or light version of a software package can be used. Should one have a large network that needs to have granular control with ease of use, then the network operator needs to look more toward enterprise-level software in which complicated tasks can be easily performed. The overall industry trend supports a software-as-a-service (SAAS) model. This particular model for software is different than putting software on a computer and then controlling a network. The SAAS model is a web-based application running on centralized servers that are usually paid for on an annual basis.

Salesforce.com is a very good example of an SAAS platform. Using this type of platform allows an operator to be future proofed. In other words, every feature that Salesforce.com adds is automatically updated and becomes part of your software. There are a number of software companies that provide digital signage software. I suggest that network operators do their research and find out what works best for their own situation.

7.5 The Future of Programming Software

Because of the very nature of the medium, one can program the network at very granular levels and provide even more local and hyperlocal content. Programming a network of this kind can be very labor intensive. This can cause the operating costs of a network to go up. The more relevant and local the content becomes, the more difficult the network is to program. Imagine, if you will, programming 2000 screens with individual content at each screen. Although some content may be the same on a national level, it is the regional and local levels that are very time consuming to program. There are a few companies that are addressing these large-scale network problems. The very idea that one can upload a piece of content and it automatically ends up at the right screen at the right time matched to the right audience is all about adding artificial intelligence (AI) to the programming of large-scale networks. It truly is the Holy Grail of integrated programming.

The use of templates will also continue to play an important part in the automation of messaging to specific geographic areas and geodemographic audiences. At Adspace, their creative team builds templates. A database basically populates the templates, and Adspace runs as many as 1050 different editorial pieces and ads per week. The software enables the company to scale their messaging in that way.

Ripple TV handles their content in more automated ways to drive community local interest. They provide events, movie information, and headlines from the local paper. McMenamin explains, "We've done a lot of focus groups and quite honestly the community content resonates very well because the viewer feels like it's their local network. So for example our weather shows a national map then regional map for cities around LA and then we show the very local weather for Manhattan Beach. Essentially web feeds enable us to distribute in a geographically targeted manner, like pulling the headlines off an RSS feed or using content partners like SIG for local traffic. This provides our viewers, especially in LA, with heads up on which highway to take to work, or in the case for entertainment which movie is playing or which band is in town and it is close to their location at the time they are watching."

7.6 Summary

After digital signage content is built, programming is the magic that brings a network together. This programming, from creating continuity on the network to making decisions about the length of ads and how many zones to apply, will make or break the network. With great content, one has the building blocks to create a powerful network. It is the network programming that becomes the vehicle for the timing and viewers' experience of the messages.

8 Measuring the Effectiveness of Content

Creating and operating a digital signage network represents a significant investment of dollars, time, and resources by the operator. So after it's up and running, the next question one faces is, How well is the network doing? Is it actually delivering the return it was designed to give?

This is not an academic question, of course. As we've seen, many digital signage networks depend on advertising revenue from external sources to provide operating capital and profits. Those advertisers, naturally, want some tangible evidence that their message is being presented effectively. Even if the resources for a network are strictly internal to an organization, that organization will want to be able to evaluate the results driven by the network. Is it engaging viewers? Is it creating favorable impressions of the products or services being marketed? Is it increasing customer satisfaction or loyalty? Is anybody actually paying attention?

These are really the first questions, given that the difference between good content and poor content is what people notice on the network in varying degrees. So far we've discussed ways to create content to make that all-important difference. Without a doubt, even in a field as new as this, we can see some excellent examples and some really poor examples of use of content. It's also obvious to even a casual observer that people will glance at almost any content—but if it doesn't seem relevant to them, they will ignore it. We've discussed the relationship of a viewer's mind-set to the type of network encountered, and we've looked at the idea of timing in terms of when the consumer encounters a piece of running content. For example, if a consumer encounters a digital display that's in the middle of a long message, and the consumer is not interested, he or she will tune it out completely. One has to create content that is relevant to the consumer and attracts his or her glance.

Even in longer, more complex messages, one has to have several points at which a viewer can pick up the message and become engaged. From studies that companies like Peoplecount have done, we know that teenagers are more likely to actually stand around and watch a whole loop of content, but not many other people demonstrate that behavior.

The issue now becomes one of providing empirical evidence we can use to evaluate the return on investment to create and maintain the digital network. That requires the use of standards and techniques to gather and interpret data that are relevant to those standards.

It also takes money. Any industry that requires some sort of formal measurement system needs to develop a sufficient revenue stream to support the cost of that process. That takes time; TV was around for about 15 years before modern measurement systems came into place (and even today, the accuracy and relevance of those systems and standards are being questioned). When one considers that the digital out-of-home network as a mass medium is really less than 5 years old, it's clear that we're in the infancy of effective metrics.

Nonetheless, there are significant efforts in this area, given the importance of measuring network effectiveness. In this chapter, we will consider measurement and the Out-of-Home Video Advertising Bureau (OVAB) standards that have been developed to date. But we also shall explore the seven areas for optimizing digital signage networks, areas that can both augment the existing standards for measurement and help operators develop more successful networks.

8.1   Foundation of Measurement

At its most basic, measurement consists of two components: proof of content delivery and proof of audience delivery. The former requires proving to the advertiser that the agreed-upon content was actually shown on the network; the latter requires proof that the agreed-upon audience was in a position to see the content.

The proof of content delivery is simply based on proof-of-play logs that are a standard part of most evolved software applications. This can be defined by what screens, locations, sites, geographic markets, and times of day the ad or message played. Those logs serve as primary proof documents to advertisers, although complete compliance can require independent audits of the software to prove to the advertiser's satisfaction that the logs represent what actually happened.

The proof of audience delivery is normally defined by demographic profiles of the audience that potentially saw the content piece. Delivering the message that matches the advertiser's demographic target is what makes digital signage such a powerful tool. Although proving that the content was shown is relatively easy, proving it was watched by the right viewers is far more difficult. OVAB has been a huge proponent of this aspect of measurement, and in late 2008 it presented the first comprehensive guidelines for audience unit measurement. It has since become the adopted standard for measuring digital signage networks for media buyers.

The Arbitron Out-of-Home Digital Video Display Study 2009 revealed that every month {2/3} of residences in the United States aged 18 years or older have seen digital signage. Of those people, some 76 percent noticed signage at multiple venues. It is this type of measurement that makes digital signage a growing media concern. Diane Williams, the Arbitron senior media research analyst who led the study, adds to the validity from her agency interaction.

"Agencies are always asking what the universe is for the DOOH [digital out-of-home] audience. We have that for TV, we have that [for] radio. It's obvious that we're used to this measurement in other types of media," she says. "But in the place-based space there was no universe number. So that's really the point of that study that we released in 2009."

One of the biggest questions agencies ask about measurement is, What are the recall rates? They vary widely from network to network, even sometimes from brand to brand, depending on the relevance of the brand to the audience. Testing for what is known as aided and unaided recall is a means to the answer. Williams explains, "Unaided recall is top of mind. Can you tell me anything you remember seeing on the screen today? And aided recall would be, 'Do you remember seeing a car ad?' And someone may say, 'Yes it was a BMW ad.' Or you just come straight out and ask, 'Do you specifically recall seeing an ad for BMW on the screen today?'"

The range of unaided and aided recall varies from network to network. One can ensure a higher recall rate by providing more relevant content. Williams gives some insight based on real cases over the 7-plus years that Arbitron has measured digital signage. "The rule of thumb that I typically use is unaided ad recall is typically 5 to 8 percent, and aided recall is usually anywhere between 20 to 40 percent. If something tests below 20 percent, I would check to see if there's a problem with the copy." Another important factor to consider for low recall rates is the relevance of the brand to this audience. "If I see that the audience is mostly teenagers and young adults but the commercial is for dish soap, then it tested poorly because these people just were not tuned in to the category of product. That's an extreme example of a bad match of advertiser to audience."

8.2 Network Accountability

When studying the three types of networks—POS, POW, and POT—it immediately becomes apparent that there are different requirements for content and how each network is programmed. What is not readily apparent is there are also differences in what is measured and how the network is measured.

8.2.1 Point of Sale

Usually in a POS network, it's all about the message that causes uplift in sales. The retailer is not usually interested in foot traffic because there are other things like transactions that are really the more important measure. When evaluating point of sale one must also look at the selling cycle of the item being sold. If it's something like toothpaste, people only buy toothpaste once every 6 to 8 weeks, so content that isn't presented across a complete sales cycle, as good as it might be, is unlikely to measure up. "So you can run the greatest toothpaste ad you want. If you're only ... looking at sell through for 3 weeks you might not see the bump that you're looking for because there's only going to be a certain amount of the audience that's going to be in the market to buy toothpaste during that period of time," Williams says. "If you extend it out further, then you can start seeing the benefits."

Similar timing applies to when the message is encountered. A shopper may view the message in the middle or catch it at the end. When the shopper does encounter the message, it is important for the message to be broken into bite-size pieces so the shopper has a chance to become engaged at any point during the message.

Kelly McGillivray, president of Peoplecount, employs a number of different processes and methods to measure the effectiveness of a digital signage network depending upon the type of network. In a POS network, for example, McGillivray looks not only at sales lift in relationship to a product but also the relevance of the product, the store, and the brand. "We'll ask people not just if they remember the message, but would they take any action, are they going to buy the product or did they try that item on or did they try it out or would they buy it or would they recommend it to friends? So it's a lot more around the specifics of their intention to purchase," he says. "It's more specific to what actions they're going to take, or have already taken if they've already bought the item. Ninety percent of the research that we do is about brand awareness, ad recall, aided and unaided recall. And people's perception of the digital signage and did that change the perception of the store."

Most of the POS network operators I spoke with use measurement to accomplish their goals of creating revenue. Dominick Porco, CEO of Adspace Networks (located in malls), is a proponent of studies and measurement. "We did qualitative research, we went and created 13 different concepts and tested them among 3000 people. We had everything in there that you could ever imagine putting on screens in a mall and most things people have tried. The Top Ten concept was one of them. And the Top Ten scored higher by a huge margin. Literally 80-plus-percent of the people who are interested in this particular concept definitely would watch it."

Ron Greenberg, vice president of marketing for TouchTunes, weighs in on measurement. "We do studies where we survey people and use Arbitron. We ask them what their experience is like. One question from our last study was, Do you agree with the statement that having a TouchTunes jukebox makes your time at the location more fun? And that's where we had 90 percent of the people said yes. We measure our performance through studies like that for both attitudes and usage."

8.2.2 Point of Transit

POT networks are usually all about the eyeballs. Reach and frequency measurements fit these types of networks very well. This is where agencies, and specifically media buyers, that try to reach a mass audience with a broad demographic work. Measurement in most of these types of networks is based on the number of people that pass and notice the digital poster or digital billboard. In some cases, looking particularly at mass transit subnetworks, these measurements can be assessed by the volume of travelers who pass the screens. Measurements include notice of the screen, intercept interviews, and even technology that counts the number of people who look at the ad.

This measurement also varies depending on the nature of the screen location—indoors or out—and weather issues. Notes McGillivray, "We have worked on the traffic audit bureaus eyes on measurement system and we developed a pedestrian model. And to count pedestrians on the street in order to get the data for the model, we did extensive work with a company who had an outdoor face recognition software and we used cameras to do some counting [to enhance] the data along with our people walking around and counting. We've used simple manual counting. Then if it's vehicle traffic, of course, there's traffic counting equipment out there that's specific to vehicles."

There are better-controlled environments indoors, and the counting techniques change. McGillivray tells us how: "Indoors we also use overhead counting equipment that uses infrared technology. They scan people by their body heat. And they're good for large open areas, like maybe the big, wide quarters of a mall. If you have people going through a doorway or up an escalator or something, you can do something simpler like an infrared beam, which breaks the beam when you're crossing. So it's just really looking at the different types of traffic and conditions and space that you're dealing with, and then you kind of choose the technology that works best."

8.2.3 Point of Wait

Point of wait networks have a different twist on what is measured and how. For example, in bank lines or in a hospital the objectives of the network are different, as is the measurement needed to meet the objectives. People arrive at a certain rate and take a certain length of time to go through the line, and there are different line-up configurations. There can be a single line delivering customers to many customer service representatives—a bank with one line feeding five tellers—or five separate lines in a grocery checkout. McGillivray gives us some insight on POW networks: "It's kind of like a flow in, flow out. So, understanding how long it takes them to get through the process in the transaction and then out the other side. That's just one way you can estimate the dwell time."

Digital signage is unique in many ways, and measurement is no exception. This is where each piece of content and its design plays a vital role in success because most consumers view the screen as entertainment and information rather than advertising. Even the companies that study digital signage and conduct the surveys agree.

Says McGillivray, "We've really discovered that you can't measure it without the consideration of the message because it plays an extremely important part in the whole process of people's awareness of the screens. For instance I've noticed that if you ask people if they saw any advertisement in the store, people often say no or they'll say yes and they'll point to maybe posters and other traditional things. They're much less likely to identify the screen as advertisement. They think of it more as entertainment." But if customers are asked if they noticed the screen, they typically reply positively. "So we find there's a very high notice of the screen throughout, and a lot of people don't identify it as being advertising."

At The University Network (TUN), CEO Peter Corrigan knows that their success is linked directly to the studies they have done, and they've used studies to track sales on special offers. "We've had about five or six different research studies done over the years. We have measured everything from wait times to ad recollection to even more like Internet type of measurement, where sales were generated as a result of the ads playing, the click through type of approach to measurement. The most recent was actually done with 1-800-Flowers and one of their key measurements was to count the new customers acquired as a result of our commercial. We ran it on…our national network with a special code that was unique to The University Network."

Of the people who responded to a Mother's Day campaign, it turned out that half of them who used the code were new customers, showing directly and in a quantifiable way how effective the digital signage had been. "All the studies we have done came back with a number better than what most digital out-of-home networks are experiencing. We're a branding-type network. We're not inside a store. We're not for the most part right in front of a point of sale. So it's going to be different from the way you'd measure something like a screen up in a Subway sandwich shop."

8.3   Audience Unit Measurement

Today the digital out-of-home industry is working to create a single set of metrics on which everyone can agree. This is a critical standard that has been driving all media buyers for decades and that digital signage has adopted. The way in which the audience is measured is not that complex, but it is not just traffic numbers. Suzanne Alecia, executive director of OVAB, and OVAB's members have worked together to formulate a model to deliver a uniform audience measurement. Networks are beginning to understand the importance of a standard that fits the agency media buying models. "I can say the good news is a lot of the networks are changing. Not too long ago, most networks were selling mostly on gross venue traffic. So in whatever venue they were in, how many people were crossing into that venue was the number. As we all know there are challenges inherent in just counting traffic and it is for the most part discounted very heavily because media buyers don't believe the numbers, and so they're not going to pay a premium or a CPM requisite to that sort of an audience measure. And gross venue traffic, or traffic isn't comparable to other media platforms."

It was this single traffic measurement that was inhibiting the growth of the industry and individual networks in their quest to command a larger share of overall ad and marketing budgets. Digital signage was always being relegated to the role of a discounted, very tactical media. So, through the formation of OVAB it became clear that this traffic measurement was a big impediment.

Alecia describes the process of how they arrived at the audience unit form of measurement. "Through a very collaborative process we created our Audience Metrics Guidelines, which is a rule book which the place-based digital and video advertising network should be using in concert with a third-party research provider in order to capture data that would allow them to report audience numbers that are basically consistent and comparable to other media." She continues, "It outlines the different dimensions and the guidelines and goes into the background of why this is the first important step."

The difference between venue traffic and what the guidelines recommend, which is audience impression, is that raw traffic is not a measure of audience. The general definition of audience is people looking at a certain media type or a certain media property. Because of the dynamic nature of venue-based networks, there are a couple of key dimensions that have to be measured to get to that sort of audience level. Alecia explains, "Certainly you have to use venue traffic as part of that math because you do have to count or substantiate how many people are going in and out of that venue. But it's only one building block. Then out of that number of people going through the venue, you then have to calculate or measure how many people are close to the screens, where the screens are placed. And of course depending on the venue and where the screens are actually hung, those dimensions are going to be different network to network and venue to venue but it is measurable" (Figure 8.1).

	SCHEDULED PERIOD (THE NETWORK'S UNIT OF SALE)		
	Network A	Network B	Network C
VENUE TRAFFIC	2000	2000	2000
% PRESENT IN THE VEHICLE ZONE	50%	50%	50%
VEHICLE TRAFFIC	1000	1000	1000
% OF NOTICE	80%	80%	80%
VEHICLE AUDIENCE	800	800	800
VEHICLE ZONE DWELL TIME	60 seconds	240 seconds	120 seconds
AD ROTATION DURATION	120 seconds	120 seconds	120 seconds
AVERAGE UNIT GROSS IMPRESSIONS FOR THE SCHEDULED PERIOD	400	1600	800

Figure 8.1 An OVAB chart equalizes one type of network versus another type of network based on loop time and dwell time, and it creates a uniform audience unit measurement. ©2009 OVAB.

In combination with the traffic, the second area of measurement is how many people actually watch or notice the screen. If one thinks of it as a step-by-step process, one has to go from the total traffic in the venue to how many of those people are close enough to the screen that they might have the opportunity to see it. Then one has to observe two things: the dwell time, meaning how long those people are in the area close to the screen; and if they notice the screen. Alecia expands on why: "One of the key differentiators with these kinds of networks is that they are networks. It is unlike static media where the message itself isn't a function of time; it's just one poster, one showing, and one piece of creative. It doesn't matter if someone looks at it for more than 30 seconds, or a minute or 2 minutes because the message is the same. But with these networks, because there's content and advertising being delivered either on a continuous basis or in a loop, it's very important to know how long those people are in that viewing zone because you have to measure their opportunity to view multiple pieces of content and/or advertising."

Measurement, then, requires that one considers all three elements: presence near the screen (what's called presence in the vehicle zone, the vehicle being the screen); dwell time (the average time that people are in that zone); and either an aggregate for how long they watched the screen or a notice rate (the percentage of those people who actually noticed the screen). One then combines all those dimensions and arrives at the audience impressions to that screen or network. Alecia helps us understand further: "And so now instead of just saying 2 million people went through my mall, the guidelines allow you to report that over the course of a month you delivered 17 million impressions to your advertising schedule. Now that's a big difference in the confidence level on what an advertiser or an agency wants to get out of a network and it allows them to compare that to what they're spending in other media. Television shows can tell them an audience, the Internet can tell them an audience based on impressions, print can tell them an audience based on impressions. And so this gives this industry the opportunity to tell the audience based on impressions."

The OVAB guidelines state the following:[1]

Average Unit Audience is defined as "the number and type of people exposed to the media vehicle with an opportunity to see a unit of time equal to the typical advertising unit." Unit in this context always means the duration of the network's typical Ad Unit.

Presence with Notice is not enough to produce a dynamic metric such as the average minute or average quarter-hour employed by traditional television. Dwell Time in the Vehicle (display) Zone must also be measured to provide a measure of Presence, with Notice, during time interval equal to the length of the typical ad unit. Vehicle Zone Dwell Time is defined as the number of seconds the viewer is in the Vehicle Zone with Notice.

The Vehicle Zone Dwell time is divided by the ad unit length to obtain the number of ad units exposed, which is then divided by the number of ad units

---

[1]2008 OVAB Audience Metrics Research Disclosure.

in the ad rotation duration to obtain the average ad unit exposure. Or more simply, the Vehicle Zone Dwell Time is divided by the Ad Rotation Duration. Averaged across the sample, this provides the average ad unit exposure for the total population, or the population segment of interest. Where the rotation length, number of ads, or individual ad frequency in the commercial rotation varies, these calculations can be done on average, or to reflect each specific variation in these factors. The Dwell Time of multiple exposure occasions within the unit of measurement, e.g. a day, or daypart, for the same person can be summed to produce an average. The dynamics underlying that average could be expressed as a frequency distribution of exposures and a net reach.

Measurement under the OVAB guidelines pertains to large and medium networks, providing agencies with comparable audience metrics that are used in other mediums. Ripple TV CEO John McMenamin adds, "You know we're measured by Nielsen under the OVAB guidelines. We have the audience numbers and our network lures about 9 million viewers a month."

Francois Beaubien, CEO and founder of Zoom Media, is also on the road educating advertisers. "I'm evangelizing on behalf of all of us, because the more of us who embrace the opportunity of having measurement, the better off we will all be. So the game plan is to be measured and have standardized measurement across the field, which is the OVAB guideline. Whether it's somebody using Nielsen or Arbitron, the important thing is that the agency and the clients trust the results. Right now it's a little bit of the Wild West in the digital world. And this is all about laying the train tracks. It's a sizable capital expenditure but it has been proven time and time again to be extremely valuable and necessary. I used to ask agency clients, what was their number one issue they're dealing with? Before, it used to be proof of performance. Did my ad go up? That's pretty much been answered. Now it's who is seeing it? Or, how many people are seeing it? I know you're reporting 300 million people are seeing your network in the United States. What is that breakdown? How does that happen? Okay, well, these are the numbers you're giving me? The agency is asking, what's the validity behind that measurement? The Nielsen study and an OVAB guideline reduce the pressure zone from the client and the agency to be able to buy our medium. The most valuable thing we're doing now is being measured. And the more networks that get measured, and the more that follow the guidelines, and the more that employ really reputable measurement firms, the better off it is for the industry. Then agencies and clients can buy across networks and feel confident with the numbers that they're getting. When you get measured, you do it right, the client and agency will embrace the validity of the measurement and the technology you use."

8.4 Seven Keys to a Successful Network

The acceptance of all these educational efforts in the industry has been absolutely remarkable. First, the industry embraced the return on investment

(ROI) factor and considered methods to measure that return, including sales uplift and actual measurement of eyeballs that are watching. As an industry there are currently several methods to accomplish this: software that ties into the sale reports, facial recognition software, and real live intercept studies.

Next the industry embraced return on objectives (ROO). This methodology is another layer that is additive to the mix. This is really understanding the objective of the network and then measuring to ensure that one has reached those objectives. ROO is a little more difficult to measure and is sometimes intangible but real, so finding ways to accomplish this measurement can be difficult.

In previous chapters we talked about applying some of the keys to successful networks to your network content. Boiling them down to seven keys will help you keep your content on track and in focus. More layers of measurement that optimize the content, the display, and the network also need to be considered. Based on my work at the Digital Signage Association and the committee I chair, Best Practices Committee on Content, my colleague Mike Foster came up with the seven keys to successful networks:

- Content
- Relevancy
- Interaction
- Scheduling
- Placement
- Refresh
- Attraction

"By taking a holistic approach one can consider a number of elements that when applied to the network, one's network will improve," says Foster. One measures and gives weighted points according to one of the three network types; therefore, the final points are scored in accordance with the purpose of the network. This is done for each of the seven keys. The following sections describe the ways in which Foster sees the optimization of these keys.

8.4.1 Content

Measuring a number of different elements of the content will help optimize the network and every message on the network. The obvious question is, How do you make this happen? The only effective method is to understand your audience and its needs. By making the content valuable to them, you will achieve the goal. There are 14 different areas that one looks at regarding content (Figure 8.2). Each network type will have a slightly different bias on the weight of each area.

8.4.2 Relevancy

Tim Manners says, "The business of marketing is promoting within the context of what is relevant to the way we live our lives today. Relevance in marketing is

				VECTOR POINT ANALYSIS				
Item#	Element	Number	Scored Value	Weight Value	Max Weight	Scored Weight	Adj. Value
1	Audience Focused	1	10	1	10	10	0.33
2	Includes "Hook"	2	10	3	30	30	1.00
3	Depth	3	10	1	10	10	0.33
4	Authenticity	4	5	1	10	5	0.17
5	Brand Awarness	5	5	3	30	15	0.50
6	Educational Content	6	10	2	20	20	0.67
7	Motion Based	7	10	2	20	20	0.67
8	Presentation Aesthetics	8	5	2	20	10	0.33
9	Optimal Duration	9	10	2	20	20	0.67
10	High-Definition	10	5	1	10	5	0.17
11	"to Do"? Call to Action	11	5	4	40	20	0.67
12	Experiental	12	5	2	20	10	0.33
13	Pre-Purposed	13	10	2	20	20	0.67
14	Message Speed	14	10	4	40	40	1.33
	Totals	14	110	30	300	235	7.83
Total Score - CONTENT							7.83

Figure 8.2 The areas to examine for content.
©2009 Image courtesy of MediaTile.

not about manipulating us as much as it is about serving us."[2] In a world of noise and chaos, the audience needs relevancy to connect with their daily lives. Of the elements that go into producing striking digital signage, one of the most important is making it relevant to your audience. The mind-set of the viewer, the venue the viewer is in, and the activity the viewer is engaged in are all elements that make content more relevant. This affects content, yet it is its own key because relevance is so critical in one's mix. Ultimately, one must connect to the very fabric of the viewers' lives.

8.4.3 Interaction

Interaction creates virtual brand channels for advertisers to run activity across online, mobile, and outdoor properties, basically enabling brands to target a wider audience. Now targeted, cross-media advertising campaigns can get directly to an audience at the point of context for the first time. It gives one the ability to do more interactive ad campaigns.

8.4.4 Scheduling

Scheduling of content is a subtle and often missed factor in messaging. Radio and television pioneered the impact of time of day on programming and messaging. They also created the standards for compliance or how the message runs as scheduled. As we discussed in previous chapters, scheduling or programming becomes a driving factor for the message's effectiveness. The time

[2]*Relevance*, Tim Manners, ©2008.

of day is a major factor for the impact of your message. Different day parts represent different viewers, needs, and interests. Dwell time is of particular importance because this will directly relate to the length of the playlist loop. In the design and maintenance of your network, it is important to always be on top of what is happening and when.

8.4.5 Placement

In real estate, the old saw is that value is based on three things: location, location, location. The same is true for digital signage. The location of the screen is relevant to the product being sold, the target audience, and the environment itself. If the screen is located in the wrong place, it will severely impact the screen's effectiveness. If the screen is located in low-traffic areas, obscured by other things, amidst a confusing jumble of visuals, or if it is just too high, it can lose major impressions. All of this affects the opportunity to see (OTS), described as "The probability of being exposed to a medium's content."[3] This is a specific measurement that is called out by OVAB and the standards it created.

Diane Williams, senior media research analyst for Arbitron, considers placement to be a key part of measurement and notice. "I've looked at screens in environments where I'm seeing less than 20 percent of the people that are visiting the store that won't pass the sign or actually notice it. Because the sign blends into the wall, it's just not eye catching. It's too high or too low to people's eye levels."

8.4.6 Refresh

Another important aspect in the message is freshness. Unlike newspaper ads, billboards, and even TV spots, digital signage must be refreshed and updated regularly. The reason? The number of visits per site is very different than the time-honored reach and frequency equation used in media planning. For digital signage, frequency of exposure within the time frame is the key. Studies show that the frequency of the message is not as important as the relevance to create action. Thus, freshness draws viewers to messages they may have already seen. Automated freshness can take the form of streaming news feeds or sports and weather updates to create relevancy and value (see Chapter 4 Figure 4.3 for refresh table).

8.4.7 Attraction

When creating content, it is equally important to consider the power of attraction. This element is less subjective than you may think. However, the primary gauge is a hybrid of expert knowledge and on-site observation. Focus areas

[3]2008 OVAB Audience Metrics Research Disclosure.

include average consumer wait time, average number of visits over time, and audience demographics. Customers who are attracted and entertained while waiting will perceive reduced wait time, an effect known as wait warping,[4] which is a context strategy that maximizes customers' attention during dwell times.

8.5 Summary

Content is the most important element of a network, but as we discussed in previous chapters, there are a lot of strategic decisions about content and the programming of the network that must be made along the way to ensure the content is right and that it is delivered to the right audience at the right time in the right place. In a world where every message counts, measurement is a critical ingredient to understand what does and what does not work. To that end, measuring the results will clarify a network's strategic direction and give one a proof point for a viable revenue source to support the network. It does not matter whether one is operating a corporate communications network or a subway station network; it will come down to justifying the resources, merchandising dollars, or ad dollars that support the efforts of the network itself. Network operators need proof of ad delivery, proof of message delivery, and proof of audience delivery.

Ultimately, great content with measurable results really makes digital signage a very powerful, valuable, and compelling medium that will be used for influencing, informing, and entertaining viewers for years to come.

[4]2008 OVAB Audience Metrics Research Disclosure.

9 Interacting with the Viewers

So far we've talked about digital signage in terms of the producer and the viewer. The former creates and presents the content; the latter absorbs it and, we hope, acts on the information. There is a way, however, to create a very different dynamic that will make your digital signage network much more engaging: shift the viewer from passive to participant. The moment one engages the viewer in this way, the entire experience changes dramatically.

Enabling the audience to manipulate and interact with the information on the screen—to alter it in some way or change its response—results in a far more personal experience. Rather than having every user view the same content, users can now choose the content that matters most to them or provide information and feedback that will affect how the content is presented to them. This is one of the most powerful aspects of the Internet and mobile screen experiences; users actively control the experience—within the limits set by the content provider—in ways that are in the moment for them. This creates a perception that the experience is unique, and it can result in a more powerful communication of brand values or motivation to purchase.

There are two primary aspects to bringing the viewer into the picture. The first is that the technology must somehow permit the interaction; there needs to be a mechanism by which the viewer can become a participant. Second, the content itself must be created from the outset with interaction in mind. In other words, the content must be built in a way that it can both recognize the user's interaction and then respond appropriately.

9.1 Engaging Through Touch

Although there are several commonly used technologies for allowing people to interact with various screens—keyboards, mice, and buttons are the most typical—they are not always applicable to digital signage. Having a keyboard or mouse in an unstaffed, public area could add costs, invite theft, and create one more thing that will need to be monitored and repaired on a regular basis.

One of the most appropriate interaction methods for most digital signage networks is touch technology. Most of us have seen this technology deployed both in public places (for example, ATMs) and private devices (for example, smart phones like the Apple iPhone or Palm Pre). The technology is proven, costs are constantly declining, and most importantly, users are generally familiar with and comfortable using it.

When digital signage becomes interactive, several things occur. The content is different, the reaction is different, and the data collected is different. First, let's consider how the content changes. Remember, digital signage is a new medium, and it is different from computers. It is encountered in different places and circumstances than computers and web sites, and its purpose is different. This means you must resist the impulse to take your web site and simply transfer it to the digital signage network to create an interactive experience. The result would be a larger, public version of a web site that does not at all provide an effective experience. (It is also unlikely that the digital signage network would have access to or allow full Internet access and browsing ability.) Therefore, micro sites would be developed specifically for digital signage implementation. Although you can adapt content from a web site for use in an interactive digital signage environment, the final content will have to be built specifically for this purpose.

First, understand that content for touch screens must be designed to both engage the viewer and lead exploration. That is, you are not simply throwing open the doors to users; you are attempting to direct them and elicit inputs and choices that will drive them toward the goal you've set for the network—finding and choosing merchandise, exploring a brand, or the like.

There are three key considerations that go into creating great interactions:

- Create the right attraction. First and foremost one needs to get viewers to participate because they may not expect to have the ability to interact with the content as they do with computers; let viewers know they have that ability. Creating an attraction loop, message, or some piece of up-front content that will motivate viewers to engage is the first step. This loop needs to be more in line with typical digital signage content following the advice in the previous chapters of this book. The one exception is the attraction loop is just that: designed to attract viewers to touch the screen.
- Present one thing at a time. When you have gotten the viewers' interest, keep them engaged and moving through a logical progression. Lead the participants in a guided manner through each step of the interaction you want to encourage. Provide focused layers of information that make it easy to comprehend what is being presented, and direct them to the layer of information that follows. A major difference between digital signage and a computer or smart phone is the amount of time that viewers will spend with each device. Because time is more limited with digital signage, you need to provide a clear, logical path for the viewers to follow. Offering too much information that is not directed will not motivate users to continue with the interaction because they will perceive it to be too time consuming and unlikely to provide them with enough value for the time invested.
- Offer choices. Interaction must be more than simple next page buttons to engage viewers and direct them toward a goal, such as a purchase. The value of interactivity comes when users are presented with choices, allowed to personalize the presented information, and perceive they are seeing something special for them.

Dr. Christopher Grey, vice president of shopper psychology at advertising giant Saatchi & Saatchi X, weighs in on the shopper experience and interactive technology. "I think that ability for digital signage to be interactive is one of the things that is going to absolutely revolutionize the shopping experience," he says.

"First of all, it gives people a sense of control. It can help them overcome a lot of obstacles that currently make shopping challenging sometimes as far as finding items and evaluating things. And then it can also be something that just creates fun and enjoyment and makes that shopping experience all the more pleasant and enjoyable."

Obviously, interactivity will only work in some categories. It will work best in a category that has fairly significant customer involvement—electronics, fashion, or cars, for example. The typical shopper will probably not engage with an interactive kiosk if the goal is buying potato chips. There is some strategy behind this approach that one needs to understand. In addition to cost effectiveness, common sense will prevail over an interactive potato chip display.

Paul Flanigan, partner at The Preset Group, who for years produced content for the Best Buy network and currently blogs at www.experiate.net, understands that interactive content is appropriate for certain types of products and situations, especially consumer electronics. "Where touch screen interactivity is going to start to have a big role is when it comes to things like electronics, especially television. But even with things as small as iPods, rarely do people just walk in the store and look at one and buy it. They've probably already done a little bit of homework. They already know someone who has one or they read about it a little bit. They already have a knowledge base," he says. "What they're looking for when they get into a retail environment is someone or something to help win that last brand decision, when you pit a Sony, versus an LG, versus a Samsung. For a Blu-ray player, TV, home theater, what you're going to want to do right then and there as a customer. You're going to want to see the rubber hit the road. You're going to want to see why Sony says it's better. Why LG says its clearer. Why Samsung says it's more, it has one-button technology."

Not only that, as Flanigan says, the shopper will also to want to be able to try the products and compare them directly—to test drive the product "at [the shopper's own] pace, which means you may not want the employees around," he says. "You may just want to do it at your own pace because you already have a set level of knowledge, and interactive digital signage is going to be able to get you there quickly."

The content for this type of engagement is specifically created for interaction. Icons or buttons are usually large and easy to see. Remember, shoppers are using their fingers to touch the screen—not a mouse. Choices are clear and simplified.

9.1.1 An Example Touch Engagement

Let's consider an example where we place touch screen technology on a network in a consumer electronics store. This particular screen is in the cell phone section of the store and is designed to provide consumers with the information (and motivation) to purchase the right phone for their needs and to present information that may upsell them to a more profitable model or service plan.

The first piece of content is the attraction loop—in this case, an eye-catching promotion for the latest RFID-equipped cell phones along with an offer for an instant coupon and a clear invitation to touch the screen to find out more.

When a viewer touches the screen and becomes a participant, the promo loop will stop running and be replaced by the next level of information. In this case, it is a brief description of three different models of RFID phones that are on offer, as well as an explanation of the benefits of RFID technology. At this point, we are not showing the viewer complete details of each phone, or even an in-depth comparison, but rather a single level of information.

Next, we offer the viewer a choice. Which model would he or she like to read more about? That delivers the next level of information, details about the individual phone. When the shopper touches the second phone on the screen, the full array of that phone's features will be displayed, including highlights of RFID uses and capabilities.

At this point, the shopper is again presented with choices. Does he or she want to look at another phone or compare two of them? Although this choice enables the shopper to have some control and direct the experience, it also guides the shopper toward the ultimate choice of one of these models.

When the shopper is finished and touches "No" when asked if he or she wants to look at details of the third phone, we move the shopper to the next level of information, which is an action call. For example, For which phone would you like an instant savings coupon? If the shopper touches "Phone 1," the screen displays the special deal on that particular phone, time stamped to be good that day, and then asks the shopper to choose whether to print the coupon, send it to the cashier electronically, or send it via text message to his or her current phone.

This approach of leading shoppers and providing choices enables them to feel good about their selection and feel informed in making the decision. But notice that, at every stage of this interaction, the number and type of choices for the shopper were limited. Had we given the shopper infinite choices in-store (like a web site), the chances of guiding him or her to a purchase decision would have been limited. Using interactive screens to show comparable models that the retailer carries, however, can be helpful and useful to the shopper.

9.2 Gesture Technology

"Witwer watches as Anderton moves his fingers across the display, 'flying through' the pre-crime scene, moving forward and back in time. ARCHITEC-TURAL REFERENCE SCREENS run side-by-side with the Prevision Screen..."[1]

---

[1]*Minority Report* script by Scott Frank.

Those who are already familiar with the film *Minority Report*, whose characters performed forensic analysis using massive, gestural-driven displays, know the kind of digital signage possibilities that come with this technology.

There are obviously two types of digital signage. There's linear digital signage, simply running content, and there's interactive signage. Today most interactive systems require viewers to come right up to the screen and interact with it through touch or possibly a small keypad. Gestural technology is quite different, and the content needs are totally different than anything that has been created for digital signage.

As a family of digital signage, it is in a class of its own. Body movements control the program, so there's no need to wear, hold, or touch anything special. A gesture-based user interface can be delivered on any surface or device. This includes floors, walls, tables, kiosks, toys, consoles, set-top boxes, desktop computers, laptops, or even cell phones. It runs on a system that uses a 3-D camera and computer to pick up gestures and interpret them so the user can enjoy a complex and natural interaction with the display.

The content is created with interactivity in mind. One can see this in airports, malls, and Las Vegas. If the image is projected onto the floor, a participant can step on or kick an image across the screen or wipe away coffee beans to reveal a logo. This type of technology is unique and fun for the participant (Figure 9.1).

I spoke with one of the foremost leaders in this area, Vincent John Vincent, cofounder of GestureTek, a company that specializes in gesture digital signage and interactivity. "What we're doing is really taking things that are catching

Figure 9.1 People interact with a gesture-based table technology in Eureka Tower, the tallest building in Australia.
©2009 GestureTek.

people's eyeballs and then letting their movement, either close to the display or from a distance, engage them in a different manner, in that they're moving things either on the floor or on a wall."

GestureTek can make the content entertaining or product focused, but the types of content that most companies are creating for interactivity is not multimedia and layer focused. Vincent explains, "You're not having to drill down through content to get the information you're looking for. In our world, you're really just affecting something as you go by and you're revealing more information as you touch it. But it's not that you're drilling down to get that information. You're just walking by."

This is what I refer to as organic entertainment. The participant is not touching on-screen buttons or icons but is directly affecting the movement of images on the screen by how they move their body—fingers, limbs, head, even eyes.

One common difference when using this technology is screen size. In a touch environment, it's largely a one-on-one experience; the interaction is personal and, because it's providing select information on a user-selected path, screens tend to be smaller. But with gesture technology, the interaction can be group as well as individual, so "we're delivering to any size screen," Vincent says. "It could be small, but it can be very large and you're having an effect and people are watching it. And so the content that we create tends to be content that it's entertaining to watch. To watch people [interact] and to do it yourself and then reveal things, find things that are hidden will also captures people's attention. They'll stay there. They'll play with it [Figure 9.2]. It's not something that is as much as very specific information as it is about just entertaining people with the information about the brand."

Figure 9.2   People interact with a gesture-based technology window in scenes from the movie *Coraline*.
©2009 Inwindow Outdoor. Image courtesy of GestureTek.

It's also very playful. That's part of the attraction. People enjoy continuing to interact with it because they are being entertained; therefore, most of the ads for this type of interaction need to be created with an entertainment component. One needs to create content that is enjoyable to see so the participant can find out what's below the next layer or how objects on-screen interact and how one is interacting with them. Because it's usually displayed on a large screen, this content acts as a billboard for other people to watch, and it delivers the branding message to others who are watching the participant's interaction. Vincent believes that it's a hybrid model in the world of digital signage. "It's really a billboard that lots of people would be able to see with the exception that we can suddenly change it up and attract their attention and add some kind of interaction and then make it for the group and make it something that's engaging is in a sense very gamelike."

9.3   Interacting with Mobile Devices

In the example earlier in this chapter, we followed a shopper who checked out different options for a new cell phone. One of the shopper's choices at the pre-purchase stage was to have an offer or coupon delivered to his or her mobile device to be used at checkout that day. Increasingly, this linkage between digital signage and the viewer's personal device will be an important consideration in content for digital signage that effectively drives purchasing.

Bluetooth and text message integration passed their experimental and pilot phases in 2008. The connection and symbiotic relationship between digital signage and personal mobile devices will continue to grow with more deployments. Consumers are ready to utilize this technology today.

Personalizing features by offering coupons and other media on handsets will further drive sales at the shelf. Tracking these interactions to measure the success of a network will also play a part in the overall success of the campaign. Digital signage will take a front seat in this area, adding value to the entire digital communications grid. Digital signage is the activator for the interaction, and when the engagement is in pursuit it is passed off to a mobile phone and the engagement continues with the consumer. So far, results appear to show that this combination is far more effective than the connection between, for example, activation via computer and final engagement with a mobile device.

"Download rates tend to be below 1 percent online, but we're seeing 3 percent [on mobile phones]," says Doug Scott, vice president of marketing for Danoo. For those users that set their mobile phones to discoverable mode, making it easier for them to receive messages via Bluetooth signals from the digital signage installation, download rates soared to 30 percent. Clearly, the consumers' ability to download additional information in easy-to-capture methods is going to drive this increase.

At some point, the interaction goes beyond just downloading information; it becomes shop anywhere, anytime. If a viewer is in front of a digital sign and then engages through his or her mobile phone and likes the product, then the next logical step is to purchase that product. This takes advantage of an essential paradigm shift in the habits of consumers that began with online shopping: see it now, buy it now.

Social media will also play a part in the engagement. Again, driving a certain promotion from the digital signage will bring attention to the product or offer itself. Digital signage as an effective promotional tool is undisputed. Having useful, helpful, relevant content is critical to get the engagement in the first place. Twitter is increasingly popular and pervasive, and digital signage vendors are moving quickly to integrate this and other social mediums. At the New York International Auto Show, Volvo used Twitter and brought the results to digital signage and YouTube. Driven for curious, core customers, Volvo became the first automaker to take over YouTube's homepage with a banner ad for a first-ever live Twitter feed on YouTube. This is a trend that is also inclusive of mobile, but with a new Twitter-twist.

As discussed in Chapter 4 User Generated Content (UGC) will also play an important role in engagement with the 4th screen and DOOH. One can see a number of applications that have been successful in integrating UGC and DOOH. One example is Show+Tell Productions work in Times Square, where the audience can participate in activities like polling or even uploading a picture to on a giant digital billboard.

I had the opportunity to catch up with Manolo Almagro, Chief Technology Officer, Show+Tell Productions. "The real challenge is to create an experience where the viewer wait time is very low," says Almagro. "People like to see immediate feedback. When you do things that involve voting and polling they work a lot better than interactive games or texting and tweeting to the screen. Even when someone comments, we can only show so much information at one time that will maintain the interest of somebody. For instance, lets say I send a tweet shout out to my friends in Times Square, I do not know when that is going to show up on the screen. It could take 15-20 minutes for it to show up, because everyone else is ahead of me." These are the type of experiences that Almagro talks about that do not receive the best reaction from the participant for the entertainment value because they have to wait and constantly keep their attention on the screen. These experiences are set up in a linear fashion and one message or one action has to be in a queue following others. Almagro explains why there are better ways to engage the user. "Voting is different, when someone votes the percentage is always changing and therefore people feel like that have affected the input and they can see the results," see Figure 9.3. Almagro also suggests that gaming works when you have a multitude of players. "Megaphone has a method where you can engage 20 people playing a game in Times Square without using the phone keyboard [which is a distraction]. So people can shout into their phone and play the game in under a minute. This type of experience has much shorter time frames, a shorter

Figure 9.3 Show+Tell Productions. The experience for UGC must be short and provide fast viewer payback.
©2009 Show+Tell Productions.

payback, more audience involvement, and shorter messages which fit the typical characteristics of DOOH." This is one area to pay close attention to when integrating the 4th screen and DOOH.

One can hardly go to a restaurant today that doesn't have a theme. A tropical-themed restaurant has drinks with coconut and umbrellas in them. That's part of branding in today's world, and it adds to the customer experience. At Atomic Props & Effects, president David Dunn is doing something a little different not only for interactive media but also bigger-than-life 3-D models for billboards. With Atomic Props's help, a network operator can dress up an LED billboard and give it that extra something. In a number of cases, that extra something is interaction.

Consumers have engaged with digital billboards through personal mobile devices. In Manhattan, viewers may have seen the controversial billboard in Figure 9.4 with an added digital element. The large billboard was a BBC installation that showed a static image of the U.S.–Mexico border with the Border Patrol and those trying to cross the border illegally. There were digital LEDs on each side, representing each side in the controversy. The sign urged viewers to send a text message on the spot to choose a side and light up an LED. Dunn gives us the details: "This is very content specific. BBC is all about sharing information and getting an opinion. So their question was, Should illegal immigrants be treated as citizens or criminals? And then you would vote in. BBC was also promoting this on their web site and on TV. It tied into the billboard as well. The BBC would direct people to the phone number to text in to. And you could see it live, so as soon as you texted the digital displays would change."

Figure 9.4 BBC Manhattan billboard where one could vote by text message. ©2009 Atomic Props & Effects.

Something common to all of these interactive displays is the technology behind them. They will always have an Internet interface on the back of the billboard or cellular data connection. In this case the BBC billboard had a web application programming interface (API) that enabled the operator to set up a web that could communicate with the billboard. Dunn says, "In this case, there is a bigger picture static content that is what really draws people in, and the LED content delivers the punch line."

Consider another billboard with interactive capabilities, a huge Sony PSP controller in Las Vegas (Figure 9.5). Says Dunn, "It is huge, 14 feet tall and 36 feet wide. And it's probably about 3 foot off the face of the building. This one is on a building in Vegas that has the white tiled background. These are high-resolution boards and were built from the CAD files from Sony."

Atomic Props is planning to create an Internet hookup between Las Vegas and New York so they can have people on the street play against one another. That will open up a new world of interest, entertainment, and interaction.

Some companies are even experimenting with personal computer interaction. Captivate Network, which offers screens in elevators in professional office buildings, recently launched a web component to provide advertisers with better metrics to understand how exposure turns into engagements. Mike DiFranza, founder and CEO, gives us the details on their thinking. "One of the reasons we launched the web site was we felt that we needed to provide advertisers with better metrics to understand how exposure turns into engagement. So if can we get our viewers to get off that elevator and walk to their desktop and start interacting with a brand once they get back to their desk and go to our web site, you'll see in our little TV-like window, there's a

Figure 9.5 Sony PSP 3-D large-scale digital billboard.
©2009 Atomic Props & Effects.

sweepstakes in this case. And now all of a sudden we can start providing advertisers with some insight to this is how many people saw your ad, this is how many people recalled your ad, and by the way this is how many people went online and either took a tour of your vehicle (if it's a car) or entered the sweepstakes to win your product. And, oh, by the way here are their names. So we can provide a tremendous amount of insight to advertisers really trying to get their arms around what happens when somebody sees my ad. So that's how we measure ourselves."

9.4   Content for Kiosks Versus Digital Signage

The content bridge between digital signage and kiosks is getting shorter and shorter. Just as the two technologies seemingly begin to merge, new methodologies and software for creating kiosk interfaces are changing. Adobe Flash has had the largest impact on the kiosk world by simplifying the complex programming that is usually required to navigate a kiosk. Now using Flash, one can create and program very integrated content.

It is not just a big button on a screen anymore. The ability to acquire data and run the kiosks has fundamentally changed in the last few years. The old-school thinking of heavy programming and layering content is over. Using programmatic tools in Flash to reach out into databases and present new user experiences with great content are rapidly replacing the thinking about kiosks. This is where kiosks meet digital signage, and the two then begin to look a lot alike.

The first self-service, interactive kiosk was developed in 1977 at the University of Illinois at Urbana-Champaign by premed student Murray Lappe. The content was created on the PLATO computer system and was accessible by plasma touch screen interface. Lappe's kiosk, called The Plato Hotline, enabled students and visitors to find movies, maps, directories, bus schedules, extracurricular activities, and courses and to email student organizations. After it first debuted at the University of Illinois student union in April 1977, more than 30,000 students, teachers, and visitors stood in line during its first 6 weeks to try their hand at a personal computer for the first time.[2]

In 1991, the first commercial kiosk with an Internet connection was displayed at COMDEX. The purpose of the application was to locate missing children. The first true documentation of a kiosk was in a 1995 report by Los Alamos National Laboratory, which detailed what the interactive kiosk consisted of. Today's kiosks bring together the classic vending machine with high-tech communications and complex robotic and mechanical internals. Such interactive kiosks can include self-checkout lanes, e-ticketing, information and wayfinding, and vending.

When is digital signage a kiosk, or when is a kiosk digital signage? This fundamental question is plaguing those on both sides of the fence. If we take digital signage and make it a touch screen with interaction and data collection, is it a kiosk? The true meaning of interactive kiosk is a stand-alone enclosure that integrates many devices (this is where the difference is really noted), includes a software GUI application and remote monitoring, and accepts user input. A kiosk is more than simply digital signage; although it has a screen, the purpose is different when it dispenses tickets or is a self checkout, for example. Digital signage begins to look like a kiosk when it is interactive and includes bar code readers or other devices that may be added to present relevant information. Remember, just because the power behind digital signage is a computer, it is not necessarily a kiosk.

The purpose sets them apart, not the type of content. Digital signage content can look a lot like kiosk content on the surface—a friendly touch screen with nicely appointed content. The content changes based on the purpose of the kiosk or digital sign. The content is relevant to the action taken by the participant. In other words, if the kiosk dispenses movie tickets, then the content is relevant to that particular action. Kiosks, unlike digital

---

[2]Interactive Kiosk Design and Consulting, http://www.arcdesignconsulting.com/custom-kiosk.php

signage, offer that type of action, and therefore the content will need to be tailored differently.

Ron Greenberg, CMO of TouchTunes—the largest out-of-home interactive entertainment network providing innovative music, game, and media solutions to more than 40,000 bars, restaurants, and retailers in North America—knows that his digital signage is more kiosklike. "It is essentially a retail kiosk in a way where we're attracting people. And I actually have likened the whole user experience to a retail experience. When people come to the screen, they're entering our store and they're finding the music that they will eventually pay to play."

TouchTunes records over 1.7 million paid music transactions every single day, second only to iTunes. TouchTunes is a digital jukebox. Is it a kiosk or digital signage? The interesting part of that question may lie in how it is used. In TouchTunes's case it is digital signage, and when the engagement occurs, it's a kiosk.

Greenberg sees it like this: "Even if you're not right at the screen, you'll notice it because we have our attract loop. So there are different messages that are cycling through. Originally it was all intended to get you to look at the screen and go over and touch it. In the beginning, people didn't know it was a touch screen. We're well beyond that now. The screen will announce new songs that are available or the top songs on the network. We've also incorporated video, so we'll have advertising or promotions that are also appearing on the screen. And this is without even touching it. So those are really akin to a digital signage impression."

The attract loop has certain content that can be local- or national-based. When viewers touch the screen, they will see a list of different albums that are available.

"You've also got what we call sticky buttons, but they're really like promotion buttons. So on the jukebox we've got a Kenny Chesney promotion and the new Green Day album being featured. And if you touch those, you go directly to the new album and the list of songs."

TouchTunes also has a banner across the bottom where it could be an advertisement or, if it's not an ad, a music promotion. For example, if a viewer wants to look at a sweepstake for the band Saving Abel, he or she would simply press the banner and could win an autographed guitar giveaway (Figure 9.6). When the viewer presses the banner, the kiosk takes him or her to a micro site where the offer is displayed. The viewer could then press the enter now button, type in his or her email address, and would then have a chance to win.

TouchTunes did this same promotion for Verizon (Figure 9.7). Greenberg explains that "we had a banner and it took you to a micro site where you could view the different phones and touch each phone and learn more about it. And then you could ask for more information and submit your email address and the result was that Verizon collected thousands of potential customers' addresses that way."

Figure 9.6 TouchTunes gave away an autographed guitar through their touch screen jukebox.
©2009 TouchTunes.

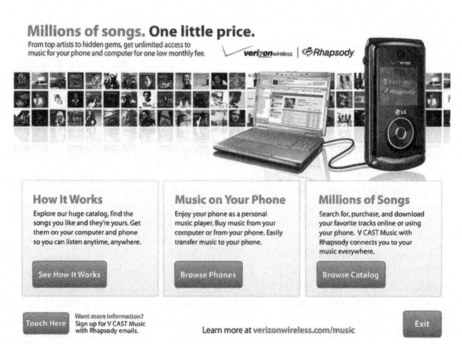

Figure 9.7 The Verizon micro site on the TouchTunes digital sign jukebox.
©2009 TouchTunes.

9.5 Summary

Digital signage is powerful, and good content makes it that way. But the next level of effectiveness comes when one truly engages users through enabling them to interact with the network. Touch screen technology today provides an excellent and proven method to let users decide the path they take through your content and personalize the experience. New technologies, such as gesture interfaces, extend that to another level and combine interaction with group entertainment. Finally, a link with the user's personal screen on a mobile device extends the interactive component of the network in a way that can stimulate longer interactions, interaction away from the digital signage itself, or motivate a purchase. In all of these cases, the content you create must account for the interactive factor and be purposefully designed for this type of network. Much more than porting a web site to the digital signage network, this requires thinking in new ways—and like a user.

10 Taking Content Across Platforms

In the previous several chapters we've discussed the path to creating content that's specific for digital signage—the art of taking advantage of the unique aspects and attributes of the 5th Screen. We've emphasized the differences in content among the various screens in the digital landscape, but it's clear that there is a sea of content designed specifically for each screen. The role of a marketing or ad agency is to deliver results across whatever medium will yield the necessary impressions or cause a sale. That presents many network operators with a daunting task of not only creating content for each of the media the consumer may encounter but also adding digital signage to the traditional mix. So it's important at this stage to consider the similarities among all five screens. Digital signage, in practice, is not necessarily a stand-alone medium, but it works in concert with all the screens.

To create a campaign that can extend across the digital landscape, one must look at a number of options that enable the marketer to accomplish a seamless transfer of assets and design elements among different media. This is one of the challenges that faces agencies and content producers across the creative continuum: taking the basic messages and elements of a campaign and moving that content across platforms as diverse as TV and digital signage.

10.1 Messages Across the Digital Landscape

As we've seen, one cannot simply apply TV thinking to digital signage. But one can't apply TV thinking to the Internet, either, nor can one apply Internet thinking to the mobile screen. Rather, one has to step back a level and consider the predesign of elements that have applicability for all screens to be able to host a campaign effectively. One can look at the creation and distribution of each piece of content as a separate element to be assembled for a particular medium at the time it is needed. As a content creator, the greatest success comes when one creates content in pieces that can be easily manipulated onto the final screen.

Take the approach the digital ad agency Razorfish employed for Microsoft Sync as I was writing this book. The assignment was pretty daunting: plan, shoot, and create content about this in-vehicle automation technology for use in five media areas, including television, computer or Internet, mobile, digital signage, and sales training. Doug Bolin, user experience and content strategy lead at Razorfish, and his team took a step back and planned the work so that the individual assets were created in such a way that they could be recombined as needed for the final medium. Instead of creating complete content for each medium, his team created elements that could be shared and customized appropriately. The result is a set of building blocks that are digitally tagged and cataloged in ways that allow automated reassembly.

"My whole way of thinking about content is as much as possible to do two things: separate it from the presentation layer or the presentation channel and also create a set of content objects," he recalls. "On a coding level, we attached the metadata to the content. We try to keep the content as granular and modular as possible so that it can be tagged and then managed and used in authoring and publish and everything else as independently as possible from the presentation channel that it's eventually going to end up in for the presentation format. Obviously you can't do that 100 percent because some content only is going to be presented in the digital signage channel and it's going to only work in a digital signage channel."

This idea of tagged building blocks is an important one, and it represents a change in the way many marketers have traditionally thought and approached this task. Creating modular granular pieces of content can be complex and cumbersome if one doesn't plan carefully. Imagine organizing all media possibilities up front. Consider if and how each piece of content might be used across television, Internet and computer, mobile, digital signage (both touch and nontouch), in kiosks, and even in print. Breaking down each piece of content that is needed, and for each medium separately, helps to wrap one's mind around the process.

Digital asset management (DAM) solutions aid in the creation, management, usage, and distribution of media content for work groups. Organizations can automate the processing and categorizing of all content while providing instant access to approved content, including photographs, logos, CAD drawings, marketing collateral, Flash, presentations, audio, and video. When dealing with a massive amount of content and a number of media platforms, using DAM is almost a necessity.

The Microsoft Sync project for Ford Motor Company, the technology's primary customer, was designed and shot based on just this approach and with DAM in mind. The team broke down each and every shot, still or motion, in advance over the course of 2 years. The reason for the time investment was the degree of complexity created by the multiple media and the need to demonstrate the technology in action from several viewpoints.

"We needed several assets that were from the point of view of the driver using Sync and several assets that were from the point of view of somebody outside of the car, or inside the car in the passenger seat watching the driver," Bolin explains. "So we needed assets around people using Sync. And there were a couple challenges. One was that Sync didn't exist yet. So we sat down—and by we I mean a big group of people, not just Razorfish. There were a lot of people. From engineering, they have a group called Team Detroit, which are eight of the largest agencies in the world who help Ford with their marketing. We started the dialogues as a team up front about what we've got to do dealer training. We've got to do this web site. We're going to have to do the auto show with this enormous digital signage presence and interactive kiosk. And that's going to have to travel all over the world to all the different auto shows. We're going to need sales support in the showrooms with digital signage and kiosks. We're going to need print ads. We're going to need broadcast ads. We're going to need YouTube videos. We're going to need stuff that people can put on their blog that all these automobile writers can refer to."

These are a lot of different assets to create, control, and publish while keeping an eye on which platform they will be published to, then the content asset objects need to be assembled to address those platforms (Figures 10.1 through 10.3). Bolin continues, "We sat down beforehand and tried to create, as much as possible, a matrix of all the different channels, all the different assets we're going to need, and the stories we [are] going to need to tell, the messages we're going to need to get across."

Figure 10.1 Background for dance scene.
©2009 Razorfish.

Figure 10.2 Dancers for dance scene.
©2009 Razorfish.

Sync with the
soundtrack
of your life.

[LEARN MORE ›]

YOUR CONNECTIONS   YOUR MUSIC   YOUR WAY   YOUR JOURNEY

Figure 10.3   Final composite for dance scene.
©2009 Razorfish.

When the matrix is complete, one can look to see where the commonalities are. Then, when it's time to commission the 3-D animation or shoot the actors, the producer has a complete list of the various ways in which cameras, actors, or point of view for the animation need to be positioned. With Sync, that meant having a number of different shots of a car's steering wheel with an actor (potentially one from each of the target groups for the Sync product) pressing the push to talk button. All of these options were determined by an analysis of the matrix. When the producer was done shooting, there was a content object for each cell in the matrix. The objects could be labeled and tagged, archived and managed, and eventually assembled into a complete content segment for a particular screen and need.

During production, the content creators needed to keep in mind the purpose of each object and the different media in which it will appear. For example, some shots (still and video) could be utilized in more than one medium; others were specific to one screen or another. Bolin continues, "We had to produce all of the assets in such a way that they can be used in different channels as well as be used in different packages in presentation formats. And then logging or tagging those assets so that they can be easily retrieved by a variety of authors who are going to be authoring the content in a variety of different contexts or a variety of different channels at a variety of different times" (Figures 10.4 through 10.9).

During the production of the content objects, Bolin and his team had challenges that were even more complex because of the way in which the Sync technology was being deployed by Ford. "Sync comes in a variety of different models, and depending upon the model of car that it comes in, the controls physically look different. The steering wheel looks different. The dash looks different. All of that stuff is different," he says. For the video of the driver's

Figure 10.4 Laura drives a car for a background composite.
©2009 Razorfish.

Figure 10.5 Escape 3-D cutout all angles.
©2009 Razorfish.

perspective, there were shots of the driver looking at the steering wheel and using Sync, or looking at the display screen and the dashboard, or using Sync and moving his or her fingers to do things and talk. In some cases, there was a passenger in the video. The combinations quickly became unwieldy, especially for a technology that was still not finished and deployed in actual cars.

"We started out with eight potential combinations by an X factor and there were 24 potential variations for every shot in a sequence. And this was just for

Figure 10.6 MLX
outlined for composite.
©2009 Razorfish.

Figure 10.7 MLX
composited into
background.
©2009 Razorfish.

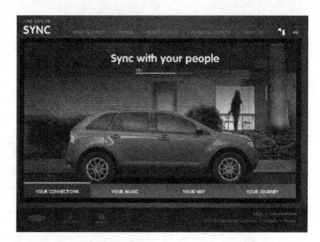

Figure 10.8 Driver composited in car.
©2009 Razorfish.

Figure 10.9 Driver composited in concert.
©2009 Razorfish.

a video, not even thinking about print yet or everything else," Bolin says. "So there were 24 different potential variations of every shot. If you were going to show the person who was thinking about buying this model of Ford, Lincoln, or Mercury, how Sync would work for them, we had to do the personalization; we had to do the content object approach. And then the other thing we did is we used a lot of green screen because we were able to shoot it in such a way that the actors could be composited into any model car, and the view out the window and the view from the driver, you could composite in any steering wheel, or any set of controls."

This is one illustration of applying compositing to production. Then one needs to use a couple of different content management systems to archive that content and all the different levels of assets. Producers need to tag each piece of content by presentation channel and all kinds of other variables. Then when the time comes to build the final presentation for each screen—or to instruct a digital signage network to display dynamically delivered content—all the pieces are there and easily identifiable. A content creator can simply search for and pull the assets from their various locations in the database and combine them with the appropriate tool. Or a programmer can write the rules for how the assets are going to be combined in certain situations and then, using XML, deliver it to the publishing platform.

By acknowledging the complexity of the Sync project in advance and producing a matrix of thousands of content objects, the marketing of the product was enabled in the salesroom, through digital signage, and at a kiosk. When a customer enters a Ford dealership, expresses interest in a certain model that has the Sync option, and wants to see how it works, the salesperson can simply say, Oh come on over here. We'll show you. Then the salesperson could call up the demo for that particular model and show the customer exactly how it works.

"The content was also used on the web site in addition to startup guides, quick start guides, and educational pieces on how to use the basic thing in Sync," Bolin says. "As part of marketing, it was an easy-to-use device. We literally created I think it was 20,000 content objects because people come into the site, either in the showroom or after they've bought the car, and they say 'Okay, I'm in this country. I bought this car, this year, this model, this version of Sync is in it and here's what I want to do. Tell me how.' And [the web site] dynamically goes into that content database and assembles all the right visuals and all the right text for every step in whatever they just asked how to do."

Obviously, one has to invest considerable time and money up front in this approach. But one saves a lot of money over the course of the campaign or the content publishing. Conducting one photo shoot that feeds 50 different presentations in six channels is less expensive in the long run than doing a separate photo shoot every time you need to do a presentation. The process creates economies of scale in content. For example, one can have a how-to video that appears in a certain zone of digital signage at a certain point in the customer's journey. The people who write the user manual for that product can use aspects of this video and its script, and the same assets can be repurposed for the web. We will continue to discover ways of leveraging content across the channels. It is simply a different way of thinking about how to create cross-platform content, and it does come with hurdles and roadblocks.

Michael Chase, president of Alchemy, takes a similar approach. "It's really about up front planning, and knowing where you're going to publish it. We manage how to leverage your assets and to get it out to all these mediums. So in our case, since we have a broad spectrum that we are creating content for, it's really about saying I'm going to take a bottle of water, or I'm going to take a product like a KitchenAid blender or mixer, and I'm going to shoot it in all the different angles I need to shoot it when I've got it in my studio. In the past the client would basically take a product like a KitchenAid mixer and with that product they would ship it to eight different vendors for example, for eight different uses and for eight different applications. We basically built a streamlined process which was item or product driven."

In contrast to the Sync project, where the product changed along with its environment, this is a case of taking a single item and shooting it from multiple angles and in many different ways so that the single shoot results in an image appropriate to any medium, from a catalog to in-store digital signage. By following this methodology and having that up front planning, one can create a database of content where it could be used by the client in home, out of home, in a catalog, on television, or on digital signage and kiosks. By planning up front one is able to reuse those assets appropriately for all these different media.

Along with this new way of approaching content is a new way of behaving within traditionally siloed ad agencies. This is where a lot of digital agencies are seeing the benefits of each group working together across all campaigns and very cost-effectively creating and publishing content across all media.

10.2   Extending the Message Across the 4th Screen, Mobile Devices

Digital signage is an activator, especially for the mobile device screen. How does it tie in? Mobile is considered by consumers to be a very personal device that exists in personal space, and thus it is very difficult for marketers to engage. The unique position that digital signage holds in the marketplace is that it is in the environment where the consumer is on the go, shopping, or waiting. Extending the initial consumer experience that is enhanced by digital signage to a mobile device can be very useful and helpful to the consumer—and generate return to the marketer. Utilizing the mobile phone in all types of networks is vital.

In a store, shoppers use their mobile devices to support their decision process through the ability of mobile devices to let shoppers search for product reviews, price comparisons, and even get recommendations from their social networks. Consider price, for example. For items that are not everyday purchases and are widely available online, a shopper is likely to use his or her mobile device and browser to check the best online price and compare it to the store's price. This can be a problem for the store because most of them will no longer adjust their prices to meet an online price. Unless the price difference is minor, there's a chance the shopper will use the retail store to try out an item and then give the sale to the lower-priced online retailer.

So the question becomes, How can digital signage change the nature of this interaction between the shopper and a mobile device or data to preserve the sale? The answer is that digital signage can initiate interaction and create an engagement on a different level about something the consumer is perhaps not even thinking about. It's very dynamic because everyone in a POS or a POW or even a POT network generally has their mobile phone, and the interaction is more top of mind than when they're sitting in their living room.

Dominick Porco, CEO of Adspace Networks, which operates POS networks in malls, agrees that mobile is going to be an essential part of doing business in digital signage. "We are very interested in the mobile application. We see in the not too distant future, you walk by one of our screens and there's a $10 coupon from a Gap T-shirt with a code and you just hit you[r] phone and you instantly have the coupon bar code on your phone. You walk over to the Gap, the cashier scans your phone and voilà, you got $10 off that purchase."

In POT networks, one needs to grab the attention of the on-the-go consumer and convert that to an engagement. Tommy Teepell, COO of Lamar Advertising, has utilized mobile applications in conjunction with digital signage. "Within our transit networks for example, I can hold a mobile device's camera up to the ad, take the picture, and if it's a movie ad, a clip of the movie is going to play on my phone. And it got that information because when I took the photograph, it sent it to whatever that deep, dark place is and notified them that I was interested. And then the movie is clipped to my phone, I can then buy tickets based on my location to the nearest theater."

At some point, the mobile device will be an engagement for shoppers to purchase anything, anytime, and anyplace and have it shipped to their home. Activating the thought process for purchase is where digital signage can have huge impacts. Simply being in the right mind-set and setting the product or service to being top of mind increases the probability for purchase.

10.3   Extending the Message to the 3rd Screen, Personal Computers

Although extending the link from digital signage to mobile devices is fairly immediate, pushing the connection back to the Internet and computer is more challenging. Consumers are rarely carrying a computer when they encounter digital signage, and even less frequently is the computer operating and connected to the Internet. Nonetheless, there are many ways in which the power of digital signage can be multiplied by the power of the Internet.

One proponent is Mike DiFranza, CEO of Captivate Network, who uses the Internet and computer in a unique way based on where Captivate's screens are located: in elevators. "One of the things that we recognized about our environment is that somebody is riding in an elevator, they're getting off and going to their desk. So we create basically an ability to provide a taste of the story on the screen in the elevators and then allow them to go get the rest of the story on our web site, which is pretty compelling. And any news story that you see running on any elevator we are in throughout the United States and Canada, you can basically go to Captivate.com [Figure 10.10] and the headline will be there and you can click on that and it will take you to the news story from the original content."

Again, navigating to a web site can also help the engagement process and become a measurement of the original engagement itself. For example, in another type of POW network, corporate communications, one can track message success by offering employees something via the digital signage for which they must visit a particular page on the corporate web site to obtain. After the offer is made, one can engage the metrics and visits to that particular web page on the site. This can also work on other networks, of course; one just needs to think across the screens.

Just as the web has used television to drive sales, digital signage can also help drive traffic to the web. This is a little more traditional approach to advertising, but having a relevant mind-set and the right message during that engagement can have significant effects on the consumer. In addition, targeting groups that are more likely to visit one's particular web site is also key. The relevant information, venue, and so forth can help target the audience for the web site itself.

10.4   Utilizing Messages from the 2nd Screen, Television

Throughout the previous chapters we have discussed how the medium of digital signage is different from television. The thumbprint of television (as well as the PC) is forever a positive influence on digital signage, but when the entire

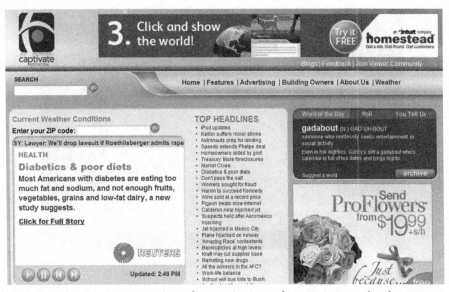

Figure 10.10 Captivate.com ties online stories into what you saw on the elevator on your ride up to the office.
©2009 Captivate Network.

handprint from television is on the back of digital signage, this is where content can go horribly wrong. There are some digital signage networks that are running visual TV spots, and they are working. How can we determine what type of television or what pieces of the television approach to content might work in digital signage, and how can one leverage those assets across these two different media?

Some TV spots may work in digital signage when there is a very visual message and it is used on the *right* network. The Ripple TV network consists of screens on a POW network in coffee and bagel shops. This network is a lifestyle network with a lot of content on the screen at once (Figure 10.11). CEO John McMenamin has his own perspective on TV spots running his digital signage networks. "I think television does work. I think that specially created ads work and I think the right TV ads also work. We did a Claritin ad in which you get a complete understanding of what's going on. There might be some ads that are extremely audio heavy that may not work as well, and in those instances we usually do something different. We find about 95 percent of our TV commercials do just fine on our network. We just finished a pretty big study with Oil of Olay on olayforyou.com, where they ran their TV ad and the level of effectiveness was super. It was fantastic piece of research."

Peter Corrigan, CEO of The University Network (TUN), also finds that some TV content works on their college campus network. "We actually produce commercials that are like TV commercials for events that are happening on campus. We have creative people that do a very nice job with it. It's a quality that you expect on a local cable channel. I think that our audience and also

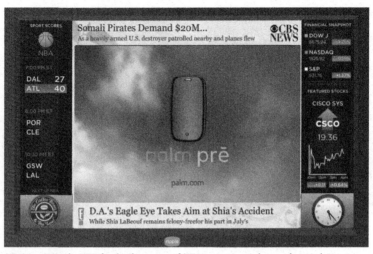

Figure 10.11 Ripple TV finds that *visual* TV commercials work on their network. ©2009 Ripple TV.

the people that control the message board don't need it to be at that level. They like content. They'll love those commercials for branding and what not, but sometimes they just want a quick message and they want to get it there right away. We have tools that allow for them to get text-based content through an RSS-type feed to the screen within seconds. And that's a new thing we're doing in addition to the television-like content that we have."

One can look at the type of network first and then determine the type of content that works. When one has a high dwell time network, TV-like advertising and content can work to the advantage of the network operator. When one has a short dwell time or even an in-store network, the content needs to change to meet the desires of the consumer who watches for a short time.

Programming that runs on cycles of 15-second ads and editorial content looks much different from a high dwell time network like a coffee and bagel network. The repurposed TV-like advertising component is radically changed. "Some clients like to repurpose television," says Jim Harris, CEO of the Wall Street Journal Office Network. "The truth in my view is that that's a mistake on all but the most static networks where you might be sitting for a long period of time because television is the kind of medium where the expectation is that you're going to be sitting and consuming a story for 30 seconds, start to finish [Figure 10.12]. With our screens and with a lot of digital out-of-home screens, sometimes your dwell time is 2 minutes."

"Sometimes your dwell time is 15 seconds. Sometimes you walk in at the end of a message. If you've architected the creative well, I mean the brand is always on, you can get value from 5 seconds of exposure or 2 seconds of exposure as opposed to expecting somebody to consume this like a 30-second TV spot," he says. "A lot of the stuff that we see on our network, I would say it's growing

Figure 10.12   The Wall Street Journal Office Network often uses repurposed TV ads. ©2009 Office Media Network.

because I think a lot more people are repurposing their television and seeing how to digitize it into a 15-second digital out-of-home play content. We're seeing a lot of stuff that has been repurposed from the web. And probably more than we're seeing repurposed television. But some of the repurposed television that we've seen customized, not just take the TV spot and run it, but actually take the TV spot and think about how you adapt it to these sorts of screens has been the best looking and some of the most powerful advertising that we've had on the network."

10.5 Summary

Planning in advance is the single most effective method for leveraging any and all assets across digital platforms. This is an industry that is a little bit TV, a little bit computer, and even a little bit print. A lot of current thinking about content is directly related to posters. Certainly now that we are in a digital age, any element can end up in the continuum of the digital landscape. Sometimes it's different graphic treatments that make the difference. If a commercial has a lot of audio and one's network does not have audio, then what might have been a voice-over can be turned into visual messages. One can sometimes use supers or text overlays and nicely tell a story graphically instead of using a voice.

Digital signage will, at some point, reach the scale of the other mediums. At that point the entire game for digital signage changes, and the industry may be feeding the other screens' content as well.

11 Legal Content Use

If the previous chapters have demonstrated anything, it's that content takes time, talent, and money to create. An individual, group of individuals, or company makes an investment in the form of time, money, and creativity to create content, whether it is text in an RSS feed or a beautifully produced video. In the United States (and in much of the rest of the world), that effort is rewarded with legal protections for the content. These protections give the creators the chance to profit from their work and the right to control (for the most part) who else can use the work, where, in what form, and for what level of compensation.

In the United States, there are three main types of legal protection for what in legal circles is called intellectual property: copyright, patent, and trademark. Of those, only two—copyright and trademark—are of general concern for digital signage content. (Patents concern inventions, like machines or formulas, rather than creative works like movies or books.) Being aware of the general concepts of copyright and trademark protection is important for you to understand because of the need to negotiate the rights to use someone else's content (even pieces of another work) in your digital signage network.

The information in this chapter is specific to the legal system in the United States. Although copyright in particular is recognized by international conventions, there are significant differences in the way different countries treat this protection. There are some countries where there is either a lack of strong protection for creative work or the widespread practice of ignoring the laws. So it's important for those contemplating content creation and protection to keep international law and practices in mind.

This chapter isn't intended to provide specific legal advice or be a substitute for consultations with appropriate legal counsel, but the information here should help you understand the general concepts about legal content use and ask more informed questions of your legal advisor. The most important rule of thumb is it's much less expensive to negotiate and secure the rights you need up front than to pay the penalties and legal costs later.

11.1 Copyright

The U.S. Copyright Office states the following:[1]

A principle of American law is that an author of a work may reap the fruits of his or her intellectual creativity for a limited period of time. Copyright is a form of protection provided by the laws of the United States for original works of authorship, including literary, dramatic, musical, architectural, cartographic, choreographic, pantomimic, pictorial, graphic, sculptural, and audiovisual creations. "Copyright" literally means the right to copy. The term has come to mean that body of exclusive rights granted by law to authors for protection of their work. The owner of copyright has the exclusive right to reproduce, distribute, and, in the case of certain works, publicly perform or display the work; to prepare derivative works; in the case of sound recordings, to perform the work publicly by means of a digital audio transmission; or to license others to engage in the same acts under specific terms and conditions. Copyright protection does not extend to any idea, procedure, process, slogan, principle, or discovery.

The United States was a pioneer of protecting the rights of creative individuals; it is such an important concept that it is enshrined in the Constitution. The basic idea is fairly straightforward: it is in the best interest of a country and its economy to have a free flow of information. At the same time, people are much more likely to invest time being creative, and to share what they have created, if they know they can profit from it. So the Constitution gave Congress the power to write laws offering copyright protection for a limited time. Congress wasted little time passing the first copyright law in 1790; Congress also gave the job of copyright registration and management to the Copyright Office, part of the Library of Congress. It took just 2 weeks for the first copyright application to arrive after the law was passed.

Since then, copyright law has undergone a significant number of changes and revisions to reflect changes in technology. When the Constitution was written, there were no telephones, phonographs, movies, or televisions, and there was certainly no Internet. In almost every case, the appearance of a major new technology by which content could be exchanged, displayed, or copied has resulted in a change to the copyright laws to keep pace. In addition, there have been a number of high-profile court cases that have helped to define how copyright applies to these new technologies, particularly the ability of people at home to make video and audio recordings, something enhanced by the Internet. (Movies, for example, came under specific copyright protection in 1912, and home recording rights were set in place by the U.S. Supreme Court's 1984 decision in the so-called Betamax case.)

Within the past few decades, there has been a sharp increase in public awareness and governmental concern over copyright issues. As the global economy in general and the American economy in particular became more dependent on the exchange of intellectual property in addition to food and manufactured

[1]http://www.copyright.gov/circs/circ1a.html. Circular 1 from the US Copyright Office

goods, these protections have become vital to economic life and the balance of trade. The degree to which creative works, such as software and entertainment (movies, music, and television), contribute to America's economy and exports is unprecedented. The ease with which the Internet has made it possible to copy entire libraries of music or movies and distribute them instantly around the world has had profound implications for a country whose economy depends on intellectual property.

As a result, U.S. copyright laws have become much tougher in recent years. The penalties for infringing on someone's copyright range as high as $250,000 per instance, with jail time added if a court determines the infringement was criminal. This came in large part at the behest of major copyright owners, particularly movie studios, television production houses, record companies, and the software industry. Newspaper and TV news reports are full of cases where these industries have used the current stringent copyright laws to sue—or press for prosecutions of—both companies and individuals who have copied works without permission.

All this should serve as a warning: whatever content you plan to use in your digital signage network, if the copyright for all or even part of it is held by someone else, pay for or negotiate the rights in advance.

11.2   What's Covered?

In the world of digital signage, pretty much everything that might appear throughout the network is subject to copyright. What the Copyright Office terms visual arts covers the gamut of "pictorial, graphic, or sculptural works, including 2-dimensional and 3-dimensional works of fine, graphic, and applied art, photographs, prints and art reproductions, maps, globes, charts, technical drawings, diagrams, architectural works and models." Movies, videos, and digitally generated images are subject to copyright as well.

Don't forget that even the ads you might display are subject to copyright protection. The rights usually belong to the company whose products or services are being advertised, but you will probably want your contracts with those providing the ads to indemnify you in case of any violation (for example, an ad that uses a song for which the rights haven't been properly obtained). The law also recognizes a concept of fair use of portions of copyrighted works for certain purposes without violating rights. Those exemptions, however, are limited. In general, the commercial use of someone else's copyrighted work requires you to obtain rights first.

For example, let's say you subscribe to a cable TV service, and one of the channels broadcasts the games of your favorite sports team. You can record those games at home using a digital video recorder so you can watch at another time at home. You can even invite your friends to watch with you, and that doesn't violate the law. But if you arrange a more public viewing of that game—putting your big screen on your front lawn, for example—or charge people admission to see the game, you've probably crossed the line. You've gone from personal use to commercial use and subjected yourself to legal liability. Putting that game, or even a short clip of that game, onto your network without permission is inviting trouble.

Indeed, in a commercial environment where cable TV programming is shown, cable operators have executed special commercial use license agreements with the company (say, a bar or an airport) to allow them to show the copyrighted material to what amounts to a paying, commercial audience. There have been instances where companies that show the content under these licenses have assumed they could run the programming, but instead of showing the on-screen commercial ad, they interrupted the signal and displayed a digital signage ad instead. This amounts to taking the creative content of the cable operator but stripping the payment—the ad. In almost every case, this would violate copyright and the commercial license agreement because it in fact alters the content coming from the cable or network channel. Altering the broadcast in any way, is illegal unless the rights are granted.

In the same fashion, simply because you can find a piece of content somewhere on the Internet, and thus easily incorporate it into your digital signage network, doesn't get you off the legal hook. There are a lot of news feeds and RSS feeds available on the web. For example, look at the fine print on a web site for FOX News or a CNN feed. Yes, you can put it on your computer for personal use. But when you take the feed and put it on a digital signage network for commercial purposes, that is a negotiated or paid-for legal right to use the content.

Some of the web's most prominent brands have found themselves in the middle of copyright troubles because of the ease with which content moves around the Internet. With your business success on the line, the most prudent path is to be thorough about securing copyright permissions for everything you don't create yourself. Incorporating provisions to build content and license content into your business models and standard operating procedures will enable you and your company to thrive and charge equally for your value adds.

Do not assume that simply because your company has the rights to use a piece of content in one form or on one screen you have the rights to use it on a digital signage network or in different ways on that network. In a world built on intellectual property protections, copyright owners slice and dice rights and permissions in myriad ways to ensure they collect the maximum revenue from their creativity. The rights a company has been granted to use an image on their web site may be limited to that use only; to put it onto a digital signage network requires another level of permission.

11.2.1 Obtaining Permission

Many content creators who routinely license their work to others for commercial purposes have standard prices and practices for this purpose. Particularly if their content has been used by others on the Internet or mobile screens, they may have form contracts spelling out the limits of use and how they will deliver the content to you. They may even have price lists so you can determine what you might have to pay for the content you want. The terms they offer will vary—widely—depending on a number of factors related to how you will make use of the work. The more unique the content resource, and the more widely you plan to employ it, the more it is likely to cost.

To allow his business to provide content to its clients, Brian Hirsh of Retail Entertainment Design licenses literally thousands of different items from hundreds of copyright owners, negotiating rights all along the way. That necessitates keeping careful track of all these rights and the uses they allow. "We probably have 300 to 500 different content owners that give us content. And I would say that we probably have 200 different ways that we've agreed to distribute content. We have to have a pretty sophisticated database that helps control and limit distribution to make sure that we're reporting based on the rights that we're given. In most cases, we are asking for the rights for an extended term, like a year or longer to get that content. And that seems to be well received."

Many of these content owners are used to licensing their works for use in broadcasting, and in that respect, digital signage is a comfortable match when it comes to rights. Like broadcast, "[W]e can tell them when we played it. You can't really prove that a consumer watched it, unlike web traffic, web media and other assets that are being distributed across that or mobile, where network owners can report based on views" and frequency. Broadcast is a good digital signage model because, Hirsh says, "it's a TV show that nobody can turn off."

Whether a creator has a significant formal licensing and pricing structure or not, you will probably need to—or want to—negotiate the terms for the specific uses you have in mind for your network. Digital signage is a new concept and offers such a wide range of possibilities that many of the licenses and pricing structures that work for more familiar screens won't be applicable for digital signage use. You may wind up negotiating a license that the creator never imagined, not unlike when other screens came on the scene. For example, movie studios were faced with the development of television, and record producers encountered the Internet and the MP3 player.

TouchTunes has digital jukeboxes in more than 40,000 bars across the United States. Ron Greenberg, CMO and SVP digital media, has some unique licensing issues. "We've got the rights issue for music across the entire 40,000 location network. So of course we have a team that focuses on nothing else but copyrights and clearance and royalty payments. A lot of what we do is based on that content, including the new advertising capability. But we pay royalties to the labels, to the publishers and to the performance rights organization for every single play. So you know in this day of people getting free downloads or using P to P systems to get music, this is one of the areas that the labels and publishers actually like because they're seeing royalty payments for this, and every single play is tracked, and those payments are growing."

The location of TouchTunes screens also presents some unique legal challenges, even after the copyright clearances are obtained: state and local alcohol laws. "There are rules based on where you serve alcohol on what sort of compensation to the bar owner can be provided. They are carefully controlled and it does vary from state to state. So for example if we were to run liquor advertising, the bar owners themselves if we're using a revenue share model would not be able to get paid for alcohol advertising based on those state alcohol beverage control laws. For nonalcoholic advertising, it's not an issue. In fact you're not even allowed to put free screens in place to show alcohol advertising. That is considered to be a payment."

Before you negotiate with a digital content owner, then, it's important that you consider all the ways in which that particular asset might be used on your network or in secondary ways as a result of creating a digital signage network. The terms surrounding rights to the content will generally be proportional to the value that content delivers to the network, including everything from how widely dispersed the network will be, to the level of revenue the network is expected to generate for its owner, to the specific role played by a piece of content. Is it a small diversion or entertainment content? Is it a direct sales aid? Does the content owner derive any direct return from the revenue generated by the network? For example, does the content being licensed help drive the actual sale of an item?

Here are a few questions you need to ask yourself and that you can expect the copyright owner to ask you:

- What do you want to do with the content?
- How often will you use the content?
- How big is the potential audience?
- When and where will the content be seen or heard?
- Will the content be made interactive?
- Will the content be needed for secondary material or uses?
- Who can use the content?

What do you Want to do with the Content?

This sounds like a simple, basic question, but it is also one that has many potential answers and therefore a lot of potential effect on the terms under which the owner will grant rights. In some cases, the plan may be to use the entire piece of content as is—let's say, a 15-second animation that will comprise a complete segment in a playlist. In other cases, however, that content will become integrated into a larger segment that the network owner is creating; it will serve as a building block rather than a complete, distinct whole. Another possible variation on the building block concept would be actually dissecting the piece of content in question and then remixing it, using parts of it in new and different ways, or making other changes to it.

In simple terms, the content will either be shown the way it was created, or it will be modified in some way. Obtaining rights to show the original content the way it was created will be simpler, in most cases, than the rights to reedit. Depending on the kind of creative work in question, the copyright owner may not consider offering rights that involve reediting to protect the integrity of the original work and hence its market value.

How Often Will you Use the Content?

Before obtaining content, a network operator has usually gone through the other steps outlined earlier in this book—assessing the kind of network, the audience, the location, and so forth. From there, decisions have been made about the size and length of playlists, how often these playlists will be shuffled or changed, and how long that collection of content will remain fresh before it is entirely replaced.

These decisions, which network operators will likely have laid out in the form of a spreadsheet or database table, will let them calculate the number of times a piece of content will be used. The more often a piece of content will be used, the more a network operator will likely have to pay.

How Big is the Potential Audience?

Copyright owners will be concerned with the number of eyeballs that your network hopes to draw by, in part, using their content. The kind of network you have will help determine whether it will draw mass viewership, such as founding a point of transit network on a freeway or busy subway platform, or a much smaller audience, such as one that occurs in a point of wait network in a modest medical practice.

Along with network type, the size of the potential audience obviously depends on the number of screens contemplated for the network. It's possible that a point of wait network for medical offices that is marketed to a large number of practices around the country will have a larger potential viewership than a point of transit network that's limited to a single city with only a few subway platforms.

Finally, audience size will be relative to the time of day and frequency with which the content is intended to be used. Content that appears only late at night in a point of transit network will capture fewer eyeballs than content on the same screens during heavy commute periods; content that appears on an in-store playlist that cycles once every 4 hours will have fewer eyeballs than the same content shown on the much faster cycling playlist of a point of sale network at a fast-food restaurant or convenience store.

Again, this calculation is one that is most easily accomplished by reference to the spreadsheet or database table that summarizes the decisions about playlists.

When and Where will the Content be Seen or Heard?

The nature of the network and its audience is another potential factor relating to rights. Some content owners may be more willing to license their content for limited viewing on networks that are not exposed to the general public. For example, a point of wait network in an educational setting that is seen mostly by students and faculty may merit a different set of rights and costs than the same content when the intent is to display it on a point of transit network in a large airport. A point of wait network for strictly internal company use, such as in cafeterias or meeting rooms, may be looked upon by the copyright holder differently than the same network when screens are in company lobbies or retail locations and are accessible to a wider audience.

Will the Content be made Interactive?

For a network that does not offer interactivity or user control, the network owner has complete control over the content and the playlist. In this case, the network owner has the ability to predict with some degree of accuracy how often a particular piece of content will be shown, what time of day it will be shown, and how many people are likely to see it. As previously noted, these are all factors that will affect the terms a content owner will offer.

If the content will be changed depending on some other factors, however, this calculation becomes more difficult. For example, when we discussed changing content based on the weather, we noted that a coffee shop might choose to market hot drinks when it is snowing and iced tea when there's baking sunshine. What if the plans for marketing those drinks call for using a piece of licensed content—perhaps a video of people on a beach enjoying the sunshine? In that case, the network owner can expect to have to come to other terms with the content owner that give permission for the content to be used as needed based on the external feed. That creates some uncertainty on the part of the content owner about how often the content will be shown and to how many people. At the same time, it introduces some uncertainty about overall costs to the network operator. If the terms of the deal involving pricing are based on usage and audience, the uncertainty will have to be addressed so both sides have some predictability and accountability regarding how often the beach video might be screened and how big the audience might be.

The same issue applies to networks in which licensed content will be shown on the screen in response to the interaction of a viewer. In our example, the beach video may not run unless a customer touches a button on the digital sign labeled "Refreshing Cold Beverages." This presents a similar issue to what happens every day on the Internet with a significant portion of advertising.

On the Internet, the most common method of pricing for advertising is the click through. An advertiser pays fees based on how many times viewers of a page click the ad, meaning that the site hosting the ad has actually delivered a prospective customer to the advertiser's site. Related to that are fees for keywords—that is, what an advertiser pays to ensure that their ad is displayed most prominently when a user searches for particular words together. The use of similar terms and similar measurement technology may be needed for a digital signage network that employs dynamic content in these ways.

Will the Content be Needed for Secondary Material or Uses?

We've discussed the concept of digital signage as a part of a larger branding, marketing, or communications effort by the network operator. Employing a network in this way is likely to multiply its effectiveness and create the kind of consistency around a brand or company that is more powerful than using a digital signage network on its own. That means that content of many kinds that appear on a digital signage network may also be appropriate to use on a company's web page or in printed material, such as advertising brochures, marketing handouts, or paper signage. In all of these cases, a network operator will need to ensure that the rights obtained for digital signage use extend to all the contemplated uses. Grabbing a still image from a licensed video source on one network may be a technically simple task, but it's not necessarily legal. So before negotiating, consider the widest possible range of uses for the content in question and determine if the appropriate licensing arrangements can be made.

Who can Use the Content?

Some copyright owners will want to ensure their work is protected from accidental or malicious misuse by placing limits on the number or identities of people who have permission to gain access. Some license agreements may even require the network operator to use passwords or security software to limit who can use the content, so the operator needs to know how the content creation process works in terms of who needs access to the raw licensed content to comply with any of these needs of the copyright owner.

11.2.2   Parts of a License

What is a license? Mark Steiner, partner and practice group leader of the Trademark and Copyright Group at Townsend and Townsend and Crew in San Francisco tells us, "A license is permission from the rights owner to use the copyrighted work pursuant to the terms of the agreement. It is the agreement that governs what use is authorized." When a network operator obtains the right to use copyrighted material, it's important to understand what that really means. The most basic idea is that, unlike purchasing a hard good, such as a pair of jeans or a sack of potatoes, this is not an outright purchase. You may do as you please with jeans or potatoes, but you have only licensed content according to specific agreed-upon terms and conditions. In fact, in the case of a pair of jeans, one thing you cannot do is to make and sell copies that directly resemble the appearance of distinctive stitching or other protected aspects of the garment. Such activity is counterfeiting, a form of intellectual property theft. Similarly, although you can take a DVD you have purchased and do what you want with the piece of plastic, the content that's on it is licensed to you under specific terms and conditions, including a prohibition on copying and, in most cases, public exhibition.

When examining a license offered for content you want to use on the network, the most important section to be carefully reviewed is usually titled Rights Granted or something similar. This section spells out the specific uses of the content in exchange for the fee or other compensation offered to the copyright owner. The rights may include (but aren't necessarily limited to) the right to relicense, view, reproduce, store or save copies, display, download, print, and forward electronically to others. These rights need to be considered against the anticipated uses of the content on the digital signage network to ensure that they are specifically covered in this section. If the anticipated uses are not specifically covered, chances are that the use being contemplated is not allowed.

Another related section that bears close examination deals with what is usually termed Authorized Uses. This section will amplify the Rights Granted language by determining, among other things, how widely you may distribute the content or in which markets you may use the content. It's not uncommon for copyright owners to segment rights according to geography. For example, this is an historic practice in the movie industry and continues to be a consideration in the release of new films on DVD; this is the purpose of region codes in DVDs. In addition to geography, copyright owners may segment rights according to the kind of audience or scope of the audience that may view the material. Corporate communications, for example, may be the only area in which your network may make use of the content.

Finally, Usage Restrictions is another important section of a license. It can have clauses that cover your rights to perform any modification of the content (for example, you may be required to show the entirety of a video clip or be prohibited from speeding it up) or how many times a piece of content may be used.

Educating your team and potential clients on the concept of licensing and the specifics of each license is absolutely critical to ensure your network hews to the letter of the license agreement. Failing to communicate these issues early in the process of network design and content creation can pose significant problems later—in particular, setting up any kind of use monitoring after the fact is much more difficult than building in the necessary monitoring up front. In addition, the difficulties faced in monitoring a network that is marketed to outside clients, rather than within a company's own facilities, is a prime reason why you should ensure there is no part of a license agreement that requires you to monitor use by your clients. Instead, have clients agree in writing to the same terms and conditions that bind the network operator.

11.2.3 Rights Agencies

Obtaining all the rights one needs may seem like an impossible task, simply because of all the variables involved. Fortunately, for many types of content, licensing agencies for intellectual property have developed over the years. Because many creative individuals don't have the time or the inclination to deal with legal matters, they are happy to turn the issuance of rights over to an outside expert in exchange for a percentage of the cost of the rights. This gives creative individuals a greater chance of getting income from their work through wider distribution and assures a more streamlined process of obtaining rights.

To see why these agencies can benefit a digital signage network operator, consider the complexities of a single piece of recorded music that a network operator is considering for use. To the operator, things may appear to be simple; all he or she wants is the ability to play a song in conjunction with an ad. But it's not at all simple because so many different individuals and entities may have rights to that particular recording. The songwriters have rights because they created the basic work. The performers have rights to that version of the song because that particular performance involves their separate creative input. Finally, the record company that furnished the studio, physically produced the recording, and distributed it also has a copyright interest in the version of the song the network operator wants to use. In addition, although the financial arrangements among the three parties may be well understood for the public sale of the song on a CD, its use in a commercial setting will likely create a different financial dynamic. Agencies can cut through all that and negotiate a package of rights that the digital signage operator needs, a much more efficient solution.

Music

If you wish to license a musical work, check with the American Society of Composers, Authors and Publishers (ASCAP), Broadcast Music Inc. (BMI), or SESAC (originally named Society of European Stage Authors & Composers). The Recording Industry Association of America (RIAA) represents most major labels and has a good explanation of the statutory licenses that are available.

Film and Video

The Motion Picture Licensing Corporation and Swank Motion Pictures Inc. grant rights to film and video. The Swank Motion Pictures Inc. is an independent copyright licensing service exclusively authorized by major Hollywood motion picture studios and independent producers to grant umbrella licenses to comply with the federal Copyright Act. Movie Licensing USA, a corporate division of Swank Motion Pictures Inc., provides exclusive licenses that suit the copyright protection needs of movie producers while offering a worry-free, liability-free movie license.

Internet Archive has educational public domain films available for download. The films are stored in MPEG format and need to be downloaded to view rather than viewing them as streaming video.

You may also need to investigate whether any rights need to be cleared that could be held by the actors, producers, writers, performers, guilds, or composers. Agent representation for living people can be found at the WhoRepresents web site.

One may research film and video copyrights using the database at the Library of Congress. This database lists claimants and copyright ownership to works registered after 1978.

Still Photos and Graphics

There are numerous online agencies that have collections of still photographs. Some of the top image sites are iStockphoto, Getty Images, Dreamstime, and Masterfile. One can purchase different levels of rights based on the use of the image.

11.3 Trademark

Trademark protection is a companion to copyright law. It is under the management of the U.S. Patent and Trademark Office. Essentially, trademarks provide protection for things like logos, brand names, distinctive color combinations, slogans and taglines, and other visual elements that identify a particular company, brand, or product. Steiner is very well versed in this area of the law and suggests, "Whether or not these are registered with the United States Patent and Trademark office, they are protected from use by others without permission and a license. Nonetheless, when you register a trademark, you do receive legal benefits, such as legal presumptions of ownership and validity of the mark as well as the ability to record it with U.S. customs and have jurisdiction in the federal courts for purposes of enforcing trademark rights in the registered mark."

Although this issue doesn't hold nearly the same significance for digital signage as copyright does, it bears consideration. The plans for digital signage content can often involve the display of the logos or product images of other companies. A point of sale network, for example, will almost certainly show the clearly identifiable trademarks of the products being promoted at the time. It's important, then, to ensure that whatever legal arrangements exist with the maker of those products allow this kind of use of their trademark.

11.4 Protecting your Original Work

We've spent most of this chapter discussing protecting the copyrights of others. But it's almost certain that along the way in creating a digital signage network a company or operator will create at least some original content themselves. This is valuable creative work that needs to be protected as well.

The most common issue that arises over this content is who actually holds the rights to it in the first place. If only company employees are involved in the creative process, there's rarely an issue because the work they do is in exchange for their paychecks, and the ownership of the material resides with the employer, not the employee.

Things can become complicated if the creative work is done in part or in whole by outside individuals or companies. In those cases, it's important to carefully examine the contracting agreements with those outsiders, including production houses, graphic artists, writers, producers, directors, and the like. The agreements should spell out that these outsiders are contractors producing work to be owned by you or your company. That is, they are creating something specifically for you in exchange for the fees paid to them, and they assign to you the copyright they might otherwise have had for their work. Right through the final product, ensure these agreements with outsiders clearly spell out that the created work belongs to the network operator or company that paid to produce it. Steiner cautions us on how the agreement is put together. "These agreements should spell out that the contracted content providers are producing works in which the copyright is to be owned by you or your company."

Steiner continues, "Basically there are three methods to obtain the rights to use the work. First, one can have the work created by full time employees of your company so that the work will be considered a work made for hire under the U.S. copyright laws; second, if one is using independent contractors, including part-time employees, to create the work, one can obtain ownership of the copyright by written assignment transferring the ownership of the copyright to you or your company; third, one can obtain an appropriate license to use the content as needed."

What if you are the content owner? Steiner suggests that "you may want to get affirmative protection if you are the copyright holder of text, visual content, or music [either through the creation of content by full-time employees or by contract]. Although you may own the copyright without registering it, it is important to understand that copyright registration is required in order to bring a lawsuit for copyright infringement. In addition, there are financial benefits to prompt registration of copyrighted works, such as statutory damages and attorney fees. With regard to trademarks, if you do have logos, taglines, brand names, or slogans that you are using on screen, then first make sure it is available by consulting with legal counsel to conduct appropriate searches. If a mark is available, then you should apply to the U.S. Patent and Trademark office to register the mark."

All the issues around intellectual property protection can appear to be daunting given the amount of content that one must create to keep feeding the beast. Original work does, however, take time to create, and high-quality content, the type that will make most networks truly effective, takes more time than slapdash work. Having rights to the assets that contribute to the final piece can help to accelerate a number of different versions that could be created for the same message, keeping it fresh on the network.

11.5 Summary

Network operators and content providers don't need to be attorneys, but they almost certainly will need the services of one early in the process of creating content. Because most operators will work with some content that is supplied by others or with components such as images or music whose rights are owned by others, getting rights wrong can be a costly mistake. For the most part, content creation involves ensuring all the copyright bases are covered through licensing agreements that spell out what rights you have—and don't have—and what you will pay. In most cases, you'll wind up working with a company's legal department that is well versed in licensing rights or a clearinghouse that serves as an agent for the rights to a wide variety of content. That will streamline the goal of making sure you respect everyone's intellectual property—your own included—as you build the best content package for your network.

12 Where Will Content Lead Us?

As I write this final chapter, the amazing potential of digital signage is just beginning to be realized as the industry begins to shift away from thinking about the technology itself and begins considering the role of content in shaping the future. Like any technology that reaches this tipping point, the changes in the industry—and the changes in daily life that will result—are bound to accelerate at a startling pace. What the industry will look like 5 years from now will be considerably different from what we see today. As one gazes into a crystal ball, the possibilities for the future of content and how we create it, interact with it, and perceive it are endless. There will be new ideas and thoughts that are, perhaps just now, being written down that will become the next big thing in our industry. The addition of new technology that delivers new ways of interacting with all this content is perhaps the most intriguing possibility on the horizon, one that could propel digital signage into every area of our lives.

12.1 The Path of Innovation

I like to think that history repeats itself, not in specific innovations, but rather in progress and patterns that lead to innovation. By looking at these patterns for the screens that have gone before, we can come to understand more about where digital signage might be in 5 years.

Let's consider the 2nd Screen, TV, for a moment. From its earliest development in the 1920s, it was seen as a way to combine two other media, motion pictures (the dominant visual medium) and radio (the dominant in-home entertainment medium and the advanced technology of the time). It was to be radio with pictures—or talking pictures sent via radio. This was not only the view of the inventors of the technology but also business pioneers like David Sarnoff, whose Radio Corporation of America (RCA) invested heavily in the development of television precisely because it offered an extension of its existing franchise in radio.

What happened eventually, of course, was that the content changed to follow what was made possible by the technology. Television became a very powerful and engaging storytelling medium that has demonstrated its ability to shape viewpoints and perceptions around the world. From the content of radio—live news, entertainment, music, and sports—sprang myriad programming choices that now pack our cable and satellite channels. Content producers learned to use what the technology made possible to deliver new ways to entice viewers and market to them.

The way in which TV and its content have changed over the years is a hint to the path along which digital signage will potentially evolve. But to get a clear view of this path, it is also necessary to think about the fact that this screen has a much more complex pedigree than TV. We are a century into technology-driven visual media and have considerable history to draw upon for instruction and inspiration. We have the knowledge gained from 25 years of the personal computer and a decade or more of mobile screen development to show us the way. The greater the number of previous influences, the more complex the potential combinations are for the medium that follows. So by shaking the ingredients and knowledge from all the previous screens, digital signage can really become something truly unlike anything that has gone before or has even been contemplated.

Therein lies the opportunity for this medium. It certainly has the potential to combine a plethora of established content creation practices, software tools, programming methods, Internet marketing metrics, and printed poster techniques. As one bakes these ingredients together in various recipes while keeping a keen eye on the expanding capabilities of digital signage, one will, with all certainty, be surprised what will come out of the oven.

Content for this medium today, of course, is in its infancy, and we have a remarkable journey ahead of us. To that end we will discuss new technologies and content practices that will have the greatest impact and ultimately will change the future of this medium as we know it.

12.2   Interaction as the Driver

One way to dive into the future is to talk about the depth of interaction between the individual and the content, looking far back down the path.

Both print media and broadcast media have one thing in common: directionally, they are only one way. Despite the recent incorporation of email and Twitter feeds to live news broadcasts or SMS text voting on reality shows, the viewer simply has no opportunity to effect any change in the content through interaction. You can change the channel on the TV, but it's the same as turning the page in a newspaper or magazine; when you get to the next page or the new channel, there's no opportunity to change it or interact with it.

Another way to think about this is that the media is always a push media; it is pushed out to us, and we watch or read in an essentially passive manner. Content is poured into us, and we receive it. Essentially the fact is that the media comes out at the consumer and nothing goes back the other way. This can be frustrating for viewers. It is equally frustrating for the content creators and the advertisers who support them because there is no truly effective way to know if you are actually delivering your content or advertising message to a consumer. A lot of methods have been developed to deliver an approximation of that knowledge, but they are simply that: approximations. And they don't deliver the vast feedback on a personalized level. It's mass marketing, mass delivery.

As we progressed to the 3rd Screen, the computer connected to the Internet, we began to have interactive experiences, and along with that came bidirectional interactivity. Initially, that interactivity was limited; there were relatively few content creators compared with content consumers, and the content creators largely determined the ways in which consumers could interact. With the advent of user-generated content and easy tools to create and publish, however, viewers have a whole new interactive experience. This does not include only text; a flip cam and an account on YouTube is all it takes to produce video about any subject.

Not a month goes by in this industry that I don't run across someone describing the future of digital signage in terms of the film *Minority Report*. It is probably the single most-used icon in the industry to represent the possibilities that lie ahead. It's no coincidence that I make that same comparison myself. One of my lifelong friends is John Underkoffler, chief scientist and a cofounder of Oblong. Underkoffler served as the chief science advisor to *Minority Report*, and he based the design of those scenes directly on his earlier work at MIT.

I had a chance to catch up him as I was finishing this book, and the work that he and his firm are doing is not only fascinating but I think will have as much impact on the future of digital signage as anything else I have seen. We are on our way to seeing that science fiction, like so many times before, becomes science fact.

To begin to understand how Underkoffler and his team will impact digital signage, we must look deep into the technology we use today to interact with various screens and content. That technology is what drives the way in which we interact with the media—and, thus, why we create media in the form as we know it today for any screen. Today, even though we think of ourselves as having very sophisticated tools and control over our interactions, in fact we're still dealing with technology that is effectively 40 years old. When it comes to manipulating the content, shifting or affecting it in some way, the majority of our interactions rely on a mouse and keyboard to manipulate a graphical user interface (GUI). All those ideas were operating in recognizable form by the early 1970s and were commercialized 10 years later. Since then, we've added the ability to manipulate that same GUI with voice in limited ways, and there has been a recent movement to add touch screen technology to that, largely in mobile. And that, Underkoffler says, has limited our sense of what we can really do with content.

"I think that once you crack the history of media open a little bit, one can see where it has to go—to a more profoundly deep interaction. I don't think you can get that far necessarily by only permitting the consumer, the recipient, the medium to have a superficial or shallow interaction." Underkoffler says, "So for us at Oblong, that's why gestural input and more generally what we're calling a spatial operating environment is really crucial."

This concept of a spatial operating environment is at the very core of what we saw in *Minority Report*, and it will change the way we think about and interact with media.

"We've got 25 years now of the mouse and keyboard as the solitary mode of interaction between humans and computers. This is the only way in any kind of commercial or broadly accessible interaction happens. We're counting basically from '84 when Steve Jobs gave us the Macintosh. That stuff is unchanged since then. So we're still using the mouse and keyboard. We're still using exactly the kind of GUI, on-screen experience that the Mac gave us and it's fundamentally unchanged, which is a strange thing 25 years on," Underkoffler says. "Now the machine itself has changed. It has a network that it didn't have before. It's got incredible graphics capabilities. Disk capacity and CPU speeds have gone up by five or six orders of magnitude. That all leaves the machine in a really good position to be able to express stuff outward toward the user, toward the operator."

Isn't that what we always celebrate when we talk about innovation and progress? So, what's the problem? It's the other direction, Underkoffler insists. "The operator is still limited to try to squeeze meaning through this tiny keyhole that is the mouse. And that's led over the last 25 years to a vastly imbalanced dialogue."

As a visionary, Underkoffler understands how one can interact with the media. He is about to literally change our point of view about digital signage by creating a new approach that vastly broadens interactions from the tiny keyhole into the broadest gestures.

"So for us, the key recognition is not even so much gestural input and gestural interaction as it is the more general idea of spatial interaction. Now we've drifted away from the one person, one computer, one screen paradigm. People are likely to have a bunch of screens around them, whether they're expressly connected to you because they're all attached to the machine or machines you're using, or you're walking through some public environment of the sort that digital signage concerns itself with."

For example, if one is in a particular environment with digital signage everywhere, then to think about coherent interaction with the entire environment (rather than a single screen), one has to take in account three-dimensional space. This is not only the placement of the screens, but also how to interact with them simultaneously.

"The computational substance behind those screens has to understand space. Fundamentally understand space in a way that's never happened before," Underkoffler explains. "If you lift up the hood on any modern day operating system, you'll see that it doesn't understand space. At best it thinks that a display is kind of an abstract collection of pixels. You talk about x and y and that's all you have. And the x and y can refer to the pixels on the screen kind of in the local coordinate system of the screen, but you know it doesn't have any sense of what happens if you turn the screen 90 degrees. Or if the screen is moving because it's a laptop and you're carrying it around with you, or it's your cell phone or your watch, or it's on the hood of a taxi."

When we consider Underkoffler's vision of expanding the operating system to not only include each screen in an environment but also consider the interface and the very depth of every screen, one can begin to expand one's vision of what future content may look like, how to interact with it, and how it may be created.

"Already the possibility of motion is kind of ignored. And then the fact that screen[s] might be arrayed around a room or arrayed in a space at a bunch of different angles, and sizes, and orientations is also something that existing operating systems just don't get."

What Oblong has been doing is essentially teaching the machine about space and its position in it, using what is essentially a new concept for an operating system. In this new world, the machine no longer thinks of the screen as a flat abstract collection of pixels but as a real object, in the real world, that exists at a particular location (Figure 12.1) and has a relationship to other things in the environment based on that location. It is also aware that the pixels it displays have a particular size based on the screen in use. There are small screens and big screens. And the screens are at a particular orientation. It's mounted on the ceiling, it's mounted on the walls, it's on the hinged top of a laptop, it's in your pocket. The point is, it has a particular location that matters with respect to the viewer.

Underkoffler believes that as soon as you have a spatially aware machine and as soon as you put the human in the same frame of reference, then all of a sudden there's a new and very important kind of connection between the person and the machine. "And at that point the gestural self, at least the way we mean it, falls out for free automatically, which is to say that you know when you point at the screen, if we know where your hand is, what your fingers are doing, where they are in space, we also know where the pixels on the screen are in the room coordinates, then the rest is really easy geometry. Because the computer and the screen and the people are all now finally understood to exist in the same space, there's a way to connect them in a really deep way. That gets us back around to the idea of deep interactions."

When one begins to think about how this relationship works within the bounds of a display and then expands the thinking beyond just one display, one then opens the mind to an even different world of content and interaction.

Back to *Minority Report*. In one scene, the character of John Anderton is walking through a mall. As he walks, he is identified and targeted with specific advertising just for him. How you or I might react to this—beyond the identity issue—really depends on how we can respond. As Underkoffler puts it, "This will get old and annoying rather quickly. I just will not want to be bothered. But, if I can talk back then it makes it more interesting. And if I can do it in such a natural human gestural manner then it becomes amazing."

Imagine a world where there are no buttons, no mice, no keyboards; instead there are gestures and spatially aware machines. How will this change content and the media for this next generation of screens? One needs only to look back a few years to see the acceleration of our times and technologies to guess that this next step is coming, and sooner than we think. Content will also catch up to the technology, just as digital signage is the new medium of today and the content understanding and development is just now catching up with the technology. The content for this vision will perhaps be modeled in 3-D worlds with layer upon layer and pieces upon pieces that are put together in cohesive combinations to make it most relevant to the viewer. That is, gestures will allow individuals to move through these virtual worlds, see things at the depth or level they choose, and create and reassemble the images to suit their needs.

This in itself is truly a demanding database of content in bits and pieces that will need to be tagged and pulled together to create a story that will define the product offering. Tomorrow's content will be created differently. If we look at

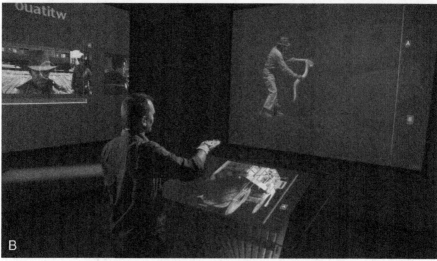

Figure 12.1 (Continued)

Figure 12.1 Oblong's G-Speak Operating System provides a new depth of interaction, including gestural movements and grabbing images from one screen and moving them to the next.
©2009 Oblong.

Doug Bolin's work at Razorfish, we see inklings of the type of media creation thinking that will absolutely be needed for the next 5 years.

"I've always had to think about marketing as TV commercials, print ads, and auto show kiosks. But it's all pretty much fixed linear static assets. It's not intelligent content where you can introduce a level of thinking into the content and how it's assembled and how it's presented," Bolin says. "The first step is to collaboratively identify what the content needs are going to be, at least at some level so that you can then start working out this sort of three-dimensional script or production schedule. What needs to be produced and how are we going to produce it so that it can be data based and tagged efficiently? And then used by the authors efficiently and then delivered efficiently?"

One can envision that the content will be layered with many dimensions. If one looks at where we are with the video game world, one can begin to envision how content will be used to deliver information and advertising in a spatial environment. Imagine putting yourself in that 3-D world and then moving around within it and then interacting with that world. Is this the first step on the way to the holodeck of *Star Trek* or the perhaps the 6th Screen?

The next innovation that will mesh with this 3-D approach to interaction is a screen that escapes the two-dimensional limits of today's displays. That's what Michael Klug, CTO of Zebra Imaging, is working on—something that will take full advantage of a spatial environment OS.

Klug explains, "We developed a dynamic...horizontal-oriented display that can create a three-dimensional volumetric image that occupies space above and below that surface, a user will be able to put their fingers into it to indicate things, point things out and eventually be able to interact with the imagery directly." Literally the concept is that one can reach in and draw in space in 3-D and also be able to reach in and grab graphic elements as if they were real objects floating in space and move them around and change them.

Klug tells us where they are with the technology. "We've demonstrated initial prototypes and alpha level prototypes of the technology and we're moving into beta level prototypes over the next year. This is a scalable display, so this display—just like our static holograms—can be tiled together to create an arbitrarily large display surface. In any orientation we've been focused mostly on horizontal, but it could be vertical, it could be inclined. And has a wide angle view capability—90 degrees in all directions. Kind of a 90-degree cone if you can imagine that coming out. And so therefore the ability to be viewed by multiple people simultaneously."

Imagine how linking a spatial environmental OS with an immersive 3-D display, advanced database technology, and new kinds of content will literally change the face of digital signage as we know it. Viewers will be able to immerse themselves as if they're inside a 3-D world and be surrounded by it. This is an experience that will be truly immersive—as opposed to exocentric, where one is standing outside the image. No longer mere viewers, people will be able to stand around these new types of displays, equipped with exciting content, and collectively interact with it—reach into it, grab objects, and interact with one another—without the need for glasses or goggles or the ability to see 3-D correctly. To me there is just one word for this: phenomenal.

There are hurdles to turning today's prototypes and plans into reality because the type of technology at work here is far more complex than today's best digital 3-D experiences in movie theaters that rely on polarized glasses to give viewers the illusion of three dimensions. That two-view binocular parallax of the movie theater, which provides the best experience in the center of the seating area and falls off toward the edges, isn't what Klug is after. He wants to create a completely immersive 3-D experience.

Klug explains that "there are all sorts of flavors of 3-D. What we do...is full parallax; no matter where you view it from you see the proper perspective [Figure 12.2]. And as you move through that continuum between binocular

Figure 12.2 Zebra Imaging creates a true 3-D experience. ©2009 Zebra Imaging.

and full parallax, there's a huge jump in the amount of data that you have to generate in order to provide even a single image, not to mention a moving image or interactive image. And so we've taken on the Holy Grail, I guess in a way, that the display we're developing is capable of doing full parallax imagery, which of course requires hundreds of gigabytes of data per frame in order to project the object and that has to be updated in 30 frames a second. We basically have a supercomputer with a display on the top in order to actually make this work and make it happen."

If this is really beginning to sound like the 25th century sci-fi of the holodeck, that's because that model is something that Klug and his colleagues have imagined, discussed, and planned. Klug helps us with the vision. "The holodeck in my mind does conjure a couple of different views. It conjures this view that you could have this exocentric viewpoint and you're interacting with a space that is distinctly different from your own, but you're interacting with it in a very natural way. And 3-D displays and interaction tools like what Oblong makes that allow you to interact. Then ultimately you could think of a future where you take our basic display technology and you create an entire wall and a floor and a ceiling and everything with that and truly create a volume in which you could have an immersive experience."

Now that's a lot of computation going on behind the scenes, and there's a lot of hardware. That would be a very expensive endeavor to accomplish given today's computing technology and costs, but it's not out of the realm of possibility. Zebra and Oblong, separately but simultaneously, have developed the fundamental technology to provide that kind of digital signage experience and reach new levels of an emotional connection that is just on the horizon. And after all, providing that emotional link we've discussed throughout this book is the most effective way to deliver a message that's memorable, actionable, and thus profitable.

We're a few years away from the kind of total immersion experience I've laid out here. But one can step back a bit from that fabulous long-term future and look to more practical but still exciting ways that content may change in the near term. One of the recent trends in digital signage is the movement toward using nonstandard shapes to present content. If one attends sports venues, one is familiar with the large LED scoreboards that also display video. The screens are made up of individual blocks tiled together to make up the entire image. In some places, like Times Square, one can see these LED blocks stacked in different basic shapes, such as an L or an O or even staircased shapes. This type of LED display technology is only suited for very large display installations where the viewer would be situated at a significant distance from the display and generally only within a narrow viewing angle.

A new technology has been designed as a versatile signage display that allows for the freedom to create nonuniform, nonstandard display configurations (Figure 12.3). It has all of the modularity and shape advantages of LED scoreboard displays and features far greater pixel resolution, producing an image that looks great at any viewing distance and angle.

Figure 12.3 "MicroTiles" provide a new design freedom for an infinite number of shapes. ©2009 Christie Digital.

Imagine creating content that is shaped based and moving. One can treat the configured shape as a digital canvas, with the freedom to design a display that can be configured to blend in perfectly, for example, with the decor, product, and printed materials in a retail or shop environment. Each MicroTile is connected to the other so that one can create content that interacts from block to block across diverse shapes (Figure 12.4). They can be configured into a wall of any shape. The wall can be part of the architecture that divides a space with live active images.

One can picture combining a number of technologies with nontraditional display shapes in a large interactive display wall that multiple people can interact with at close range. Coupled with appropriate content, this type of display in a point of transit network provides a compelling way to engage and entertain consumers for an extended period of time.

The content itself will improve dramatically over the next few years. The quality and understanding of what works and what does not is a moving target. What we think works today may change in the next few years, as we have seen in every screen that has come before, while many people experiment with different approaches and observe which of them is most effective. One thing is for certain: continuity is an important part of the look and feel of the network, as are individual pieces of content. The important industry benchmarks have been

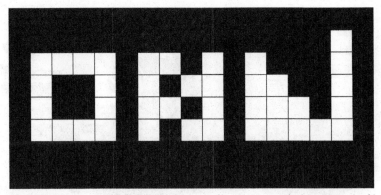

Figure 12.4 Content created for these shapes will open up a whole new way of looking at digital signage.

set, and I expect to see millions of screens in the marketplace. If one thinks about a million screens with each in need of fresh, relevant content, that adds up to billions of pieces of content that need to be customized, prepurposed, and created. In large-scale networks, automation of content will be key. The ability to use data-driven content that has visual components and data-driven delivery will impact our medium in new and grand ways that we never thought of before. Creating content in a manner where one is able to leverage the assets in many different venues and for many different uses will help in keeping content costs down. The reuse of content pieces and drawing those pieces from a database will help the industry reach a more sustainable future. As we discussed with Michael Chase, president of Alchemy, he sees this as a must for the success of creating content for this medium. "If I want to supply digital signage with content then I am going to believe that this incredibly dynamic asset management database will need to track those assets. And from there I can pull and push appropriately out to any medium and in the end create a greater return on investment for us."

Layering content and being able to reach in and pull out assets in small bite-size pieces may very well be some of the next changes we see in creating relevant content. For example, let's take a hypothetical airline with two routes: San Francisco to Hawaii and New York to the Caribbean. If one wants to have an advertisement for this airline, the service and branding messages are the same in all four destinations. However, one will want to make the ad in each of these destinations completely relevant to that particular market. So one may have the San Francisco advertisement layered with Hawaii call to action messages and the New York call to action messages layered with Caribbean images. To do that one will draw from the database and assemble the final advertisement automatically with the right pricing information and destination wrapped around the main service and branding message.

This is already being done in less sophisticated but data-managed manners in the billboard industry. Tommy Teepell, CMO of Lamar Advertising, tells us how they currently drive a change in messaging for BMW on their large roadside

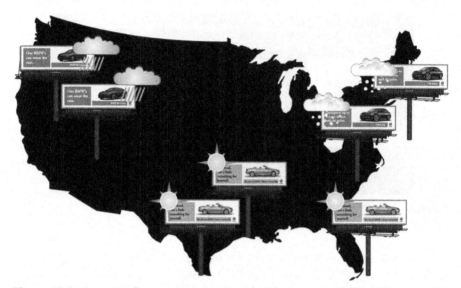

Figure 12.5 Lamar Adverting is managing the changes on BMW billboards with automated data like weather reports.
©2009 Lamar Advertising.

digital billboards (Figure 12.5). "In the South every time after April, when the temperatures reach over 68 degrees, BMW advertisements are all about convertibles and we rotate different convertible models every time the ad shows. And above the Mason-Dixon Line in the winter every time it gets below 35 degrees, BMW will show X5 and other models emphasizing heated seats."

An example of data-driven content can be valuable to ongoing content generation. Greg Argyle, COO of GoGo Cast, a narrowcaster in advertising-based networks, takes a completely hands-off approach to updating screens in sports complex arenas. In combination with RSports, who manages complex game results for team sports, GoGo Cast takes the data and makes it viewer friendly. Argyle gives us more details, "So the schedule for let's say 500 games and the locker room assignment is on screen so [that] everyone who needs to get dressed and ready for the game can see which locker room to go to. Then we show the results of every game on that digital sign [Figure 12.6]. We have a skin that show[s] all this plus…the time and the date and it only shows the games that are coming up. It doesn't show past games. And a lot of these games are seeded. So if there's a round-robin tournament, so one seed has to play another, it's actually fed from the RSports system. All the data loads up into the skin every 3 minutes or every time the digital sign calls home. On screen it will show an upcoming game. And as soon as that game results are in the system from the scoreboard, it automatically refreshes the data and those teams are displayed. It's pretty amazing actually. It also shows in a ticker form at the bottom as every game finishes, it scrolls across the screen and says 12 and under Team USA beat Great Britain 3 to 2. So it shows the schedule of

Figure 12.6 Automated data displayed in templates will keep labor to a minimum and provide scale.
©2009 GoGo Cast.

all the games, the locker rooms and then it shows the results of the games via the ticker throughout the day."

12.3 Neuromarketing

Neuroscience meets the marketer, this is the latest in the biological study of the human brain and advertising. The goal is to understand how the brain produces behaviour, and how people choose and how the beginning of that choice is a process that is purely biological. And according to neuromarking researchers, it is the act of deciding whether to make that purchase in 2.5 seconds.

This is type of testing of content can be invaluable in large scale campaigns. Brands are using these types of studies to help refine their messages and the images that are used. One can use brain imaging such as an MRI to gain insight into the mechanisms behind people's decisions. Each time there is a decision the brain doesn't run through a list of risks, benefits and value judgments. Whenever it can, the brain takes advantage of past experience and stored information that acts as sort of an index to quickly make the decision. Knowing what type of image triggers pleasure as opposed to pain is the first step. One can measure emotional engagement, attention and memory retention on advertising. One can measure the components of the ad that a shopper pays attention to and discover the point in the ad that they become emotionally engaged. In addition one can find out which portion of the ad the shopper retains in long term memory. In using the neuromarketing information the advertiser can get to the core of what makes their ad effective.

Some research conducted at a London hospital for Viacom Brand Solutions, measured brain activity amongst people aged 18-34, while TV ads were screened. The research discovered that the more advertising content is relevant to the program environment in which it appears the higher probability to generate brain activity in the areas of the brain commonly associated with advertising effectiveness. Research has found out that advertising generates more brain activity than the programming in which it appears, if it is relevant. Once can extend this thinking to DOOH and how the more relevant the content is to the consumer experience and the venue the more effective the advertising will be.

12.4 Summary

Within our reach is the ability to expand digital signage that will be self-healing, data-driven, hands-off machines that will ultimately shift content templates slightly to keep refresh costs down, high-quality content up, and be more relevant than ever. It will, however, take the inspiration and guidance of keen artists and technologists to bring this to fruition. As one contemplates this extraordinary medium, we are on the precipice of something big, something so powerful and so engaging that one has to ponder its impact on our daily lives. Is it the *Minority Report* experience or is our vision better than that? I, for one, say that in our wildest dreams for digital signage it has some of *Minority Report* and some of *Blade Runner*, but a lot more common sensibility of usefulness to each and every viewer. The business models will drive what the technology has brought to us, and content will drive the experience and value to all of us.

Experience and engagement will effectively put digital signage in a category of its own. Digital signage will be added to our daily lives and create new experiences for each and every person that can literally change every time one comes in contact with that particular screen. The use for digital signage is in an ever-expanding flight of the imagination. The type of network subcategories and how we will encounter digital signage may creep up on us in unassuming ways. It may be as contradictory as when we order a mouthwatering cheeseburger and fries with a thirst-quenching cola and an ice cream sundae from the drive-through window then work out at the local gym and watch inspirational fitness messages as we work off lunch from the day before. Or it may be as simple as waiting in line at our local bank and realizing that time flies when you're having fun or it is time to take out a loan for that new convertible car I just saw on the billboard on a warm summer day because my bank is offering great rates on new cars.

Content that is done well will seep into our experience from the moment we walk out our door to the time we return to our abode. The ultimate landscape of content that this medium offers will be some of the most influential, meaningful experiences we can provide for our fellow humankind as we rush into the future with each and every deployment that will impact the viewer for the good, sometimes the bad, and hopefully never the ugly.

Glossary

1st Screen Motion pictures, the first in the historic progression of communication screens.

2nd Screen Television, the second in the historic progression of communication screens.

3rd Screen Computers, especially in combination with the World Wide Web.

4th Screen Mobile handheld devices, such as cellular telephones.

5th Screen Digital signage and other digital out-of-home displays.

Ad rotation duration The amount of time it takes for all digital signage announcements in one rotation to display.

Aided recall A research method often used to measure audience retention of advertising content. In an aided recall study, subjects might be shown an advertisement and asked if they've seen it before.

Animation A series of images captured on still frames that create the impression of fluid movement when presented in sequence at the proper speed.

Antialiasing A digital processing technique used to create the appearance of greater visual clarity in computer graphics and digital photographs. Also applicable for reducing distortion in audio files.

API (application programming interface) A computer interface that manages the interaction between an application program and a library or operating system.

Artificial intelligence A field of science devoted to creating computers with the capacity to think, reason, and learn at a level that approaches that of the human brain.

Aspect ratio The horizontal and vertical dimensions of an image or electronic screen, written as a ratio with the horizontal dimension (width) first and the vertical dimension (height) second. Often indicated as 16:9.

Attraction loop A media presentation designed to draw users' attention to a kiosk or touch screen and to repeat itself indefinitely until stopped by user input.

Audience Metrics Guidelines A set of guidelines created by the Out-of-Home Video Advertising Bureau (OVAB) to provide digital signage networks and their advertisers with an industry standard formula for calculating the impact of digital signage advertising on the target audience.

Audio component An element of sound incorporated into digital signage in both content and displays.

Average unit audience (AUA) A measure of the number and type of people who had the opportunity to view a particular advertising vehicle (display) for an amount of time equal to the vehicle network's standard advertising unit.

AVI (audio video interlace or audio video interleave) A container format for files with synchronized audio and video; also used for multiple streaming audio or video presentations. Files using AVI format are named with the .avi extension, for example, "Customer Greeting.avi."

Banner ad An electronic advertisement or promotional announcement, often running horizontally along the top or bottom of the screen as part of a digital signage display.

Behavioral attitude The psychological, emotional, and experiential factors that influence consumer behavior.

Billboard Large-scale signage traditionally placed outdoors and used for advertising.

Bitmap A graphics format that stores pixel-by-pixel information about a specific image.

Blu-ray Disc A data storage unit often used for high-definition video and computer games. Blu-ray Discs are the same physical size as DVDs but have roughly six times more data storage capacity.

BMP (basic multilingual plane) A bitmap file format.

Brand identity The public perception of the character and quality of a particular organization or product.

Broadband A type of high-speed Internet or wireless connection achieved by high-frequency signal transmission across a wide bandwidth.

CAD (computer aided design) drawings A type of commercial drafting and design using computer-generated graphics to create two- and three-dimensional schematics as well as animation and special effects.

Cellular technology A form of communications technology that relies on a series of radio cells served by base stations to transmit and receive signals wirelessly.

Copyright The legal ownership of an original work. Copyright ownership includes the right to create copies of the original work for sale and the right to license the work for use by others. These rights expire after a set time and can be sold to others.

Copyright infringement The unlawful use or reproduction of copyrighted work without the permission of the copyright holder.

CPM requisite Cost per thousand. The basic formula used to determine the success of a digital signage advertising campaign is the cost to the client per 1000 impressions or times the ad is viewed. (CPM stands for cost per mille, which is the Latin word for thousand.)

Cross-platform media A media application designed to run on multiple computer platforms.

Demographic A distinct segment of the population identified by a particular trait or set of traits, such as gender, age, marital status, or income.

Digital A term that applies to any media asset created or reproduced through the computerized binary code of 1s and 0s.

Digital asset management (DAM) The process of storing, cataloging, organizing, safeguarding, and maintaining digital material, such as video, audio, photographs, and computer-generated graphics.

Digital billboard An outdoor electronic large-scale billboard screen, frequently timed to change on a specific schedule.

Digital landscape An abundance of digital media networks and screens for placement of creative information and advertising content.

Digital out-of-home (DOOH) Digital advertising that takes place outside of the home, including digital signage. The nomenclature comes from the advertising industry's term OOH (Out of Home) advertising.

Digital poster An electronic sign placed on a wall that can display dynamic content.

Digital signage The presentation of targeted information or advertising content via a network of electronic screens, projectors, or other types of display devices.

Digital video recorder (DVR) A device used to record, store, and play back video input digitally. The term commonly refers to machines designed for in-home use, though it also applies to handheld video cameras and other devices that record video digitally.

Digitally tagged Tags are keywords used to describe a piece of data. Content is tagged in such a way that the content can be cataloged as a set of building blocks that allow automated reassembly into a final presentation.

Dwell time The amount of time an audience member spends viewing a digital signage display.

Dynamic content Flash technologies are frequently used to orchestrate media types (sound, animations, changing text, etc.) in a presentation. The scripting also allows a technique by which a Flash file requests additional information from a server using XML requests. For example, when the temperature falls below 55 degrees Fahrenheit, the advertisement changes to sell hot chocolate; when the temperature climbs above 76 degrees Fahrenheit, it advertises iced tea.

Electronic screen A smooth, clear glass or plastic surface used to display electronically generated images as part of a computer, television, cell phone, or other device.

Flash content A graphics application frequently used to create animation or other dynamic visual effects for web sites, digital signage, and multimedia presentations.

Frenetic motion Frantic or frenzied movement.

Full parallax Term for a hologram that appears to be three-dimensional from any angle, rather than only when the viewer's eyes are on the horizontal plane with respect to the image.

Gestural technology The development of computers with the capacity to recognize and respond appropriately to human gestures, including body language and facial expressions.

Gesture interaction Software that enables a computer display to recognize and respond to a user's gestures.

GUI (graphical user interface) The graphics and imagery used to illustrate the functions of a computer program.

High-definition (HD) Technology that enables images to be broadcast and displayed in sharper detail and greater clarity than images presented in standard-definition (SD). The resolutions are 1280 × 720 and 1920 × 1080 pixels.

High resolution Often used as a pixel count in digital imaging for presenting images on an electronic screen where the first number is the number of pixel columns (width) and the second is the number of pixel rows (height); for example, 1280 × 720. Higher numbers of pixels create greater clarity and sharper detail.

IMAX (Image MAXimum) A format used for motion picture film that features larger image size and sharper resolution than traditional film formats.

In-store media Promotional, advertising, and informational content played on an in-store network.

In-store network A coordinated multiscreen advertising and merchandising presentation network housed inside a store.

Intellectual property An original creative work, such as a musical composition, scientific invention, or graphic design. Intellectual property is safeguarded through laws regulating trademarks, copyrights, and patents, among others.

Interactive Term for computer applications that offer varied responses depending on user input.

Interactive kiosk An electronic display device that allows users to obtain information or complete a transaction through the use of buttons, a touch screen, a mouse, or another input mechanism.

Interactive screen A screen that provides information to users and also asks for users to input information or responses to questions, often through a touch screen or button pad.

Internet The global collective of computer networks that share and transmit data using a common set of communication protocols.

Intranet A private, internal computer communications network used by a specific organization.

JPEG (Joint Photographic Experts Group) A file format for storing and transferring still images and digital photographs.

Kilobyte (KB) A digital information storage unit equal to roughly 1000 bytes.

Kiosk A stall or terminal device set up in a public space, often equipped with interactive technology to help users obtain information.

LCD (liquid crystal display) screen A flat-panel display screen that incorporates liquid crystals between two transparent panes of glass or plastic. The images produced by electrically stimulating the liquid crystals are brighter and clearer than those created by a standard television screen or computer monitor.

Letterboxing The insertion of black lines (known as mattes) on the top and bottom of the screen when transferring video filmed in widescreen to standard video format. Preserves the aspect ratio and scene composition of the film.

Metrics The science of measurement often used in business to quantify the impact or success of a program, product, or initiative.

MPEG (Moving Picture Experts Group) A file format used for storing and transferring digital video and audio.

MRSS feed (media really simple syndication) Web-based protocol that allows more than one visual element within an RSS feed.

Net reach The number of people who were exposed to a particular digital signage display during a set time frame.

Network In digital signage, a system of multiple connected computers or displays capable of sharing data and displaying content across multiple locations.

Neuromarketing A new field of marketing that studies the brains primal process of thought and affective response to marketing and advertising.

Notice rate Percentage of passersby who notice a digital advertising display.

On-demand screen In telecommunications, a screen that offers the user a variety of options for completing a particular transaction, such as ordering a movie from a list of titles. The user inputs a selection through a remote control, button panel, touch screen, or other device.

Orthographic A two-dimensional representation of a three-dimensional object or scene rendered from one observer's point of view.

Pillarboxing The insertion of black lines (known as mattes) on the left and right sides of the screen when transferring video filmed in standard video format to a widescreen display.

Pixel The smallest data unit that makes up a computer-generated or displayed image; a shortened version of the term "picture element." The resolution of a high-definition image consists of 1920 × 1080 pixels.

Playlist In digital signage, a list of programming elements scheduled to run in sequence as part of an advertising or informational display.

Point of sale network (POS) One of three main categories of digital signage network types. These networks are positioned to sell more product in-store, establish branding, and enhance the shopper experience.

Point of transit network (POT) One of three main categories of digital signage network types. These networks are usually found where people are on the go. These networks are used primarily for branding. Subcategories include airports, train stations, subway stations, etc.

Point of wait network (POW) One of three main categories of digital signage network types. This type of network is where people are waiting for a service or product or have high dwell time; for example, a bank line, a break room in a corporate environment, an elevator, or a doctor's office waiting area.

Pop-up ad An advertisement that appears on web sites, often covering a portion of the screen for a given period of time or until the user clicks on, minimizes, or deletes the pop-up image.

Pop-up blocker A software tool that prevents pop-up ads from displaying.

Portable Network Graphics (PNG) A bitmapped file format used for computer-generated images.

Qualitative research A field of psychological study that explores the motivation and rationale behind an individual's decision-making process.

Relevancy Pertinence or level of significance, especially in a particular situation or to attract a particular audience.

RFID (radio frequency identification) phone A cellular phone equipped with RFID technology that enables it to send and receive signals from RFID tags, such as those placed on retail items.

ROI (return on investment) Benefit earned as a result of the resources allocated to achieving a particular business objective.

ROO (return on objectives) An analysis of the return provided by business activities that don't generate immediate or tangible benefits, such as meetings, conference presentations, or product demonstrations.

RSS feeds (really simple syndication) Web-based protocol that allows subscribers to automatically receive updated content from their preferred web sites. Digital signage displays can also be updated via RSS feed.

Screen zones Designated sections of a digital signage screen, each of which can potentially feature its own content and programming.

Search engine A computer program that reviews pages on the World Wide Web in response to search parameters (such as keywords) provided by a user and then displays a list of links to corresponding web pages.

SMS text messages (short message service or silent messaging service) A data application designed to facilitate the exchange of brief, text-only messages across cellular telephone communication systems.

Social network The collection of family, friends, colleagues, and acquaintances known personally by an individual. Often used to describe online networks of the same type.

Spam Unsolicited electronic messages, frequently of a commercial nature.

Spatial interaction Technology-enabled interactivity between a person and screens placed around them, whether they're expressly connected to a person or all attached to a machine or machines a person is using.

Static billboard A billboard featuring a still image or text.

Static hologram A three-dimensional projected image designed to appear still.

Static media In digital signage, a form of messaging that features still images, such as photos or graphic designs that are at times combined with text.

Statutory damages An amount of money awarded in a lawsuit in which the plaintiff claims the defendant's unlawful actions resulted in a loss of income for the plaintiff. Statutory damages are set by law and often used in intellectual property or other cases where the exact dollar amount owed the plaintiff is difficult to estimate.

Store zones Designated areas of a retail outlet that are separate categories of specific product groups, such as the produce or deli section of a grocery store. Often referred to as the area to be covered by digital signage displays.

Storyboard A drawing or other still image created as part of the process of preparing a film, animation, interactive display, or other dynamic media presentation. The storyboarding process involves the creation of numerous such images to help creators of dynamic media content map out a sequence of images in advance.

Tagline In advertising, a memorable turn of phrase that helps reinforce the brand identity of a product or organization.

Template A file or document containing an established design format to which customized content can be added for purposes of creating a presentation.

Three-dimensional Occupying, or appearing to occupy, the three dimensions of height, width, and depth.

Three-dimensional space The physical (as opposed to virtual) world where objects have height, width, and depth.

Ticker A message or series of messages streamed across the bottom of a television or other digital signage during a program. Sometimes referred to as a crawl.

TiVo A digital video recording device that connects to a user's television and Internet service, providing extensive scheduling information and recording options, primarily for TV programs and movies.

Touch screen A screen equipped with software enabling it to sense contact on its surface, often used for interactive kiosk displays.

Trademark A form of intellectual property, such as a logo, name, slogan, graphic image, or design. A trademark's owner is the only entity legally entitled to its use and may take legal action to prevent or curtail unauthorized exploitation.

Twitter A social networking site founded in 2006 that allows users to connect to one another by sending and receiving short messages (known as Tweets).

Twitter feed Web-based protocol that allows subscribers to automatically receive updated Twitter messages (or Tweets) from preferred Twitter users.

Two-dimensional Having, or appearing to have, height and width while lacking depth.

User Generated Content (UGC) Content that is generated by viewers who are participating in the content origination, i.e., YouTube, Twitter, Amazon.com reader reviews, and UGC for DOOH.

Unaided recall A research method often used to measure audience retention of advertising content. For example, subjects may be asked to name all the advertising for a particular kind of product or service that they've seen in the last month. A particular ad's unaided recall rate is the percentage of respondents who named that ad (or the subject of the ad) without prompting.

Vehicle zone The area of a retail outlet or other public space where people can see or hear the content of an advertising vehicle set up in a fixed space.

Vehicle zone dwell time The amount of time a potential customer spends in the vehicle zone while paying attention to the advertisement.

Venue The specific location where a digital signage display is placed, such as a department store, a bank, or the lobby of an office building.

Venue-based network A network of linked advertisements, such as digital signage screens, set up in a specific venue, such as a university student center or an airport.

Videography Traditionally, the process of recording moving images using a video camera (digital or analog), as distinct from the process of recording moving images on film, known as cinematography. Changing technology has broadened the definition of videography beyond capturing video to the creation of computer-based moving images for web, cell phone, and digital signage applications.

Wait-warping Attracting consumers' attention to a digital signage display while they are waiting. It causes them to view the display for a period of time, thereby reducing the level of dissatisfaction associated with waiting.

Web banner A form of Internet messaging in which an announcement or advertisement is embedded into a web page. The embedded image is often rectangular in shape and may contain promotional information about a particular product, service, or event as well as a link to a web site with additional information.

Web-based A program, application, or service designed to be accessed exclusively through the World Wide Web.

Web browser A software application that enables a user to access the World Wide Web as well as receive and transmit data through the Internet.

Widescreen An image presented on a film, television, or computer screen that features a wider aspect ratio than the standard 4:3.

Wi-Fi (wireless fidelity) network A local area network (LAN) that enables remote Internet access by broadcasting a radio signal on the IEEE 802.11 protocol.

Windows Media Video (WMV) A container format for files with compressed audio and video. Files using WMV format are named with the .wmv extension, such as "August Promotion.wmv."

Wireless network A network in which computers are connected to one another through a centralized wireless access point (WAP).

Index

Note: Page numbers followed by f indicates figures, b indicates boxes and t indicates tables.

CPSIA information can be obtained
at www.ICGtesting.com
Printed in the USA
BVOW03s2034050118

504600BV00001B/21/P